Cambridge Sketches

Frank Preston Stearns

Contents

CAMBRIDGE SKETCHES

BY

Frank Preston Stearns

PREFACE

It has never been my practice to introduce myself to distinguished persons, or to attempt in any way to attract their attention, and I now regret that I did not embrace some opportunities which occurred to me in early life for doing so; but at the time I knew the men whom I have described in the present volume I had no expectation that I should ever write about them. My acquaintance with them, however, has served to give me a more elevated idea of human nature than I otherwise might have acquired in the ordinary course of mundane affairs, and it is with the hope of transmitting this impression to my readers that I publish the present account. Some of them have a world-wide celebrity, and others who were distinguished in their own time seem likely now to be forgotten; but they all deserve well of the republic of humanity and of the age in which they lived.

THE EVERGREENS,
JANUARY 4, 1905.

THE CLOSE OF THE WAR

Never before hast thou shone
So beautifully upon the Thebans;
O, eye of golden day:
  --Antigone of Sophocles.

One bright morning in April, 1865, Hawthorne's son and the writer were coming forth together from the further door-way of Stoughton Hall at Harvard College, when, as the last reverberations of the prayer-bell were sounding, a classmate called to us across the yard: "General Lee has surrendered!" There was a busy hum of voices where the three converging lines of students met in front of Appleton Chapel, and when we entered the building there was President Hill seated in the recess between the two pulpits, and old Doctor Peabody at his desk, with his face beaming like that of a saint in an old religious painting. His prayer was exceptionally fervid and serious. He asked a blessing on the American people; on all those who had suffered from the war; on the government of the United States; and on our defeated enemies. When the short service had ended, Doctor Hill came forward and said: "It is not fitting that any college tasks or exercises should take place until another sun has arisen after this glorious morning. Let us all celebrate this fortunate event."

On leaving the chapel we found that Flavius Josephus Cook, afterwards Rev. Joseph Cook of the Monday Lectureship, had collected the members of the Christian Brethren about him, and they were all singing a hymn of thanksgiving in a very vigorous manner.

There were some, however, who recollected on their way to breakfast the sad procession that had passed through the college-yard six months before,--the military funeral of James Russell Lowell's nephews, killed in General Sheridan's victory at Cedar Run. There were no recent graduates of Harvard more universally beloved than Charles and James Lowell; and none of whom better things were expected. To Lowell himself, who had no other children, except a daughter, they were almost like his own sons, and the ode he wrote on this occasion touches a depth of pathos not to be met with elsewhere in his poetry. There was not at that time another family in Cambridge or Boston which contained two such bright intellects, two such fine characters. It did not seem right that they should both have left their mother, who was bereaved already by a faithless husband, to fight the battles of their country, however much they were needed for this. Even in the most despotic period of European history the only son of a widow was exempt from conscription. Then to lose them both in a single day! Mrs. Lowell became the saint of Quincy Street, and none were so hardened or self-absorbed as not to do her reverence.

But now the terrible past was eclipsed by the joy and pride of victory. The great heroic struggle was over; young men could look forward to the practice of peaceable professions, and old men had no longer to think of the exhausting drain upon their resources. Fond mothers could now count upon the survival of their sons, and young wives no longer feared to become widows in a night. Everywhere there was joy and exhilaration. To many it was the happiest day they had ever known.

President Hill was seen holding a long and earnest conversation with Agassiz on the path towards his house. The professors threw aside their contemplated work. Every man went to drink a glass of wine with his best friend, and to discuss the fortunes of the republic. The ball-players set off for the Delta, where Memorial Hall now stands, to organize a full match game; the billiard experts started a tournament on Mr. Lyon's new tables; and the rowing men set off for a three-hours' pull down Boston harbor. Others collected in groups and discussed the future of their country with the natural precocity of youthful minds. "Here," said a Boston cousin of the two young Lowells, to a pink-faced, sandy-haired ball-player, "you are opposed to capital punishment; do you think Jeff. Davis ought to be hung?" "Just at present," replied the latter, "I am more in favor of suspending Jeff. Davis than of suspending the law,"--an opinion that was greeted with laughter and applause. The general sentiment of the crowd was in favor of permitting General Lee to retire in peace to private life; but in regard to the president of the Southern Confederacy the feeling was more vindictive.

We can now consider it fortunate that no such retaliatory measures were taken by the government. Much better that Jefferson Davis, and his confederates in the secession movement, should have lived to witness every day the consequences of that gigantic blunder. The fact that they adopted a name for their newly-organized nation which did not differ essentially from the one which they had discarded; that their form of government, with its constitution and laws, differed so slightly from those of the United States, is sufficient to indicate that their separation was not to be permanent, and that it only required the abolition of slavery to bring the Southern States back to their former position in the Union. If men and nations did what was for their true interests, this would be a different world.

* * * * *

At that time the college proper consisted of three recitation buildings, and four or five dormitories, besides Appleton Chapel, and little old Holden Chapel of the seventeenth century, which still remains the best architecture on the grounds. The buildings were mostly old, plain, and homely, and the rooms of the students simply furnished. In every class there were twelve or fifteen dandies, who dressed in somewhat above the height of the fashion, but they served to make the place more picturesque and were not so likely to be mischievous as some of the rougher country boys. It was a time of plain, sensible living. To hire a man to make fires in winter, and black the boots, was considered a great luxury. A majority of the students blacked their own boots, although they found this very disagreeable. The college pump was a venerable institution, a leveller of all distinctions; and many a pleasant conversation took place about its wooden trough. No student thought of owning an equipage, and a Russell or a Longworth would as soon have hired a sedan chair as a horse and buggy, when he might have gone on foot. Good pedestrianism was the pride of the Harvard student; and an honest, wholesome pride it was. There was also some good running. Both Julian Hawthorne and Thomas W. Ward ran to Concord, a distance of sixteen miles, without stopping, I believe, by the way. William Blaikie, the stroke of the University crew, walked to New York during the

Thanksgiving recess--six days in all.

The undergraduates had not yet become acquainted with tennis, the most delightful of light exercises, and foot-ball had not yet been regulated according to the rules of Rugby and Harrow. The last of the pernicious foot-ball fights between Sophomores and Freshmen took place in September, 1863, and commenced in quite a sanguinary manner. A Sophomore named Wright knocked over Ellis, the captain of the Freshman side, without reason or provocation, and was himself immediately laid prostrate by a red-headed Scotch boy named Roderick Dhu Coe, who seemed to have come to college for the purpose, for he soon afterwards disappeared and was never seen there again. With the help of Coe and a few similar spirits, the Freshmen won the game. It was the first of President Hill's reforms to abolish this brutal and unseemly custom.

The New York game of base-ball, which has since assumed such mammoth proportions, was first introduced in our colleges by Wright and Flagg, of the Class of '66; and the first game, which the Cambridge ladies attended, was played on the Delta in May of that year with the Trimountain Club of Boston. Flagg was the finest catcher in New England at that time; and, although he was never chosen captain, he was the most skillful manager of the game. It was he who invented the double-play which can sometimes be accomplished by muffing a fly-catch between the bases. He caught without mask or gloves and was several times wounded by the ball.

Let us retrace the steps of time and take a look at the old Delta on a bright June evening, when the shadows of the elms are lengthening across the grass. There are from fifty to a hundred students, and perhaps three or four professors, watching the Harvard nine practise in preparation for its match with the formidable Lowell nine of Boston. Who is that slender youth at second base,--with the long nose and good-humored twinkle in his eye,--who never allows a ball to pass by him? Will he ever become the Dean of the Harvard Law School? And that tall, olive-complexioned fellow in the outfield, six feet two in his ball-shoes,--who would suppose that he is destined to go to Congress and serve his country as Minister to Spain! There is another dark-eyed youth leaning against the fence and watching the ball as it passes to and fro. Is he destined to become Governor of Massachusetts? And that sturdy-looking first-baseman,--will he enter the ministry and preach sermons in Appleton Chapel? These young men all live quiet, sensible lives, and trouble themselves little concerning class honors and secret societies. If they have a characteristic in common it is that they always keep their mental balance and never go to extremes; but neither they nor others have any suspicion of their several destinies. Could they return and fill their former places on the ground, how strangely they would feel! But the ground itself is gone; their youth is gone, and the honors that have come to them seem less important than the welfare of their families and kindred.

Misdemeanors, great and small, on the part of the students were more common formerly than they have been in recent years, for the good reason that the chances of detection were very much less. Some of the practical jokes were of a much too serious character. The college Bible was abstracted from the Chapel and sent to Yale; the communion wine was stolen; a paper bombshell was exploded behind a curtain in the Greek recitation-room; and Professor Pierce discovered one morning that all his black-boards had been painted white. All the copies of Cooke's Chemical Physics suddenly disappeared one afternoon, and next morning the best scholars in the Junior Class were obliged to say, "Not prepared."

A society called the Med. Fac. was chiefly responsible for these performances; but so secret was it in its membership and proceedings that neither the college faculty nor the great majority of the students really knew whether there was such a society in existence or not. A judge of the United States Circuit Court, who had belonged to it in his time, was not aware that his own son was a member of it.

Some of the members of this society turned out well, and others badly; but generally an inclination for such high pranks shows a levity of nature that bodes ill for the future. A college class is a wonderful study in human nature, from the time it enters until its members have arrived at forty or fifty years of age. There was one young man at Harvard in those days who was so evidently marked out by destiny for a great public career that when he was elected to Congress in 1876 his classmates were only surprised because it seemed so natural that this should happen. Another was of so depraved a character that it seemed as if he was intended to illustrate the bad boy in a Sunday-school book. He was so untrustworthy that very soon no one was willing to associate with him. He stole from his father, and, after graduating, went to prison for forgery and finally was killed by a tornado. There was still another, a great fat fellow, who always seemed to be half asleep, and was very shortly run over and killed by a locomotive. Yet if we could know the whole truth in regard to these persons it might be difficult to decide how much of their good and evil fortune was owing to themselves and how much to hereditary tendencies and early influences. The sad fact remains that it is much easier to spoil a bright boy than to educate a dull one.

The undergraduates were too much absorbed in their own small affairs to pay much attention to politics, even in those exciting times. For the most part there was no discrimination against either the Trojans or Tyrians; but abolitionists were not quite so well liked as others, especially after the close of the war; and it was noticed that the sons of pro-slavery families commonly seemed to have lacked the good moral training (and the respect for industry) which is youth's surest protection against the pitfalls of life. The larger proportion of suspended students belonged to this class.

During the war period Cambridge social life was regulated by a coterie of ten or twelve young ladies who had grown up together and who were generally known as the "Spree,"--not because they were given to romping, for none kept more strictly within the bounds of a decorous propriety, but because they were accustomed to go off together in the summer to the White Mountains or to some other rustic resort, where they were supposed to have a perfectly splendid time; and this they probably did, for it requires cultivation and refinement of feeling to appreciate nature as well as art. They decided what students and other young ladies should be invited to the assemblies in Lyceum Hall, and they arranged their own private entertainments over the heads of their fathers and mothers; and it should be added that they exercised their authority with a very good grace. They had their friends and admirers among the collegians, but no young man of good manners and pleasing address, and above all who was a good dancer, needed to beg for an invitation. The good dancers, however, were in a decided minority, and many who considered themselves so in their own habitats found themselves much below the standard in Cambridge.

Mrs. James Russell Lowell was one of the lady patronesses of the assemblies, and her husband sometimes came to them for an hour or so before escorting her home. He watched the performance with a poet's eye for whatever is graceful and charming, but sometimes also with a humorous smile playing upon his face. There were some very good dancers among the ladies who skimmed the floor almost like swallows; but the finest waltzer in Cambridge or Boston was Theodore Colburn, who had graduated ten years previously, and with the advantage of a youthful figure, had kept up the pastime ever since. The present writer has never seen anywhere another man who could waltz with such consummate ease and unconscious grace. Lowell's eyes followed him continually; but it is also said that Colburn would willingly dispense with the talent for better success in his profession. Next to him comes the tall ball-player, already referred to, and it is delightful to see the skill with which he adapts his unusual height to the most *petite* damsel on the floor. Here the "Spree" is omnipotent, but it does not like Class Day, for then Boston and its suburbs pour forth their torrent of beauty and fashion, and Cambridge for the time being is left somewhat in the shade.

Henry James in his "International Episode" speaks as if New York dancers were the best in the world, and they are certainly more light-footed than English men and women; but a New York lady, with whom Mr. James is well acquainted, says that Bostonians and Austrians are the finest dancers. The true Bostonian cultivates a sober reserve in his waltzing which, if not too serious, adds to the grace of his movement. Yet, when the german is over, we remember the warning of the wealthy Corinthian who refused his daughter to the son of Tisander on the ground that he was too much of a dancer and acrobat.

*   *   *   *   *

From 1840 to 1860 Harvard University practically stagnated. The world about it progressed, but the college remained unchanged. Its presidents were excellent men, but they had lived too long under the academic shade. They lacked practical experience in the great world. There were few lectures in the college course, and the recitations were a mere routine. The text-books on philosophical subjects were narrow and prejudiced. Modern languages were sadly neglected; and the tradition that a French instructor once entertained his class by telling them his dreams, if not true, was at least characteristic. The sons of wealthy Bostonians were accustomed to brag that they had gone through college without doing any real studying. To the college faculty politics only meant the success of Webster and the great Whig party. The anti-slavery agitation was considered inconvenient and therefore prejudicial.

During the struggle for free institutions in Kansas, the president of Harvard College undertook to debate the question in a public meeting, but he displayed such lamentable ignorance that he was soon obliged to retire in confusion.

The war for the Union, however, waked up the slumbering university, as it did all other institutions and persons. Rev. Thomas Hill was chosen president in 1861, and was the first anti-slavery president of the college since Josiah Quincy; and this of itself indicated that he was in accord with the times,--had not set his face obstinately against them. He was not so practical a man as President Quincy, but he was one of the best scholars in America. His administration has not been looked upon as a success, but he served to break the ice and to open the way for future navigation. He accepted the position with definite ideas of reform; but he lacked skill in the adaptation of means to ends. He was determined to show no favoritism to wealth and social position, and he went perhaps too far in the opposite direction. One day when the workmen were digging the cellar of Gray's Hall, President Hill threw off his coat, seized a shovel, and used it vigorously for half an hour or more. This was intended as an example to teach the students the dignity of labor; but they did not understand it so. At the faculty meetings he carried informality of manner to an excess. He depended too much on personal influence, which, as George Washington said formerly, "cannot become government." He wrote letters to the Sophomores exhorting them not to haze the Freshmen, and, as a consequence, the Freshmen were hazed more severely than ever. Then he suspended the Sophomores in a wholesale manner, many of them for slight offences. However, he stopped the foot- ball fights, and made the examinations much more strict than they had been previously. He endeavored to inculcate the true spirit of scholarship among the students,--not to study for rank but from a genuine love of the subject. The opposition that his reforms excited made him unpopular, and Freshmen came to college so prejudiced against him that all his kindness and good will were wasted upon them.

"There goes the greatest man in this country," said a fashionable Boston youth, one day in the spring of 1866. It was Louis Agassiz returning from a call on President Hill. Such a statement shows that the speaker belonged to a class of people called Tories, in 1776, and who might properly be called so still. As a matter of fact, Agassiz had long since passed the meridian of his reputation, and his sun was now not far from setting. He had returned from his expedition to South America with a valuable collection of fishes and other scientific materials; but his theory of glaciers; which he went there to substantiate, had not been proven. Darwin's "Origin of Species" had already swept his nicely- constructed plans of original types into the fire of futile speculation. Yet Agassiz was a great man in his way, and his importance was universally recognized. He had given a vigorous and much-needed impetus to the study of geology in America, and as a compendium of all the different branches of natural history there was nobody like him. In his lifelong single-minded devotion to science he had few equals and no superiors. He cared not for money except so far as it helped the advancement of his studies. For many years Madam Agassiz taught a select school for young ladies (to which Emerson, among others, sent his daughters), in order to provide funds for her husband to carry on his work. It is to be feared that the Commonwealth of Massachusetts was rather stingy to him. Edward Everett once made an eloquent address in his behalf to the legislature, but it had no effect. Louis Napoleon's munificent offers could not induce him to return to Paris, for he believed that more important work was to be done in the new world,-- which, by the way, he considered the oldest portion of the globe.

In height and figure Agassiz was so much like Doctor Hill that when the two were together this was very noticeable. They were both broad- shouldered, deep-chested men, and of about the same height, with large, well-rounded heads; but Agassiz had an elastic French step, whereas Doctor Hill walked with something of a shuffle. One might even imagine Agassiz dancing a waltz. Lowell said of him that he was "emphatically a man, and that wherever he went he made a friend." His broad forehead seemed to smile upon you while he was talking, and from his simple- hearted and genial manners you felt that he would be a friend whenever you wanted one. He was the busiest and at the same time one of the most accessible persons in the university.

On one occasion, happening to meet a number of students at the corner of University Building, one of them was bold enough to say to him: "Prof. Agassiz, would you be so good as to explain to us the difference between the stone of this building and that of Boylston Hall? We know that they are both granite, but they do not look alike." Agassiz was delighted, and entertained them with a brief lecture on primeval rocks and the crust of the earth's surface. He told them that Boylston Hall was made of syenite; that most of the stone called granite in New England was syenite, and if they wanted to see genuine granite they should go to the tops of the White Mountains. Then looking at his watch he said: "Ah, I see I am late! Good day, my friends; and I hope we shall all meet again." So off he went, leaving each of his hearers with the embryonic germ of a scientific interest in his mind.

Longfellow tells in his diary how Agassiz came to him when his health broke down and wept. "I cannot work any longer," he said; and when he could not work he was miserable. The trouble that afflicted him was congestion of the base of the brain, a disorder that is not caused so frequently by overwork as by mental emotion. His cure by Dr. Edward H. Clarke, by the use of bromides and the application of ice, was considered a remarkable one at the time; but five years later the disorder returned again and cost him his life.

He believed that the Laurentian Mountains, north of the St. Lawrence River, was the first land which showed itself above the waste of waters with which the earth was originally surmounted.

Perhaps the most picturesque figure on the college grounds was the old Greek professor, Evangelinus Apostolides Sophocles; a genuine importation from Athens, whom the more imaginative sort of people liked to believe was descended from the Greek poet Sophocles of the Periclean age. He was much too honest himself to give countenance to this rumor, and if you inquired of him concerning it, he would say that he should like very well to believe it, and it was not impossible, although there were no surnames in ancient Greece before the time of Constantine; he had not found any evidence in favor of it. He was a short, thick-set man with a large head and white Medusa-like hair; but such an eye as his was never seen in an Anglo-Saxon face. It reminded you at once of Byron's Corsair, and suggested contingencies such as find no place in quiet, law-abiding New England,--the possibility of sudden and terrible concentration. His clothing had been long since out of fashion, and he always wore a faded cloth cap, such as no student would dare to put on. He lived like a hermit in No. 3 Holworthy, where he prepared his own meals rather than encounter strange faces at a boarding-house table. Once he invited the president of the college to supper; and the president went, not without some misgivings as to what his entertainment might be. He found, however, a simple but well-served repast, including a French roll and a cup of black coffee with the grounds in it. The coffee loosened Sophocles's usually reticent tongue, and after that, as the president himself expressed it, they had a delightful conversation. Everybody respected Sophocles in spite of his eccentric mode of life, and the Freshmen were as much afraid of him as if he had been the Minotaur of Crete.

The reason for his economy did not become apparent until after his death. When he first came to the university he made friends with a gentleman in Cambridge to whom he was much attached, but who, at the time we write of, had long since been dead. It was to support the daughters of his friend, who would have otherwise been obliged to earn their own living, that he saved his money; and in his will he left them a competency of fifty thousand dollars or more.

On one occasion a Freshman was sent to him to receive a private admonition for writing profane language on a settee; but the Freshman denied the accusation. Sophocles's eyes twinkled. "Did you not," said he, "write the letters d-a-m-n?" "No," said the boy, laughing; "it must have been somebody else." Sophocles laughed and said he would report the case back to the college faculty. A few days later he stopped the youth in the college yard and, merely saying "I have had your private admonition revoked," passed on. Professor Sophocles was right. If the Freshman had tried to deceive him he would not have laughed but looked grave.

The morning in April, 1861, after President Lincoln had issued his call for 75,000 troops, a Harvard Senior mentioned it to Sophocles, who said to him: "What can the government accomplish with 75,000 soldiers? It is going to take half a million of men to suppress this rebellion."

He was a good instructor in his way, but dry and methodical. Professor Goodwin's recitations were much more interesting. Sophocles did not credit the tradition of Homer's wandering about blind and poor to recite his two great epics. He believed that Homer was a prince, or even a king, like the psalmist David, and asserted that this could be proved or at least rendered probable by internal evidence. This much is morally certain, that if Homer became blind it must have been after middle life. To describe ancient battle-scenes so vividly he must have taken part in them; and his knowledge of anatomy is very remarkable. He does not make such mistakes in that line as bringing Desdemona to life after she has been smothered.

How can we do justice to such a great-hearted man as Dr. Andrew P. Peabody? He was not intended by nature for a revolutionary character, and in that sense he was unsuited, like Everett, for the time in which he lived. If he had been chosen president of the university after the resignation of Doctor Hill, as George S. Hillard and other prominent graduates desired, the great broadening and liberalizing of the university, which has taken place since, would have been deferred for the next fifteen years. He had little sympathy with the anti-slavery movement, and was decidedly opposed to the religious liberalism of his time; but Doctor Peabody's interest lay in the salvation of human souls, and in this direction he had no equal. He felt a personal regard in every human being with whom he was acquainted, and this seemed more important to him than abstract schemes for the improvement of the race in general. He was a man of peace and wished all others to be at peace; the confusion and irritation that accompanies reform was most disagreeable to him. Many a Harvard student who trembled on the brink of an abyss, far from home and left to his own devices, afterwards looked back to Doctor Peabody's helping hand as to the hand of a beneficent providence held out to save him from destruction; and those whom he was unable to save thought of him no less gratefully.

In the autumn of 1864 a strange sort of student joined the Sophomore class. He soon proved that he was one of the best scholars in it; but to judge from his recitations it was long since he had been to school or received any regular instruction. He lived chiefly on bread and milk, and seemed not to have learned how to take exercise. It is feared that he suffered much from loneliness in that busy hive, where everyone has so many small affairs of his own to attend to. Just before the annual examinations he was seized with brain-fever and died. Doctor Peabody conducted the funeral services at the boarding-house of the unfortunate youth, and the plainness of the surroundings heightened the eloquence of his address. His prayer on that occasion was so much above the average character of his religious discourses that it seemed to come from a secret fountain of the man's nature, which could only be drawn upon for great occasions.

With all his tenderness of feeling Doctor Peabody could be a very vigorous debater. He once carried on a newspaper argument with Rev. Dr. Minor, of Boston, on the temperance question, in which he took the ground that drinking wine and beer did not necessarily lead to intemperance,-- which, rightly considered, indicates a lack of self-control; and he made this point in what his friends, at least, considered a satisfactory and conclusive manner.

It is pleasant to think that such a man should have met with unusual prosper-

ity in his old age--and the person to whom he owed this improvement of his affairs was Nathaniel Thayer, of Boston. Mr. Thayer took charge of Doctor Peabody's
property and trebled or quadrupled it in value. Mr. Thayer was very fond of doing such kindnesses to his friends, especially to clergymen. He liked the society of
clergymen, and certainly in this he showed excellent judgment. During the last ten
years of his life he spent his summers at the Isles of Shoals, and generally with one
or more reverend gentlemen in his company. He was besides a most munificent
patron of the university. He provided the means for Agassiz to go on his expedition
to South America, and in conjunction with Doctor Hill reestablished commons for
the students--a reform, as he once stated, as advantageous to their morals as to their
purses. He afterwards built the dormitory which is known by his name. He was so
kind-hearted, that he was said to have given up banking because he was not hard-
hearted enough for the profession. After his death his family received letters upon
letters from persons of whom they had never heard, but who wished to express
their gratitude for his generosity.

Prof. Benjamin Pierce, the mathematician, was rather an awe-inspiring figure
as he strolled through the college grounds, recognizing few and speaking to none-
-apparently oblivious to everything except the internal life which he led in the
"functions of curves" and "celestial mechanics." He was a fine-looking man, with his
ashen-gray hair and beard, his wide brow and features more than usually regular.
When he was observed conversing with President Hill the fine scholars shook their
heads wisely as if something remarkable was taking place. The president had said
in one of his addresses to the Freshmen that it would require a whole generation to
utilize Professor Pierce's discoveries in algebra; and I believe, at last accounts, they
have not been utilized yet. He would often be seen in the horse-cars making figures
on scraps of paper, which he carried with him for the purpose, oblivious as ever to
what was taking place about him. To "have a head like old Benny Pierce" has become a proverb in Boston and Cambridge.

Neither did he lack independence of character. In his later years he not unfre-
quently attended the meetings of the Radical Club, or Chestnut Street Club, at Mrs.
John T. Sargent's, in Boston, a place looked upon with pious horror by good Doctor
Peabody, and equally discredited by the young positivists whom President Eliot had
introduced in the college faculty. His remarks on such occasions were fresh, origi-

nal, and very interesting; and once he brought down the house with laughter and applause by explaining the mental process which prevented him from appreciating a joke until after all others had done so. This naive confession made his audience like him.

It is a curious geneological fact that Professor Pierce had a son named after him who would seem to have been born in mirth, to have lived in comedy, and died in a jest. He was a college Yorick who produced roars of laughter in the Dicky and Hasty Pudding clubs. Another son, called affectionately by the students "Jimmy Mills," was also noted for his wit, and much respected as an admirable instructor.

Doctor Holmes says, in Parson Turell's Legacy:

"Know old Cambridge? Hope you do,--
Born there? Don't say so! I was too.
Born in a house with a gambrel-roof,--
Standing still, if you must have proof.--

    *   *   *   *   *

--Nicest place that ever was seen,--
Colleges red and Common green,
Sidewalks brownish with trees between."

This describes Cambridge as it was forty years since. In spite of its timid conservatism and rather donnish society, as Professor Child termed it, it was one of the pleasantest places to live in on this side the Atlantic. It was a community of a refined and elegant industry, in which every one had a definite work to do, and seemed to be exactly fitted to his or her place,--not without some great figures, too, to give it exceptional interest. There was peace and repose under the academic shade, and the obliviousness of its inhabitants to the outside world only rendered this more restful.

How changed is it now! The old Holmes house has been long since pulled down to make way for the new Law-School building. Red-gravel paths have been replaced by brick sidewalks; huge buildings rise before the eye; electric cars whiz in every direction; a tall, bristling iron fence surrounds the college yard; and an enormous clock on the tower of Memorial Hall detonates the hours in a manner which is by no means conducive to the sleep of the just and the rest of the weary. The elderly graduate, returning to the dreamland of his youth, finds that it has actually become a dreamland and still exists only in his imagination.

The university has broadened and extended itself wonderfully under the present management, but the simple classic charm of the olden time is gone forever.

FRANCIS J. CHILD

Fifty years ago it was the fashion at Harvard, as well as at other colleges, for professors to cultivate an austere dignity of manner for the purpose of preserving order and decorum in the recitation-room; but this frequently resulted in having the opposite effect and served as a temptation to the students to play practical jokes on their instructors. The habitual dryness of the college exercises in Latin, Greek, and mathematics became still more wearisome from the manner in which these were conducted. The youthful mind thirsting for knowledge found the road to it for the most part a dull and dreary pilgrimage.

Professor Francis J. Child would seem to have been the first to break down this barrier and establish more friendly relations with his classes. He was naturally well adapted to this. Perfectly frank and fearless in his dealings with all men, he hated unnecessary conventionality, and at the same time possessed the rare art of preserving his dignity while associating with his subordinates on friendly terms. Always kindly and even sympathetic to the worst scapegraces in the division, he could assert the superiority of his position with a quickness that often startled those who were inclined to impose on him. He did not call out the names of his class as if they were exceptions to a rule in Latin grammar, but addressed each one of them as if he felt a personal interest in the man; so that they felt encouraged to speak out what they knew and even remembered their lessons so much the better. As a consequence he was universally respected, and there were many who felt an affection for him such as he could never have imagined. His cordial manner was sufficient of itself to make his instruction effective.

Francis J. Child was the first scholar in his class at the Boston Latin School, and afterwards at Harvard. That first scholars do not come to much good in the world is an illusion of the envious. It is true that they sometimes break down their health by too strenuous an effort, but this may happen to an ambitious person in any undertaking. In Professor Child's case, as in many another, it proved the making of his fortune, for which he did not possess any exceptional advantages. Being of an amiable disposition and good address, he was offered a tutorship on graduation, and rose from one position in the university to another until he became the first authority on the English language in America. His whole life was spent at Harvard College, with the exception of a few short expeditions to Europe; and his influence there steadily increased until it became a power that was universally recognized.

He was a short, thick-set man, like Sophocles, but as different as possible in general aspect. Sophocles was always slow and measured, but Professor Child was quick and lively in all his movements; and his face wore an habitual cheerfulness which plainly showed the sunny spirit within. Most characteristic in his appearance was the short curly yellow hair, so light in color that when it changed with age, his friends scarcely noticed the difference.

During his academic years he created a sensation by declining to join the Hasty Pudding Club. This was looked upon as a piece of inordinate self- conceit; whereas, the true reason for it was that he had little money and preferred to spend it in going to the theatre. He said afterwards, in regard to this, that he was not sorry to have done it, for "the students placed too much importance on such matters."

Through his interest in fine acting, he became one of the best judges of oratory, and it was always interesting to listen to him on that subject. He considered Wendell Phillips the perfection of form and delivery, and sometimes very brilliant, but much too rash in his statements. Everett was also good, but lacked warmth and earnestness. Choate was purely a legal pleader, and outside of the court-room not very effective. He thought Webster one of the greatest of orators, fully equal to Cicero; but they both lacked the poetical element. Sumner's sentences were florid and his delivery rather mechanical, but he made a strong impression owing to the evident purity of his motives. The general public, however, had become suspicious of oratory, so that it was no longer as serviceable as formerly.

"After all," he would say, "the main point for a speaker is to have a good cause. Then, if he is thoroughly in earnest, we enjoy hearing him." He once illustrated his subject by the story of a Union general who tried to rally the fugitives at Pittsburg Landing, and said, waving his sword in the air: "In the name of the Declaration of Independence, I command, I exhort you," etc., while a private soldier leaning against a tree, with a quid of tobacco in his mouth, remarked, "That man can make a good speech," but showed no intentions of moving. This summary, however, gives no adequate idea of the brightness of Professor Child's conversation. He was an animated talker, full of wit and originality.

When the classes at Harvard were smaller than at present, he would arrange them in University Hall for declamation, so as to cover as much space as possible. They did not understand this until he said, "Now we have a larger audience, if not more numerous;" and this placed every one in the best of humor.

Besides his regular college duties, Professor Child had three distinct interests to which he devoted himself in leisure hours with all the energy of an ardent nature. The first of these, editing a complete edition of the old English ballads, was the labor of his life, and with it his name will always be associated, for it is a work that can neither be superseded nor excelled. He was the first to arouse English scholars to the importance of this, as may be read in the dedication of a partial edition taken from the Percy manuscripts and published in London in 1861. He recognized in them the true foundation of the finest literature of the modern world, and he considered them so much the better from the fact that they were not composed to be printed, but to be recited or sung. Matthew Arnold wrote in a letter from America: "After lecturing at Taunton, I came to Boston with Professor Child of Harvard, a very pleasant man, who is a great authority on ballad poetry," very warm praise, considering the source whence it came. Late in life Professor Child edited separate versions in modern English of some curious old ballads, and sent them as Christmas presents to his friends. It is not surprising that he should have been interested as well in the rude songs of the British sailors, which he heard on crossing the ocean. He was mightily amused at their simple refrain:

"Haul in the bowlin', long-tailed bowlin',   Haul in the bowlin' Kitty, O, my darlin'."

"That rude couplet," he said, "contains all the original elements of poetry. Firstly, the anthropomorphic element; the sailor imagines his bowline as if it had life. Secondly, the humorous element, for the bowline is all tail. Thirdly, the reflective element; the monotonous motion makes him think of home,--of his wife or sweetheart,--and he ends the second line with 'Kitty, O, my darlin'.' I like such primitive verses much better than the 'Pike County Ballads,' a mixture of sentiment and profanity."

Then he went on to say: "I want my children, when they grow up, to read the classics. My boy will go to college, of course; and he will translate Homer and Virgil, and Horace,--I think very highly of Horace; but the literal meaning is a different thing from understanding the poetry. Then my daughters will learn French and German, and I shall expect them to read Schiller and Goethe, Moliere and Racine, as well as Shakespeare and Milton. After that they can read what they like, but they will have a standard by which to judge other authors." He was afraid that the students wasted too much time in painting play-bills and other similar exercises of ingenuity, which lead to nothing in the end.

He gave some excellent advice to a young lady who was about visiting Europe for the first time, who doubted if she could properly appreciate the works of art and other fine things that she would be called upon to admire. "Don't be afraid of that," said Professor Child; "you will probably like best just those sights which you do not expect to; but if you do not like them, say so, and let that be the end of it. Now, I am so unfortunate as not to appreciate Michel Angelo. His great horned Moses is nothing more to me than a Silenus in a garden. The fact does not trouble me much, for I find enough to interest me as it is, and I can enjoy life without the Moses."

After mentioning a number of desirable expeditions, he added: "You will go to Dresden, of course, to see Raphael's Madonna and Titian's 'Tribute Money'; and then there are the Green Vaults. I have known the Green Vaults to have an excellent effect on some ladies of my acquaintance. They did not care one-quarter as much for a diamond ring as they did before they went into the Green Vaults. You will see a jewelled fireplace there which is worth more than all I own in the world." The young lady looked, however, as if it would take more than the Green Vaults to cure her love for jewelry.

*   *   *   *   *

Professor Child's second important interest was politics, and as a rule he much preferred talking on this to literary subjects.

Josiah Quincy was the most distinguished president that Harvard College has had, unless we except President Eliot; and his admirers have been accustomed to refer to his administration as "Consule Planco." His politics did not differ widely from those of John Quincy Adams, who was the earliest statesman of the anti-slavery struggle, and a true hero in his way. After Quincy, the presidents of the university became more and more conservative, until Felton, who was a pronounced pro-slavery Whig, and even attempted to defend the invasion of Kansas in a public meeting. The professors and tutors naturally followed in the train of the president, while a majority of the sons of wealthy men among the undergraduates always took the southern side. The son of an abolitionist who wished to go through Harvard in those days found it a penitential pilgrimage. He was certain to suffer an extra amount of hazing, and to endure a kind of social ostracism throughout the course.

For many years before the election of Lincoln, Professors Child, Lowell, and Jennison were the only pronounced anti-slavery members of the faculty; and this left Francis J. Child to hear the brunt of it almost alone, for Lowell's connection with the university was semi-detached, and although he was always prepared to face the enemy in an honest argument, he was not often on the ground to do so.

Now that the most potent cause of political agitation resides in the far-off problem of the Philippine Islands it is difficult to realize the popular excitement of those times, when both parties believed that the very existence of the nation depended on the result of the elections. Professor Child was not the least of an alarmist, and deprecated all unnecessary controversy. In 1861 he even cautioned Wendell Phillips Garrison against introducing too strong an appeal for emancipation in his commencement address; but he was as firm as a granite rock on any question of principle, and when he considered a protest in order he was certain to make one. He did not trust party newspapers for his information, but obtained it from persons who were in a position to know, and his facts were so well supported by the quick sallies of his wit that those who interfered with him once rarely attempted it again. Moreover, as we all see now, he had the right on his side.

He was proud of having voted twice for Abraham Lincoln. What he thought of John Brown, at the time of the Harper's Ferry raid, is uncertain; but many years later, when one of his friends published a small book in vindication of Brown against the attack of Lincoln's two secretaries, he wrote to him:

"I congratulate you on the success of your statement, which I have read with very great interest. John Brown was like a star and still shines in the firmament. We could not have done without him."

He considered Governor Andrew's approbation of John Brown as more important than anything that would be written about him in the future.

He did not trouble himself much in regard to Lincoln's second election, for he saw that it was a foregone conclusion; but after Andrew Johnson's treachery in 1866, he felt there was a need of unusual exertion. When the November elections arrived, he told his classes: "Next Tuesday I shall have to serve my country and there will be no recitations." When Tuesday came we found him on the sidewalk distributing Republican ballots and soliciting votes; and there he remained until the polls closed in the afternoon. He had little patience with educated men who neglected their political duties. "Why are you discouraged?" he would ask. "Times will change. Remember the Free-soil movement!" He attended caucuses as regularly as the meetings of the faculty, and served as a delegate to a number of conventions. More than once he aroused the good citizens of Cambridge to the danger of insidious plots by low demagogues against the public welfare. The poet Longfellow took notice of this and spoke of him as an invaluable man.

On another occasion Professor Child was discoursing to his class on oratory and mentioned the fact that Webster and Choate both came from Dartmouth; that Wendell Phillips graduated at Harvard, but the university had not seen much of him since. At the mention of Wendell Phillips some of the boys from pro-slavery families began to sneer. Professor Child raised himself up and said determinedly, "Wendell Phillips is as good an orator as either of them!" He was chagrined, however, at Phillips's later public course,--his support of Socialism and General Butler. Neither did he like Phillips's Phi Beta Kappa oration, in which he advocated the dagger and dynamite for tyrants. "A tyrant," said Professor Child, "is what anyone chooses to imagine. My hired man may consider me a tyrant and blow me up according to Mr. Phillips's principle." The assassins of Garfield and McKinley evidently supposed that they were ridding the earth of two of the worst tyrants that ever existed. Professor Child was exceptionally liberal. He even supported Woman Suffrage for a time, but he held Socialism in a kind of holy horror,--such as one feels of a person who is always making blunders.

In 1878 Professor Child and some other political reformers were elected to a Congressional convention and went with the hope of securing a candidate who would represent the educated classes,--the incumbent at that time being a shoe manufacturer. They argued and worked hard all day, but without success. Late in the afternoon the shoe manufacturer, a worthy man but very ignorant, who afterwards became governor of the State, was renominated; and when it was proposed to make the nomination unanimous Professor Child called out such an emphatic No that it seemed to shake the whole assembly. Not content with this he entered a protest next day in the Boston *Advertiser*. He was so much used up by the exertion that he was unable to attend to his classes. Some years later he enjoyed the satisfaction of seeing his candidate, Theodore Lyman, nominated and elected.

Emerson once delivered a lecture in Boston on university life in which he made the rather bold statement that "in the course of twenty years the rank-list is likely to become inverted." One of Professor Child's class paraphrased this lecture for a theme, and against the sentence above quoted the Professor wrote: "A statement frequently made, but what is the fact?" I do not think he liked Emerson quite so well after this, and he can hardly be blamed for feeling so. It was not only a disparagement of good scholarship but like a personal slight upon himself. That Emerson graduated near the foot of his class ought not to prove that an idle college life is a sign of genius.

Professor Child talked freely in regard to the meetings of the college faculty, for he believed that graduates had a right to know about them. He quoted some amusing anecdotes of a certain professor who led the opposition against President Eliot and praised the dignified manner with which Eliot regarded him. In 1879 he said one day:

"We are in the half-way stage between a college and a university, and there is consequently great confusion. If we once became a university, pure and simple, all that would be over; but the difficulty is that the material which comes to us is so poor. I do not mean that the young men are lacking in intelligence, but the great majority of them do not brace themselves to the work. As Doctor Hedge says, the heart of the college is in the boating and ball-playing and not in its studies."

His third occupation and chief recreation was his rose-garden. The whole space between his front piazza and Kirkland Street was filled with rose- bushes which he tended himself, from the first loosening of the earth in spring until the straw sheaf-caps were tied about them in November. What more delightful occupation for a scholar than working in a rose-garden! There his friends were most likely to find him in suitable weather, and when June came they were sure to receive a share of the bountiful blossoms; nor did he ever forget the sick and suffering.

He was greatly interested to hear of a German doctor at Munich who had a rose-garden with more than a hundred varieties in it. "I should like to know that man," he said; "wouldn't we have a good talk together?" He complained that although everybody liked roses few were sufficiently interested in them to distinguish the different kinds. Naturally rose- bugs were his special detestation. "Saving your presence," he said to President Felton's daughter, "I will crush this insect;" to which she aptly replied, "I certainly would not have my presence save him." When he heard of the Buffalo-bug he exclaimed: "Are we going to have another pest to contend with? I think it is a serious question whether the insect world is not going to get the better of us."

After his painful death at the Massachusetts Hospital in September, 1896, the president and fellows of the university voted to set apart little Holden Chapel, the oldest building on the college grounds, and yet one of the most dignified, for an English library dedicated to the memory of Francis J. Child. Such an honor had never been decreed for president or professor before; and it gives him the distinction that we all feel he deserved. It is much more appropriate to him, and satisfactory than a marble statue in Saunders Theatre would have been, or a stained-glass window in Memorial Hall. Yet his presence still lingers in the memory of his friends, like the fragrance of his own roses, after the petals have fallen from their stems.

LONGFELLOW

It has been estimated that there were four hundred poets in England in the time of Shakespeare, and in the century during which Dante lived Europe fairly swarmed with poets, many of them of high excellence. Frederick II. of Germany and Richard I. of England were both good poets, and were as proud of their verses as they were of their military exploits. Frederick II. may be said to have founded the vernacular in which Dante wrote; and Longfellow rendered into English a poem of Richard's which he composed during his cruel imprisonment in Austria. A knight who could not compose a song and sing it to the guitar was as rare as a modern gentleman of fashion who cannot play golf. When James Russell Lowell resigned the chair of poetry at Harvard no one could be found who could exactly fill his place, and it was much the same at Oxford after Matthew Arnold retired.

The difference between then and now would seem to reside in the fact, that poetry is more easily remembered than prose. From the time of Homer until long after the invention of printing, not only were ballad-singers and harpers in good demand, but the recital of poetry was also a favorite means of livelihood to indigent scholars and others, who wandered about like the minstrels. The "article," as Tom Moore called it, was in active request. Poetry was recited in the camp of Alexander, in the Roman baths, in the castles on the Rhine, and English hostelries. Now it is replaced by novel-reading, and there are few who know how much pleasure can be derived on a winter's evening by impromptu poetic recitations. If a popular interest in poetry should revive again, I have no doubt that hundreds of poets would spring up, as it were, out of the ground and fill the air with their pleasant harmonies. The editor of the *Atlantic* informed Professor Child that he had a whole barrelful of poetry in his house, much of it excellent, but that there was no use he could make of it.

Henry Wadsworth Longfellow was as irrepressible a rhymer as John Watts himself, and fortunately he had a father who recognized the value of his talent and assisted him in a judicious manner, instead of placing obstacles in his way, as the father of Watts is supposed to have done. The account that Rev. Samuel Longfellow has given us of the youth of his brother is highly instructive, and ought to be of service to all young men who fancy they are destined by nature for a poetic career. He tells us how Henry published his first poem in the Portland *Gazette*, and how his boyish exultation was dashed with cold water the same evening by Judge ----, who said of it in his presence: "Stiff, remarkably stiff, and all the figures are borrowed."

The "Fight at Lovell's Pond" would not have been a remarkable poem for a youth of nineteen, but it showed very good promise for the age at which it was written. Few boys at that age can write anything that will hang together as a poem. Young Longfellow was a better poet at thirteen than his father's friend, the Judge, was a critic. His verses were by no means stiff, but on the contrary showed indications of that natural grace and facility of expression for which he became afterwards distinguished. As for the originality of his comparisons it is doubtful also if the Judge could have proved his point on that question. They were original to Henry, if to nobody else.

Fortunately for Henry he was also a fine scholar. The following year saw him enter as a Freshman at Bowdoin College, which was equal to entering Harvard at the age of fifteen. Look out for the youngest members of a college class! They may not distinguish themselves at the university, but they are the ones who, if they live, outstrip all others. But Longfellow did distinguish himself. In his Junior year he composed seventeen poems which were published, then and afterwards, in the *United States Literary Gazette*, where his name appeared beside that of William Cullen Bryant. This was quite exceptional in the history of American literature, and as the editor of the *Literary Gazette* stated it: "A young tree which puts forth so many blossoms is likely to bear good fruits."

With the close of his college course came the important question of Longfellow's future occupation. His father, with good practical judgment, foresaw that poetry alone would not serve to make his son self-supporting and independent; but the boy hated to give this up for a more prosaic employment. While the discussion was going on between them, the authorities of Bowdoin solved the problem for them both by offering young Longfellow a professorship of modern languages on condition that he would spend two years in Europe preparing himself for the position. He had graduated fourth in his class.

Does not this prove the advantage of good scholarship? Was the rank list inverted in Longfellow's case? I think not. He had lived a virtuous and industrious life, not studying for rank or honor, but because he enjoyed doing what was right and fit for a young man to do; and now the reward had come to him, like the sun breaking through the clouds which seemed to obscure his future prospects. Still, there was a hard road before him. It is very pleasant to travel rapidly through foreign countries, seeing the best that is in them and to return home with a multitude of fresh impressions; but living and working a long time in another country seems too much like exile. The loneliness of the situation becomes a weary burden, and it is dangerous from its very loneliness. Many have died or lost their health under such conditions (in fact Longfellow came near losing his life from Roman fever), and he wrote from Paris: "Here one can keep evil at a distance as well as elsewhere, though, to be sure, temptations are multiplied a thousand-fold if he is willing to enter into them." A young man's first experience in London or Paris is a dangerous sense of freedom; for all the customary restraints of his daily life have been removed.

Mrs. Stowe says of her beautiful character, "Eva St. Clair," that all bad influences rolled off from her like dew from a cabbage leaf, and it was the same with Longfellow throughout. He lived in France, Spain, Italy, and Germany, and then returned to Portland, the same true American as when he left there, without foreign ways or modes of thinking, and with no more than the slight aroma of a foreign air upon him. Longfellow and his whole family were natural cosmopolitans. There was nothing of the proverbial Yankee in their composition.

Whittier was a Quaker by creed, but he was also much of a Yankee in style and manner. Emerson looked like a Yankee, and possessed the cool Yankee shrewdness. Lowell's "Biglow Papers" testified to the fundamental Yankee; but the Longfellows were endowed with a peculiar refinement and purity which seemed to distinguish them as much in Cambridge or London as it did in Portland, where there has always been a rather superior sort of society. It was like French refinement without being Gallic. No wonder that a famous poet should emanate from such a family.

What we notice especially in the Longfellow Letters during this European sojourn is the admonition of Henry's father, that German literature was more important than Italian,--and the poet was always largely influenced by this afterwards; that Henry did not find Paris particularly attractive, and on the whole preferred the Spanish character to the French on account of its deeper under-currents; that he did not seem to realize the danger that menaced him from Spanish brigands, in spite of the black crosses by the roadside; and that he was not vividly impressed by the famous works of art in the Louvre gallery. He only notices that one of Correggio's figures resembles a young lady in Portland.

Longfellow would seem to have been always the same in regard to his appreciation of art. When he was in Italy, in 1869, he visited all the picture galleries and evidently enjoyed doing so; but it was easy to see that his brother, Rev. Samuel Longfellow, felt a much livelier interest in the subject than he did; and injured frescos or mutilated statues, like the Torso of the Belvidere, were objects of aversion to him. Poets and musical composers see more with their ears than they do with their eyes.

The single work of art that attracted him strongly at this time was a statue of Venus, by Canova, which he compares to the Venus de' Medici, and his brother Samuel remarks that he was always more attracted by sculpture than painting. Canova was a genius very similar to Longfellow himself, as nearly as an Italian could be made to match an American, and he was then at the height of his reputation.

In 1829 Longfellow returned to Portland and was immediately chosen a professor at Bowdoin College, where he remained for the next seven years. When, in 1836, Professor Ticknor retired from his position as instructor of modern languages at Harvard, his place was offered to Longfellow and accepted. This brought him into the literary centre of New England, and one of the first acquaintances he made there was Charles Sumner, who was lecturing before the Harvard Law-School.

The friendship between these two great men commenced at once and only ceased at Sumner's death in 1874, when Longfellow wrote one of the finest of his shorter poems in tribute to Sumner's memory. It was as poetic a friendship as that between Emerson and Carlyle; but whereas Emerson and Carlyle had differences of opinion, Sumner and Longfellow were always of one mind. When Sumner made his Fanueil Hall speech against the fugitive slave law, which was simply fighting revolution with revolution, and Harvard College and the whole of Cambridge turned against him, Longfellow stood firm; and it may be suspected that he had many an unpleasant discussion with his aristocratic acquaintances on this point. It was considered bad enough to support Garrison, but supporting Sumner was a great deal worse, for Sumner was an orator who wielded a power only inferior to Webster. Fortunately for Longfellow, his connection with the university ceased not long after Sumner's election to the Senate; and the unpleasantness of his position may have been the leading cause of his retirement.

Sumner was the best friend Longfellow had, and perhaps the best that he could have had. There was Emerson, of course, and Longfellow was always on friendly terms with him; but Emerson had a habit of catechising his companions which some of them did not altogether like; and this may have been the case with Longfellow, for they never became very intimate. Sumner, on the contrary, had always a large stock of information to dispense, not only concerning American affairs but those of other nations, in which Longfellow never lost his interest. More important to him even than this is the fact that Sumner's statements were always to be trusted. It may be surmised that it was not so much similarity of opinion as the purity of their motives that brought the poet and statesman together.

As soon as Sumner returned from Washington, in spring or summer, he would go out to call on Longfellow; and it was a pleasant sight to see them walking together on a June evening beneath the overarching elms of historic Brattle Street. They were a pair of majestic-looking men; and though Longfellow was nearly a head shorter than Sumner, his broad shoulders gave him an appearance of strength, as his capacious head and strong, finely cut features evidently denoted an exceptional intellect. He wore his hair poetically long, almost to his coat collar; and yet there was not the slightest air of the Bohemian about him. They seemed to be oblivious of everything except their conversation; and if this could have been recorded it might prove to be as interesting as the poetry of the one and the orations of the other. They were evidently talking on great subjects, and the earnestness on Sumner's face was reflected on Longfellow's as in a mirror.

Hawthorne was a classmate of Longfellow, and in the biography of the latter there are a number of letters from one to the other which are always friendly,--but never more than that on Hawthorne's side,--with one exception, where he thanks Longfellow for a complimentary review of "Twice-Told Tales" in the *North*

American. At that time the *North American* was considered an authority which could make or unmake an author's reputation; and Longfellow may be said to have opened the door for Hawthorne into the great world. Hawthorne's friendship for President Pierce proved an advantage to him financially, but it also became a barrier between him and the other literary men of his time. Of course he believed what his friend Pierce told him concerning public affairs, and when he found that his other friends had not the same faith in Pierce's veracity he became more strongly a partisan of the pro- slavery cause on that account. Longfellow frankly admitted that he did not understand Hawthorne, and he did not believe that anyone at Bowdoin College understood him. He was the most secretive man that he ever knew; but so far as genius was concerned, he believed that Hawthorne would outlive every other writer of his time. He had the will of a great conqueror.

Goethe has been called the pampered child of genius, of fortune, and the muse; but if Goethe had greater celebrity he never enjoyed half the worldly prosperity of Longfellow. While Emerson was earning a hard livelihood by lecturing in the West, and Whittier was dwelling in a country farm-house, Longfellow occupied one of the most desirable residences in or about Boston, and had all the means at his command that a modest man could wish for. The Craigie House was, and still remains, the finest residence in Cambridge,--"formerly the head-quarters of Washington, and afterwards of the Muses." Good architecture never becomes antiquated, and the Craigie House is not only spacious within, but dignified without.

One could best realize Longfellow's opulence by walking through his library adjacent to the eastern piazza, and gazing at the magnificent editions of foreign authors which had been presented to him by his friends and admirers; especially the fine set of Chateaubriand's works, in all respects worthy of a royal collection. There is no ornament in a house that testifies to the quality of the owner like a handsome library.

Byron would seem to have been the only other poet that has enjoyed such prosperity, although Bryant, as editor of a popular newspaper, may have approached it closely; but a city house, with windows on only two sides, is not like a handsome suburban residence. Longfellow could look across the Cambridge marshes and see the sunsets reflected in the water of the Charles River.

Here he lived from 1843, when he married Miss Appleton, a daughter of one of the wealthiest merchant-bankers of Boston, until his death by pneumonia in March, 1882. The situation seemed suited to him, and he always remained a true poet and devoted to the muses:

Integer vitae scelerisque purus.

He did not believe in a luxurious life except so far as luxury added to refinement, and everything in the way of fashionable show was very distasteful to him. His brother Samuel once said, "I cannot imagine anything more disagreeable than to ride in a public procession;" and the two men were more alike than brothers often are. We notice in the poet's diary that he abstains from going to a certain dinner in Boston for fear of being called upon to make a speech. Craigie House gave Longfellow the opportunity in which he most delighted,--of entertaining his friends and distinguished foreign guests in a handsome manner; but conventional dinner parties, with their fourteen plates half surrounded by wine- glasses, were not often seen there. He much preferred a smaller number of guests with the larger freedom of discourse which accompanies a select gathering. Many such occasions are referred to in his diary,--as if he did not wish to forget them.

He was the finest host and story-teller in the country. His genial courtesy was simply another expression of that mental grace which made his reputation as a poet, and his manner of reciting an incident, otherwise trivial, would give it the same additional quality as in his verses on Springfield Arsenal and the crooked Songo River, which without Longfellow would be little or nothing. Then his fund of information was what might be expected from a man who had lived in all the countries of western Europe.

He had humble and unfortunate friends whom he seemed to think as much of as though they were distinguished. He recognized fine traits of character, perhaps real greatness of character, in out-of-the-way places,--men whose chief happiness was their acquaintance with Longfellow. It was something much better than charity; and Professor Child spoke of it on the day of Emerson's funeral as the finest flower in the poet's wreath.

Longfellow was one of the kindest friends that the Hungarian exiles found when they came to Boston in 1852. Longfellow helped Kossuth, subscribed to Kalapka's riding-school, and entertained a number of them at his house. Afterwards, when one of the exiles set up a business in Hungarian wines, Longfellow made a large purchase of him, which he spoke of twenty years later with much satisfaction. He liked Tokay, and also the white wine of Capri, which he regretted could not be obtained in America.

Those who supposed that Longfellow was easily imposed upon made a great mistake. He had the reputation among his publishers of understanding business affairs better than any author in New England; but he was almost too kind-hearted. Somewhere about 1859 a photographer made an excellent picture of his daughters--indeed, it was a charming group--and the man begged Mr. Longfellow for permission to sell copies of it as it would be of great advantage to him. Longfellow complied and the consequence was that in 1860 one could hardly open a photograph album anywhere without finding Longfellow's daughters in it. Then a vulgar story originated that the youngest daughter had only one arm, because her left arm was hidden behind her sister. It is to be hoped that Longfellow never heard of this, for if he did it must have caused him a good deal of pain, in return for his kindness; but that is what one gets. Fortunately the photographs have long since faded out.

Much in the same line was his interest in the children of the poor. A ragged urchin seemed to attract him much more than one that was nicely dressed. Perhaps they seemed more poetic to him, and he could see more deeply into the joys and sorrows of their lives.

Where the Episcopal Theological School now stands on Brattle Street there was formerly a sort of tenement-house; and one day, as we were taking a stroll before dinner, we noticed three small boys with dirty faces standing at the corner of the building; and just then one of them cried out: "Oh, see; here he comes!" And immediately Longfellow appeared leaving the gate of Craigie House. We passed him before he reached the children, but on looking back we saw that he had stopped to speak with them. They evidently knew him very well.

It is remarkable how the impression should have been circulated that Longfellow was not much of a pedestrian. On the contrary, there was no one who was seen more frequently on the streets of Cambridge. He walked with a springy step and a very slight swing of the shoulders, which showed that he enjoyed it. He may not have walked such long distances as Hawthorne, or so rapidly as Dickens, but he was a good walker.

His sister, Mrs. Greenleaf, built a memorial chapel in North Cambridge for the Episcopal society there, and from this Longfellow formed the habit of walking in that direction by way of the Botanic Garden. Somewhere in the cross streets he became acquainted with two children, the son and daughter of a small shop-keeper. They, of course, told their mother about their white-haired acquaintance, and with the fate of Charlie Ross before her eyes, their mother warned them to keep out of his way. He might be a tramp, and tramps were dangerous!

However, it was not long before the children met their white-haired friend again, and the boy asked him: "Are you a tramp? Mother thinks you're a tramp, and she wants to know what your name is." It may be presumed that Mr. Longfellow laughed heartily at this misconception, but he said: "I think I may call myself a tramp. I tramp a good deal; but you may tell your mother that my name is Henry W. Longfellow." He afterwards called on the mother in order to explain himself, and to congratulate her on having such fine children.

When the Saturday Club, popularly known as the Atlantic Club, was organized, one of the first subjects of discussion that came up was the question of autographs. Emerson said that was the way in which he obtained his postage stamps; but Longfellow confessed that he had given away a large number of them. And so it continued to the end. "Why should I not do it," he would say, "if it gives them pleasure?" Emerson looked on such matters from the stoical point of view as an encouragement to vanity; but he would have been more politic to have gratified his curious, or sentimental admirers; for every autograph he gave would have made a purchaser for his publishers.

Harmony did not always prevail in the Saturday Club, for politics was the all-embracing subject in those days and its members represented every shade of political opinion. Emerson, Longfellow, and Lowell were strongly anti-slavery, but they differed in regard to methods. Lowell was what was then called a Seward man, and differed with Emerson in regard to John Brown, and with Longfellow in regard to Sumner. Holmes was still more conservative; and Agassiz was a McClellan Democrat. William Hunt, the painter, believed that the war was caused by the ambition of the leading politicians in the North and South. Longfellow had the advantage of more direct information than the others, and enjoyed the continued successes of the Republican party.

In the spring of 1866 a number of Southerners came to Boston to borrow funds in order to rehabilitate their plantations, and were introduced at the Union League Club. Finding themselves there in a congenial element they made speeches strongly tinged with secession doctrines. Sumner, of course, could not let this pass without making some protest against it, and for this he was hissed. The incident was everywhere talked of, and came under discussion at the next meeting of the Saturday Club. Otto Dresel, a German pianist, who had small reason for being there, said, "It was not Mr. Sumner's politics but his bad manners that were hissed." Longfellow set his glass down with emphasis, and replied: "If good manners could not say it, thank heaven bad manners did;" and Lowell supported this with some pretty severe criticism of the Union League Club. In justice to the Union League Club, however, it ought to be said that there was applause as well as hisses for Sumner.

Longfellow had a leonine face, but it was that of a very mild lion; one that had never learned the use of teeth and claws. Yet those who knew him felt that he could roar on occasion, if occasion required it. Once at Longfellow's own table the conversation chanced upon Goethe, and a gentleman present remarked that Goethe was in the habit of drinking three bottles of hock a day. "Who said he did?" inquired the poet. "It is in Lewes's biography," said the gentleman. "I do not believe it," replied Longfellow, "unless," he added with a laugh, "they were very small bottles." A few days afterwards Prof. William James remarked in regard to this incident that the story was quite incredible.

In his youth Longfellow seems to have taken to guns and fishing-rods more regularly than some boys do, but pity for his small victims soon induced him to relinquish the sport. His eldest son, Charles, also took to guns very naturally, and in spite of a severe wound which he received from the explosion of a badly loaded piece, he finally became one of the most expert pigeon-shooters in the State. At the intercession of his father, who considered the game too cruel, he afterwards relinquished this for target-shooting, in which he succeeded equally well. I was talking one day with him on this subject and remarked that I had recently shot two crows with my rifle. "What did you do it for?" interposed his father, in a deprecatory tone. So I explained to him that crows were outside of the pale of the law; that they not only were a pest to the farmers but destroyed the eggs and young of singing birds,--

in fact, they were bold, black robbers, whose livery betokened their evil deeds. This evidently interested him, and he finally said with a laugh: "If that is the case, we will give you and Charlie a commission to exterminate them."

There was a story that when young Nicholas Longworth came to Harvard College in the autumn of 1862 and called on Mr. Longfellow, who had been entertained at his father's house in Cincinnati, the poet said to him: "It is ***worth*** that makes the man; the want of it the ***fellow***" --a compliment that almost dumfounded his young acquaintance. It is certain that Longfellow addressed a poem to Mrs. Longworth which will be found in the collection of his minor poems, and in which he speaks of her as--

"The Queen of the West in her garden dressed,
By the banks of the beautiful river."

In the midst of this unrivalled prosperity, this distinction of genius, and public and private honor, on the ninth of July, 1861, there came one of the most harrowing tragedies that has ever befallen a man's domestic life. Longfellow was widowed for the second time, and five children were left without a mother. It seemed as if Providence had set a limit beyond which human happiness could not pass. It was after this calamity that Longfellow undertook his metrical translation of Dante's "Divina Commedia," a much more difficult and laborious work than writing original poetry. As his brother said, "He required an absorbing occupation to prevent him from thinking of the past."

No wonder that in later years he said, in his exquisite verses on the Mountain of the Holy Cross in Colorado, these pathetic words, "On my heart also there is a cross of snow." In Longfellow's diary we meet with the names of many books that he read, and these as well as the pertinent comments on them tell much more of his intellectual life than we derive from his letters. "Adam Bede," which took the world by storm, did not make so much of an impression on him as Hawthorne's "Marble Faun," which he read through in a day and calls a wonderful book. Of "Adam Bede" he says: "It is too feminine for a man; too masculine for a woman." He says of Dickens, after reading "Barnaby Rudge": "He is always prodigal and ample, but what a set of vagabonds he contrives to introduce us to!" "Barnaby Rudge" is certainly the most bohemian and esoteric of Dickens's novels. He liked much better Miss Mu-loch's "John Halifax,"--a popular book in its time, but not read very much since. He calls Charles Reade a clever and amusing writer. We find nothing concerning Dis-raeli, Trollope, or Wilkie Collins. Neither do we hear of critical and historical writ-ers like Ruskin, Matthew Arnold, Carlyle, and Froude. He went, however, to call on Carlyle in England, and was greatly impressed by his conversation. The scope of Longfellow's reading does not compare with that of Emerson or Marian Evans; but the doctors say that "every man of forty knows the food that is good for him," and this is true mentally as well as physically.

He refers more frequently to Tennyson than to any other writer, and always in a generous, cordial manner. Of the "Idyls of the King" he says that the first and third Idyls could only have come from a great poet, but that the second and fourth are not quite equal to the others.

Once, at his sister's house, he held out a book in his hand and said: "Here is some of the finest dramatic poetry that I have ever read." It was Tennyson's "Queen Mary;" but there were many who would not have agreed with his estimate of it. Rev. Samuel Longfellow considered the statement very doubtful.

In the summer of 1868 Longfellow went to Europe with his family to see what Henry James calls "the best of it." Rev. Samuel Longfellow and T. G. Appleton ac-companied the party, which, with the addition of Ernest Longfellow's beautiful bride, made a strong impression wherever they were seen. In fact their tour was like a triumphal procession.

Longfellow was everywhere treated with the distinction of a famous poet; and his fine appearance and dignified bearing increased the reputation which had al-ready preceded him. His meeting with Tennyson was considered as important as the visit of the King of Prussia to Napoleon III., and much less dangerous to the peace of Europe. It was talked of from Edinburgh to Rome.

Longfellow, however, hated lionizing in all its forms, and he avoided ceremo-nious receptions as much as possible. He enjoyed the entertainment of meeting dis-tinguished people, but he evidently preferred to meet them in an unconventional manner, and to have them as much to himself as possible. Princes and savants called on him, but he declined every invitation that might tend to give him publicity.

His facility in the different languages was much marvelled at. While he was in

Florence a delegation from the mountain towns of Tuscany waited upon him and he conversed with them in their own dialect, greatly to their surprise and satisfaction.

From a number of incidents in this journey, related by Rev. Samuel Longfellow, the following has a permanent interest:

When the party came to Verona in May, 1869, they found Ruskin elevated on a ladder, from which he was examining the sculpture on a monument. As soon as he heard that the Longfellow party was below, he came down and greeted them very cordially. He was glad that they had stopped at Verona, which was so interesting and so often overlooked; he wanted them to observe the sculptures on the monument,--the softly-flowing draperies which seemed more as if they had been moulded with hands than cut with a chisel. He then spoke in grievous terms of the recent devastation by the floods in Switzerland, which had also caused much damage in the plains of Lombardy. He thought that reservoirs ought to be constructed on the sides of the mountains, which would stay the force of the torrents, and hold the water until it could be made useful. He wished that the Alpine Club would take an interest in the matter. After enjoying so much in Switzerland it would be only fair for them to do something for the benefit of the country. Mr. Appleton then said: "That is a work for government to do;" to which Ruskin replied: "Governments do nothing but fill their pockets, and issue this,"--taking out a handful of Italian paper currency, which was then much below par.

Everyone has his or her favorite poet or poets, and it is a common practice with young critics to disparage one in order to elevate another. Longfellow was the most popular American poet of his time, but there were others besides Edgar A. Poe who pretended to disdain him. I have met more such critics in Cambridge than in England, Germany, or Italy; and the reason was chiefly a political one. At a distance Longfellow's politics attracted little attention, but in Cambridge they could not help being felt. In 1862 a strong movement emanated from the Harvard Law-School to defeat Sumner and Andrew, and the lines became drawn pretty sharply. As it happened, the prominent conservatives with one or two exceptions all lived to the east and north of the college grounds, while Longfellow, Lowell, Doctor Francis (who baptized Longfellow's children), Prof. Asa Gray, and other liberals lived at the west end; and the local division made the contest more acrimonious. The conservatives afterwards felt the bitterness of defeat, and it was many years before they recovered from this. A resident graduate of Harvard, who was accustomed to converse on such subjects as the metaphysics of Hamilton's quaternions, once said that Longfellow was the paragon of schoolgirls, because he wrote what they would like to so much better than they could. This was contemptible enough; but how can one expect a man who discourses on the metaphysics of Hamilton's quaternions to appreciate Longfellow's art, or any art pure and simple. "Evangeline," which is perhaps the finest of Longfellow's poems, is not a favorite with youthful readers.

He was greater as a man, perhaps, than as a poet. Future ages will have to determine this; but he was certainly one of the best poets of his time. Professor Hedge, one of our foremost literary critics, spoke of him as the one American poet whose verses sing themselves; and with the exception of Bryant's "Robert of Lincoln," and Poe's "Raven," and a few other pieces, this may be taken as a judicious statement.

Longfellow's unconsciousness is charming, even when it seems childlike. As a master of verse he has no English rival since Spenser. The trochaic meter in which "Hiawatha" is written would seem to have been his own invention;[1] and is a very agreeable change from the perpetual iambics of Byron and Wordsworth. "Evangeline" is perhaps the most successful instance of Greek and Latin hexameter being grafted on to an English stem. Matthew Arnold considered it too dactylic, but the lightness of its movement personifies the grace of the heroine herself. Lines like Virgil's

"Illi inter sese multa vi brachia tollunt   In numerum, versantque tenaci forcipe massam,"

would not have been suited to the subject.

It has often been said that "Hiawatha" does not represent the red man as he really is, and this is true. Neither does Tennyson represent the knights of King Arthur's court as they were in the sixth century A.D. They are more like modern English gentlemen, and when we read the German Neibelungen we recognize this difference. Virgil's Aeneid does not belong to the period of the Trojan war, but this does not prevent the Aeneid from being very fine poetry. The American Indian is not without his poetic side, as is proved by the squaw who knelt down on a flowery Brussels carpet, and smoothing it with her hands, said: "Hahnsome! hahnsome!

---

1   At least I can remember no other long poem composed in it.

heaven no hahnsomer!" There is true poetry in this; and so there is in the Indian cradle-song:

"The poor little bee that lives in the tree;
The poor little bee that lives in the tree;
Has but one arrow in his quiver."

Either of these incidents is sufficient to testify to Longfellow's "Hiawatha."

The best poetry is that which forces itself upon our memories, so that it becomes part of our life without the least effort of recollection. Such are Emerson's "Problem," Whittier's "Barbara Frietchie," and Longfellow's "Santa Filomena."

"Whene'er a noble deed is wrought,
Whene'er is spoken a noble thought,
Our hearts in glad surprise
To higher levels rise."

Those are fortunate in this life who feel the glad surprise of Longfellow.

"Hiawatha" is equally universal in its application to modern life. The questions of the Indian boy and the replies of his nurse, the good Nikomis, are not confined to the life of the aborigines. Every spirited boy is a Hiawatha, and in one form or another goes through the same experiences that Longfellow has represented with such consummate art in his American epic-idyl.

LOWELL

The Lowell family of Boston crossed over from England towards the middle of the seventeenth century. One of their number afterwards founded the city of Lowell, by establishing manufactures on the Merrimac River, late in the eighteenth century; and in more recent times two members of the family have held the position of judge in the Supreme Court of Massachusetts. They are a family of refined intellectual tastes, as well as of good business and professional ability, but of a retiring disposition and not often conspicuous in public life,--a family of general good qualities, nicely balanced between liberal and conservative, and with a poetic vein running through it for the past hundred years or more. In the Class of 1867 there was an Edward J. Lowell who was chosen class odist, and who wrote poetry nearly, if not quite, as good as that of his distinguished relative at the same period of life.

James Russell Lowell was born at Elmwood, as it is now called, on Washington's birthday in 1819,--as if to make a good staunch patriot of him; and, what is even more exceptional in American life, he lived and died in the same house in which he was born. It was not such a house as the Craigie mansion, but still spacious and dignified, and denoted very fair prosperity for those times.

Elmwood itself extends for some thirty rods on Brattle Street, but the entrance to the house is on a cross-road which runs down to the marshes. Beyond Elmwood there is a stonecutter's establishment, and next to that Mount Auburn Cemetery, which, however, was a fine piece of woodland in Lowell's youth, called Sweet Auburn by the Harvard students, much frequented by love-sick swains and strolling parties of youths and maidens.

The Lowell residence was well into the country at that time. There were few houses near it, and Boston could only be reached by a long detour in a stage; so that an expedition to the city exhausted the better part of a day. It was practically further in the country than Concord is at present; and it was here that Lowell enjoyed that repose of mind which is essential to vigorous mental development, and could find such interests in external nature as the poet requires for the embellishment of his verse.

He went to college at the age of fifteen, two years older than Edward Everett, but sufficiently young to prove himself a precocious student. Cambridge boys of good families have always been noted at Harvard for their gentlemanly deportment. Besides this, Lowell had an immense fund of wit and good spirits, and the two together served to make him very popular--perhaps too much so for his immediate good. His father had great hopes of his promising son,--that he would prove a fine scholar and take a prominent part in the commencement exercises. He even offered the boy a reward of two hundred dollars in case this should happen; but the attractions of student and social life proved too strong for James. He was quick at languages, but slow in mathematics, and as for Butler's analogy he cannot be blamed for the aversion with which he regarded it. He writes a letter in which he confesses to peeping over the professor's shoulder to see what marks have been given for his recitations, so that his father's exhortation would seem at one time to have been seriously felt by him; but the effort did not last long, and we find him repeatedly reprimanded for neglect of college duties.

He did not live the life of a roaring blade, but more like the humming- bird that darts from one plant to another, and gathers sweetness from every flower in the garden. Finally he was rusticated, just after he had been elected poet of his class, with directions not to return until commencement. We recognize the Puritanic severity of President Quincy in this sentence, which robbed young Lowell of the pleasantest term of college life, as well as the honor of appearing on the stage on Class Day. That his poem should have been read by another to the assembled families of his classmates, served to make his absence more conspicuous. Nor can we discover any sufficient reason for such hard statement.

At the same age that Longfellow was writing for the ***United States Literary Gazette***, Lowell was scribbling verses for an undergraduates' periodical called ***Harvardiana***. They were not very serious productions, and might all be included under the head of bric-a-brac; but there was a-plenty of them. While Longfellow's verse at nineteen was remarkable for its perfection of form, Lowell's suffered chiefly from a lack of this. He had an idea that poetry ought to be an inspiration of the moment; a good foundation to begin with, but which he found afterwards it was necessary to modify.

In the preface to one of his Biglow Papers he speaks of his life in Concord as being

> "As lazy as the bream
> Which only thinks to head up stream."

The men whom he chiefly associated with there were named Barziliai and Ebenezer, and the hoar frost of the Concord meadows would seem to have had a chilling effect on Lowell's naturally tolerant and amiable disposition. He was not attracted by Emerson at this time, but, on the contrary, would seem to have felt an aversion to him. The following lines in his class poem could not have referred to anyone else:

> "Woe for Religion, too, when men who claim
> To place a 'Reverend' before their name
> Ascend the Lord's own holy place to preach
> In strains that Kneeland had been proud to reach;
> And which, if measured by Judge Thatcher's scale,
> Had doomed their author to the county jail!
> Alas that ***Christian ministers*** should dare
> To preach the views of Gibbon and Voltaire!"

To confound the strong spiritual assertion of Emerson with the purely negative attitude of the French satirist was a common mistake in those days, and the Lowell of 1838 needs small excuse for it. He must have been in a biting humor at this time, for there is a cut all round in his class poem, although it is the most vigorous and highly-finished production of his academic years.

After college came the law, in which he succeeded as well as youthful attorneys commonly do; and at the age of twenty-five he entered into the holy bonds of matrimony.

The union of James Russell Lowell to Maria White, of Watertown, was the most poetic marriage of the nineteenth century, and can only be compared to that of Elizabeth Barrett and Robert Browning. Miss White was herself a poetess, and full of poetical impulse to the brim. Maria would seem to have been born in the White family as Albinos appear in Africa,--for the sake of contrast. She shone like a single star in a cloudy sky,--a pale, slender, graceful girl, with eyes, to use Herrick's expression, "like a crystal glasse." A child was born where she did not belong, and Lowell was the chivalrous knight who rescued her.

It must have been Maria White who made an Emersonian of him. Margaret Fuller had stirred up the intellectual life of New England women to a degree never known before or since, and Miss White was one of those who came within the scope of her influence.[2] She studied German, and translated poems from Uhland, who might be called the German Longfellow. Certain it is that from the time of their marriage his opinions not only changed from what they had been previously, but his ideas of poetry, philosophy, and religion became more consistent and clearly defined. The path that she pointed out to him, or perhaps which they discovered together, was the one that he followed all through life; so that in one of his later poems, he said, half seriously, that he was ready to adopt Emerson's creed if anyone could tell him just what it was.

The life they lived together was a poem in itself, and reminds one of Goethe's saying, that "he who is sufficiently provided for within has need of little from without." They were poor in worldly goods, but rich in affection, in fine thoughts, and courageous endeavor. It is said that when they were married Lowell had but five hundred dollars of his own. They went to New York and Philadelphia, and soon discovering that they had spent more than half of it, they concluded to return home.

The next ten years of Lowell's life might be called the making of the man. He worked hard and lived economically; earning what he could by the law, and what he could not by magazine writing, which paid poorly enough. Publishers had not then discovered that what the general public desires is not literature, but information on current topics, and this is the last thing which the true man of letters is able to provide. A magazine article, or a campaign biography of General Grant, could

---

2   Lowell himself speaks of her as being "considered transcendental."

be written in a few weeks, but a solid historical biography of him, with a critical examination of his campaigns, has not yet been written, and perhaps never will be. A literary venture of Lowell and his friends in 1843, to found a first-rate literary magazine, proved a failure; and it is to be feared that he lost money by it. [3]

However the world might use him he was sure of comfort and happiness at his own fireside, where he read Shelley, and Keats, and Lessing, while Mrs. Lowell studied upon her German translations. The sympathy of a true- hearted woman is always valuable, even when she does not quite understand the grievance in question, but the sympathy that Maria Lowell could give her husband was of a rare sort. She could sympathize with him wholly in heart and intellect. She encouraged him to fresh endeavors and continual improvement. Thus he went on year by year broadening his mind, strengthening his faculties, and improving his reputation. The days of frolicsome gaiety were over. He now lived in a more serious vein, and felt a deeper, more satisfying happiness. It was much more the ideal life of a poet than that of Thoreau, paddling up and down Concord River in search of the inspiration which only comes when we do not think of it.

It may be suspected that he read more literature than law during these years, and we notice that he did not go, like Emerson, to the great fountain-heads of poetry,--to Homer or Dante, Shakespeare or Goethe,--but courted the muse rather among such tributaries as Virgil, Moliere, Chaucer, Keats, and Lessing. It may have been better for him that he began in this manner; but a remark that Scudder attributes to him in regard to Lessing gives us an insight into the deeper mechanism of his mind. "Shelley's poetry," he said, "was like the transient radiance of St. Elmo's fire, but Lessing was wholly a poet." This is exactly the opposite of the view he held during his college life, for Lessing worked in a methodical and painstaking manner and finished what he wrote with the greatest care.

More than this, Lessing was as Lowell realized afterwards, too critical and polemical to be wholly a poet. His "Emilia Galotti" still holds a high position on the German stage and has fine poetic qualities, but it is written in prose. His "Nathan the Wise" was written in verse, but did not prove a success as a drama. In one he attacked the tyranny of the German petty princes, and in the other the intolerance of the Established Church. We may assume that is the reason why Lowell admired

---

3　See Scudder's Life of Lowell, iii. 109.

them; but Lowell was also too critical and polemic to be wholly a poet,--except on certain occasions. In 1847 he published the "Fable for Critics," the keenest piece of poetical satire since Byron's "English Bards and Scotch Reviewers,"--keen and even saucy, but perfectly good-humored. About the same time he commenced his "Biglow Papers," which did not wholly cease until 1866, and were the most incisive and aggressive anti-slavery literature of that period. Soon afterwards he wrote "The Vision of Sir Launfal," which has become the most widely known of all his poems, and which contains passages of the purest a priori verse. Goethe, who exercised so powerful an influence on Emerson, does not appear to have interested Lowell at all.

The most plaintive of Beethoven scherzos,--that in the Moonlight Sonata, --says as if it were spoken in words:

> "Once we were happy, now I am forlorn;
> Fortune has darkened, and happiness gone."

Lowell's poetic marriage did not last quite ten years. Maria White was always frail and delicate, and she became more so continually. Longfellow's clear foresight noticed the danger she was in years before her death, which took place in the autumn of 1853. She left one child, Mabel Lowell, slender and pale like herself, and with poetical lines in her face, too, but fortunately endowed with her father's good constitution. Only ten years! But such ten years, worth ten centuries of the life of a girl of fashion, who thinks she is happy because she has everything she wants. If the truth were known we might find that in the twilight of his life Lowell thought more of these ten years with Maria White than of the six years when he was Ambassador to England,--with twenty-nine dinner-parties in the month of June.

What would poets do without war? The Trojan war, or some similar conflict, served as the ground-work of Homer's mighty epic; Virgil followed in similar lines; Dante would never have been famous but for the Guelph and Ghibeline struggle. Shakespeare's plays are full of war and fighting; and the wars of Napoleon stimulated Byron, Schiller, and Goethe to the best efforts of their lives. In dealing with men like Emerson, Longfellow, and Lowell, who were the intellectual leaders of their time, it is impossible to escape their influence in the anti-slavery movement, and its influence upon them, unpopular as that subject is at present. That was the heroic age of American history, and the truth concerning it has not yet been written. It was as heroic to the South as to the North, for, as Sumner said, the slaveholders would never have made their desperate attack on the Government of this country if they had not been themselves the slaves of their own social organization.

It was the solution of a great historical problem, like that of Constitutional Government **versus** the Stuarts, and it ought to be treated from a national and not a sectional stand-point.

The live men of that time became abolitionists as inevitably as their forefathers became supporters of the Declaration of Independence. If Webster and Everett had been born twenty years later, they must needs have become anti-slavery, too. Those of Lowell's friends, like George S. Hillard and George B. Loring, who for social or political reasons took the opposite side, afterwards found themselves left in the lurch by an adverse public opinion.

It was the Mexican war that first aroused Lowell to the seriousness of the extension of slavery, and it was meeting a recruiting officer in the streets of Boston, "covered all over with brass let alone that which nature had set on his countenance," which inspired his writing the first of the "Biglow Papers." They were hastily and carelessly written, and Lowell himself held them in slight estimation as literature; but they became immediately popular, as no poetry had that he had published previously. Their freshness and directness appealed to the manliness and good sense of the average New Englander, and the whole community responded to them with repeated applause. There is, after all, much poetry in the Biglow Papers, the more genuine because unintentional; but they are full of the keenest wit and a proverbial philosophy which, if less profound than Emerson's, is more capable of a practical application.

The vernacular in which they are written must have been learned at Concord,--perhaps on the front stoop of the Middlesex Hotel,--while Lowell was listening to the pithy conversation of Yankee farmers, not only about their crops and cattle, but also discussing church affairs and politics, local and national. It was the grandfathers of these men who drove the British back from Concord bridge, and it was their sons who fought their way from the Rapidan to Richmond. With the help of country lawyers they sent Sumner and Wilson to the Senate, and knew what they were about when they did this. For wit, humor, and repartee,--and, it may be added, for decent conversation,--there is no class of men like them. Both Lowell and Emerson have testified to their intrinsic worth.

On one occasion a Concord farmer was driving a cow past Sanborn's school-house, when an impudent boy called out, "The calf always follows the cow." "Why aren't you behind here, then?" retorted the man, with a look that went home like the stroke of a cane. If Lowell had been present he would have been delighted.

The Yankee dialect which he makes use of as a vehicle in these verses is not always as clear-cut as it might be. He says, for instance,

> "Pleasure doos make us Yankee kind of winch
> As if it was something paid for by the inch."

The true New England countryman never flattens a vowel; if he changes it he always makes it sharp. He would be more likely to say: "Pleasure does make us Yankee kind er winch, as if 'twas suthin' paid for by the inch." There are other instances of similar sort; but, nevertheless, if the primitive Yankee should become extinct, as now seems very probable, Lowell's masterly portrait of him will remain, and future generations can reconstruct him from it, as Agassiz reconstructed an extinct species of mammal from fossil bones.

Lowell did not join the Free-soilers, who were now bearing the brunt of the anti-slavery conflict, but attached himself to the more aristocratic wing of the old abolitionists, which was led by Edmund Quincy, Maria Chapman, and L. Maria Child. Lowell was far from being a non-resistant. In fact, he might be called a fighting-man, although he disapproved of duelling; and this served to keep him at a distance from Garrison, of whom he wisely remarked that "the nearer public opinion approached to him the further he retreated into the isolation of his own private opinions." He wrote regularly for the ***Anti-Slavery Standard*** until 1851, when the death of his father-in-law supplied the long-desired means for a journey to Italy,--more desired perhaps for his wife's health than for his own gratification. It may be the fault of his biographers, but I cannot discover that Lowell took any share in the opposition to the Fugitive Slave bill, or in the election of Sumner, which was the signal event that followed it. In his whole life Lowell never made the acquaintance of a practical statesman, while Whittier was in constant communication with prominent members of the Free-soil and Republican parties. Sumner went to hear Lowell's lecture on Milton, and praised it as a work of genius.

I have heard the "Vision of Sir Launfal" spoken of more frequently than any other of Lowell's poems. Some of the descriptive passages in it would seem to have flowed from his pen as readily as ink from a quill; and there are others which appear to have been evolved with much thought and ingenuity. One cannot help feeling the sudden change from a June morning at Elmwood to a mediaeval castle in Europe as somewhat abrupt; but when we think of it subjectively as a poetic vision which came to Lowell himself seated on his own door-step, this disillusion vanishes, and we sympathize heartily with the writer. There is no place in the world where June seems so beautiful as in New England, on account of the dismal, cutthroat weather in the months that precede it. Perhaps it is so in reality; for what nature makes us suffer from at one time she commonly atones for it another.

The "Fable for Critics" is written in an easy, nonchalant manner, which helps to mitigate its severity. Thoreau could not have liked very well being called an imitator of Emerson; but the wit of it is inimitable. "T. never purloins the apples from Emerson's trees; it is only the windfalls that he carries off and passes for his own fruit." Emerson remarked on this, that Thoreau was sufficiently original in his own way; and he always spoke of Lowell in a friendly and appreciative manner. The whole poem is filled with such homely comparisons, which hit the nail exactly on the head. The most subtle piece of analysis, however, is Lowell's comparison between Emerson and Carlyle:

> "There are persons, mole-blind to the soul's make and style,
> Who insist on a likeness 'twixt him and Carlyle;
> To compare him with Plato would be vastly fairer,
> Carlyle's the more burly, but E. is the rarer;
> He sees fewer objects, but clearlier, truelier,
> If C.'s as original, E.'s more peculiar;
> That he's more of a man you might say of the one,
> Of the other he's more of an Emerson;
> C.'s the Titan, as shaggy of mind as of limb,--

E. the clear-eyed Olympian, rapid and slim;
The one's two-thirds Norseman, the other half Greek,
Where the one's most abounding, the other's to seek."

It was the fashion in England at that time to disparage Emerson as an imitator of Carlyle; and this was Lowell's reply to it.

He told Professor Hedge an amusing incident that happened during his first visit to Rome. Lowell and his wife took lodgings with a respectable elderly Italian woman whose husband was in a sickly condition. One morning she met him in the passageway with tearful eyes and said: "Un gran' disgrazie happened last night,--my poor husband went to heaven." Lowell wondered why there was a pope in Rome if going to heaven was considered a disgrace there.

Longfellow's resignation of his professorship at Harvard was a rare piece of good fortune for Lowell; for it was the only position of the kind that he could have obtained there or anywhere else. In fact, it was a question whether the appointment would be confirmed on account of his transcendental tendencies, and his connection with the ***Anti-slavery Standard***; but Longfellow threw the whole weight of his influence in Lowell's favor, and this would seem to have decided it. From this time till 1873 Lowell was more of a prose-writer than a poet, and his essays on Chaucer, Shakespeare, Milton, and other English poets are the best of their kind,--not brilliant, but appreciative, penetrating, and well- considered. Wasson said of him that no other critic in the English tongue came so near to expressing the inexpressible as Lowell.

One could wish that his studies in Shakespeare had been more extended. He treats the subject as if he felt it was too great for him; but he was the first to take notice that the play of Richard III. indicated in its main extent a different hand, and it is now generally admitted to have been the work of Fletcher. With the keenest insight he noticed that the magician Prospero was an impersonation of Shakespeare himself; and George Brandes, the most thoroughgoing of Shakespearean scholars, afterwards came to the same conclusion.

Lowell was the gentlemanly instructor. He appealed to the gentleman in the students who sat before him, and he rarely appealed in vain. Like Longfellow he carried an atmosphere of politeness about him, which was sufficient to protect him from everything rude and common. He would say to his class in Italian: "I shall not mark you if you are tardy, but I hope you will all be here on time." This was a safer procedure with a small division of Juniors than it would have been with a large division of Freshmen or Sophomores. Neither did he take much personal interest in his classes. He always invited them to an entertainment at Elmwood in June, but two or three years later he could not remember their faces unless they remained in or about Cambridge. In regard to his efficiency as an instructor and lecturer there was a difference of opinion.

He attended the meetings of the college faculty quite regularly considering the distance of Elmwood from the college grounds; and he was once heard to say that there seemed to be more bad weather on Monday nights than at any other time in the week. His presence might have been dispensed with for the most part. He rarely spoke in conclave, and when the question came up in regard to the suspension of students he often declined to vote. His decorum was perfect, but now and then a humorous look could be observed in his eyes, and it may be suspected that he had a quiet laugh all to himself on the way homeward. On one occasion, before the meeting had been called to order, Professor Cutler said to him: "Do you not dread B.'s forthcoming translation of the Iliad?" But Lowell, seeing that he was watched, replied: "Oh, no, not at all," at the same time nodding to Cutler with his brows.

He was always well-dressed, and pretty close to the conventional in his ways,--noted specially for the nicety of his gloves. This was a kind of safeguard to him. Insidious persons suggested that he perfumed his beard, but I do not believe it. He does not appear to have been fond of walking, for we never met him in any part of Cambridge except on the direct road from Elmwood to the college gate. He had a characteristic gait of his own--walking slowly in rather a dreamy manner, and keeping time to the movement of his feet with his arms and shoulders. He was not, however, lost in contemplation, for he often scrutinized those who passed him as closely as a portrait painter might.

If one could meet Lowell in a fairly empty horse-car, he would be quite sociable and entertaining; but if the horse-car filled up, he would become reticent again. He clung to his old friends, his classmates, and others with whom he had grown up, and did not easily make new ones. The modesty of his ambition is conspicuous in the fact that he was quite satisfied with the small salary paid him by the college,--at first only twelve hundred dollars. He evidently did not care for luxury.

Lowell's second marriage was as simple and inevitable as the first. Miss Dunlap was not an ordinary housekeeper, but the sister of one of Maria Lowell's most intimate friends, and she was such a pleasant, attractive lady that the wonder is rather he should have waited four years before concluding to offer himself. She was compared to the Greek bust called Clyte, because her hair grew so low down upon her forehead, and this was considered an additional charm.

Louisa Alcott had a story that at first she refused Lowell's offer on account of what people might say; and that then he composed a poem answering her objections in the form of an allegory, and that this finally convinced her. If he had considered material interests he would have married differently.

In November, 1857, the firm of Phillips & Sampson issued the first number of the ***Atlantic Monthly*** in the cause of high-minded literature,--a cause which ultimately proved to be their ruin. Lowell accepted the position of editor, and such a periodical as it proved to be under his guidance could not have been found in England, and perhaps not in the whole of Europe; but it could not be made to pay, and two years later Phillips & Sampson failed,--partly on that account, and partially the victims of a piratical opposition.

Lowell published Emerson's "Brahma" in spite of the shallow ridicule with which he foresaw it would be greeted; but when Emerson sent him his "Song of Nature" he returned it on account of the single stanza:

"One in a Judaean manger,   And one by Avon stream,   One over against the mouths of Nile,   And one in the Academe."

which he declared was more than the ***Atlantic*** could be held responsible for. Emerson, who really knew little as to what the public thought of him, was for once indignant. He said: "I did not know who had constituted Mr. Lowell my censor, and I carried the verses to Miss Caroline Hoar, who read them and said, that she considered those four lines the best in the piece." He permitted Lowell, however, to publish the poem without them, as may be seen by examining the pages of the ***Atlantic***, and afterwards published the original copy in his "May Day."

Lowell's editorship of the ***North American Review***, which followed after this, was not so successful. It was chiefly a political magazine at that time, and to understand politics in a large way--that is, sufficiently to write on the subject--one must not only be a close observer of public affairs, but also a profound student of history; and Lowell was neither. He was not acquainted with prominent men in public life, and depended too much on information derived at dinner-parties, or similar occasions. During the war period Sumner, Wilson, and Andrew were almost omnipotent in Massachusetts, for the three worked together in a common cause; but power always engenders envy and so an inside opposition grew up within the Republican party to which Lowell lent his assistance without being aware of its true character. His articles in the ***North American*** on public affairs were severely criticised by Andrew and Wilson, while Frank W. Bird frankly called them "giving aid and comfort to the enemy." It was certainly a doubtful course to pursue at such a critical juncture--when all patriots should have been united--and it offended a good many Republicans without conciliating the opposition. Lowell's successor in this editorial chair was an old Webster Whig who had become a Democrat.

In 1873 he resigned his professorship and went to Italy for a holiday. He said to some friends whom he met in Florence: "I am tired of being called Professor Lowell, and I want to be plain Mr. Lowell again. Eliot wanted to keep my name on the catalogue for the honor of the university, but I did not like the idea." This was true republicanism and worthy of a poet.

Lowell was little known on the continent, and he travelled in a quiet, unostentatious manner. He went to dine with his old friends, but avoided introductions, and remained at Florence nearly two months after other Americans had departed for Rome. The reason he alleged for this was that Rome was a mouldy place and the ruins made him feel melancholy; also, because he preferred oil paintings to frescos. He had just come from Venice, and spoke with enthusiasm of the mighty works of Tintoretto,-- especially his small painting of the Visitation, above the landing of the staircase in the Scuola of San Rocco. He did not like the easel-paintings of Raphael on account of their hard outlines; those in the Vatican did him better justice. This idea he may have derived from William Morris Hunt, the Boston portrait-painter. He considered the action of the Niobe group too strenuous to be represented in marble.

Miss Mary Felton liked the Niobe statues; so Lowell said, "Now come back with me, and I will sit on you." Accordingly we all returned to the Niobe hall, where Lowell lectured us on the statues without, however, entirely convincing Miss Felton. Then we went to the hall in the Uffizi Palace, which is called the *Tribune*. Mrs. Lowell had never been in the *Tribune*, where the Venus de' Medici is enshrined; so her husband opened the door wide and said, "Now go in"--as if he were opening the gates of Paradise.

At Bologna he wished to make an excursion into the mountains, but the 100 veturino charged about twice the usual price, and though the man afterwards reduced his demand to a reasonable figure Lowell would not go with him at all, and told him that such practices made Americans dislike the Italian people. It is to be feared that a strange Italian might fare just as badly in America.

Readers of Lowell's "Fireside Travels" will have noticed that the first of them is addressed to the "Edelmann Storg" in Rome. The true translation of this expression is "Nobleman Story;" that is, William W. Story, the sculptor, who modelled the statue of Edward Everett in the Boston public garden. Lowell's biographer, however, does not appear to have been aware of the full significance of this paraphrase of Story's name.

When King Bomba II. was expelled from Naples by Garibaldi he retired to Rome with his private possessions, including a large number of oil paintings. Wishing to dispose of some of these, and being aware that Americans paid good prices, he applied to William Story to transact the business for him. This the sculptor did in a satisfactory manner; whereupon King Bomba, instead of rewarding Story with a cheque, conferred on him a patent of nobility. It seems equally strange that Story should have accepted such a dubious honor, and that Lowell should recognize it.

On his return to Cambridge the following year, Lowell found himself a grandfather, his daughter having married a gentleman farmer in Worcester county. He was greatly delighted, and wrote to E. L. Godkin, editor of *The Nation*:

"If you wish to taste the real bouquet of life, I advise you to procure yourself a grandson, whether by adoption or theft.... Get one, and the *Nation* will no longer offend anybody."[4]

This was a pretty broad hint, but E. L. Godkin was not the man to pay much attention to the advice of Lowell or anybody. In fact, he seems to have won Lowell over after this to his own way of thinking.

Lowell certainly became more conservative with age. He did not support the

---

4 Scudder's biography, ii., 186.

movement for negro citizenship, and had separated himself in a manner from the other New England poets. After 1872 Longfellow saw little of him, except on state occasions. In 1876 he made a political address that showed that if he had not already gone over to the Democratic party he was very close upon the line. Charles Francis Adams had already gone over to Tilden, and had carried the ***North American Review*** with him. It would not do to lose Lowell also, so the Republican leaders hit upon the shrewd device of nominating him as a presidential elector, an honor which he could not very well decline. When the disputed election of Hayes and Tilden came, Godkin proposed that, in order to prevent "Mexicanizing the government," one of the Hayes electors should cast his vote for General Bristow, which would throw the election of President into the House of Representatives; and he endeavored to persuade Lowell to do this. Lowell went so far as to take legal advice on the subject, but his counsellor informed him that since the election of John Quincy Adams it had been virtually decided that an elector must cast his vote according to the ticket on which he was chosen. When the electors met at the Parker House in January, 1877, Lowell deposited his ballot for Hayes and Wheeler, and the slight applause that followed showed that his colleagues were conscious of the position he had assumed.

When President Hayes appointed Lowell to be Minister to Spain, Lowell remarked that he did not see why it should have come to him. It really came to him through his friend E. E. Hoar, of Concord, who was brother- in-law to Secretary Evarts. His friends wondered that he should accept the position, but the truth was that Lowell at this time was comparatively poor. His taxes had increased, and his income had diminished. He complained to C. P. Cranch that the whole profit from the sale of his books during the preceding year was less than a hundred dollars, and he thought there ought to be a law for the protection of authors. The real trouble was hard times.

He did not like Madrid, and at the end of a year wrote that it seemed impossible for him to endure the life there any longer. Evarts gave him a vacation, and at the end of the second year Hayes promoted him to the Court of St. James.

Such an appointment would have been dangerous enough in 1861, but at the time it was made the relations between the United States and Great Britain were sufficiently peaceable to warrant it. Lowell represented his country in a highly creditable manner. The only difficulty he experienced was with the Fenian agitation, and he managed that with such diplomatic tact that no one has yet been able to discover whether he was in favor of home rule for Ireland or not.

He made a number of excellent addresses in England, besides a multitude of after-dinner speeches. Perhaps the best of them was his address at the Coleridge celebration, in which he levelled an attack on the English canonization of what they call "common sense," but which is really a new name for dogmatism. Lowell, if not a transcendentalist, was always an idealist, and he knew that ideality was as necessary to Cromwell and Canning as it was to Shakespeare and Scott.

He was certainly more popular in England than he had ever been in America, and he openly admitted that he disliked to resign his position. Professor Child said, in 1882: "Lowell's conversation is witty, with a basis of literary cramming; and that seems to be what the English like. He went to twenty-nine dinner parties in the month of June, and made a speech at each one of them."

In the last years of his life he was greatly infested with imitators who, as he said of Emerson in the "Fable for Critics," stole his fruit and then brought it back to him on their own dishes. Some of them were too influential to be easily disposed of, and others did not know when they were rebuffed. An old man, failing in strength and vigor, he had to endure them as best he could.

The story of Lowell's visions rests on a single authority, and if there was any truth in it, it seems probable that he would have confided the fact to more intimate friends. There are well-authenticated instances of visions seen by persons in a waking condition--this always happens, for instance, in *delirium tremens*--but they are sure to indicate nervous derangement, and are commonly followed by death. If there was ever a poet with a sound mind and a sound body, it was James Russell Lowell.

Edwin Arnold considered him the best of American poets, while Matthew Arnold did not like him at all. Emerson, in his last years, preferred him to Longfellow, but it is doubtful if he always did so. The strong point of his poetry is its intelligent manliness,--the absence of affectation and all sentimentality; but it lacks the musical element. He composed neither songs nor ballads,--nothing to match Hiawatha, or Gray's famous Elegy. America still awaits a poet who shall combine the *savoir faire* of Lowell with the force of Emerson and the grace and purity of Longfellow.

Emerson had an advantage over his literary contemporaries in the vigorous life he lived. You feel in his writing the energy of necessity. The academic shade is not favorable to the cultivation of genius, and Lowell reclined under it too much. His best work was already performed before he became a professor. What he lacks as a poet, however, he compensates for as a wit. He is the best of American humorists--there are few who will be inclined to dispute that--even though we regret occasional cynicisms, like his jest on Milton's blindness in "Fireside Travels."

CRANCH.

Christopher Pearce Cranch was born March 9, 1813, at Alexandria, Virginia, and was the son of Judge William Cranch, of the United States Circuit Court. His father came originally from Weymouth, Massachusetts, and had been appointed to his position through the influence of John Quincy Adams. His mother, Anna Greenleaf, belonged to a well known Boston family. Pearce, as he was always called by his relatives, indicated a talent for the fine arts, as commonly happens, at an early age, and united with this a lively interest in music, singing and playing on the flute. These side issues may have prevented him from entering college so early as he might otherwise have done. He graduated at Columbia College, in 1832, after a three-year course. He wished to make a profession of painting, but Judge Cranch was aware how precarious this would be as a means of livelihood, and advised him to study for the ministry,--for which his quiet ways and grave demeanor seemed to have adapted him. He accordingly entered the Harvard Divinity-School, and was ordained as a Unitarian clergyman.

For the next six years Cranch lived the life of an itinerant preacher. He preached all over New England, making friends everywhere, and receiving numerous calls without, however, settling down to a fixed habitation. This would seem to have been a peculiarity of his temperament; for in 1875 George William Curtis wrote to Mr. and Mrs. Cranch a letter which began with "O ye Bedouins"; and it is true that until that time he can hardly be said to have had a habitation of his own. He extended his migration as minister-at-large from Bangor, Maine, to Louisville, Kentucky. His varied accomplishments made him attractive to the younger members of the parishes for which he preached, but he never remained long enough in one place for their interest to take root.

The wave of German thought and literary interest was now sweeping over England and America. Repelled by doctors of divinity and the older class of scholars, it was seized upon with avidity by the more susceptible natures of the younger generation. Its influence was destined to be felt all through the coming period of American literature. C. P. Cranch was affected by it, as Emerson, Longfellow and even Hawthorne, were affected by it. This, however, did not take place at once, and when Emerson's "Nature" was published, Cranch was at first repelled by the peculiarity of its style. At the house of Rev. James Freeman Clark, in Cincinnati, he drew some innocently satirical illustrations of it. One was of a man with an enormous eye under which he wrote: "I became one great transparent eye-ball"; and another was a pumpkin with a human face, beneath which was written: "We expand and grow in the sunshine." In another sketch Emerson and Margaret Fuller were represented driving "over hill and dale" in a rockaway.[5]

He would make these humorous sketches to entertain his friends at any time, seizing on a half-sheet of paper, or whatever might be at hand; but he did not long continue to caricature Emerson. His first volume of poetry, published in 1844, was dedicated to Emerson, and in Dwight's "Translations from Goethe and Schiller," there are a number of short pieces by Cranch, almost perfect in their rendering from German to English. Among these the celebrated ballad of "The Fisher" is translated so beautifully as to be slightly, if at all, inferior to the original. The stanza,

> "The water in dreamy motion kept,
> As he sat in a dreamy mood,
> A wave hove up, and a damsel stept
> All dripping from the flood,"

may have appealed strongly to Cranch at this time; for we find that in October, 1841, he was married at Fishkill-on-the-Hudson to a young lady of an old Knickerbocker family, Miss Elizabeth De Windt. If she did not come to him out of the Hudson, there can be no doubt that he courted her by the banks of the most beautiful river in North America.

Cranch had given up the clerical profession six months before this, and had

---

5   Sanborn's Life of Alcott.

adopted that of a landscape painter, for which he would seem to have studied with some artist in New York City,--unknown to fame, and long since forgotten. He continued to sketch and paint, and write prose and verse on the Hudson until 1846, when he embarked with his wife on a sailing packet for Marseilles. He had the good fortune to find a fellow- passenger in George William Curtis, and during the voyage of seven weeks, a lifelong friendship grew up between these two highly gifted men.

The volume of poems which he published in 1844 is now exceedingly rare; yet many of the pieces belong to a high order of excellence. In ease and grace of versification they resemble Longfellow, but in thought they are more like Emerson or Goethe. Consider this opening from "The Riddle":

"Ye bards, ye prophets, ye sages,
　　Read to me, if ye can,
That which hath been the riddle of ages,
　　Read me the riddle of *Man*.

Then came the bard with his lyre,
　　And the sage with his pen and scroll,
And the prophet with his eye of fire,
　　To unriddle a human soul.

But the soul stood up in its might;
　　Its stature they could not scan;
And it rayed out a dazzling mystic light,
　　And shamed their wisest plan.

Yet sweetly the bard did sing,
　　And learnedly talked the sage,
And the seer flashed by with his lightning wing,
　　Soaring beyond his age."

This is sonorous. It has a majesty of expression and a greatness of thought which makes Longfellow's "Psalm of Life" seem weak and even common-place. The whole poem is pitched in the same key, and Cranch never equalled it again, excepting once, and then in a very different manner. Rev. Gideon Arch, a Hungarian scholar, philologist, and exile of 1849, said of his "Endymion" that there were Endymions in all languages, but that Cranch's was the best. To resuscitate it from the oblivion into which it has fallen, it is given entire:

"Yes, it is the queenly moon
Walking through her starred saloon,
Silvering all she looks upon:
I am her Endymion;
For by night she comes to me,--
O, I love her wondrously.

She into my window looks,
As I sit with lamp and books,
And the night-breeze stirs the leaves,
And the dew drips down the eaves;
O'er my shoulder peepeth she,
O, she loves me royally!

Then she tells me many a tale,
With her smile, so sheeny pale,
Till my soul is overcast
With such dream-light of the past,
That I saddened needs must be,
And I love her mournfully.

Oft I gaze up in her eyes,
Raying light through winter skies;
Far away she saileth on;
I am no Endymion;
O, she is too bright for me,

And I love her hopelessly!

Now she comes to me again,
And we mingle joy and pain,
Now she walks no more afar,
Regal with train-bearing star,
But she bends and kisses me--
O, we love now mutually!"

This has the very sheen of moonlight upon it, and certainly is to be preferred to Dr. Johnson's scholastic "Endymion":

"Diana, huntress chaste and fair,
Now thy hounds have gone to sleep,"--

If Cranch had continued in this line, and perhaps have improved upon it, he would surely have become one of the foremost American poets, but a poet cannot live by verse alone, and after he began to be thoroughly in earnest with his painting, his rhythmic genius fell into the background. From Marseilles George W. Curtis proceeded to Egypt, where he wrote his well known book of Nile travels, while Cranch set out for Rome to perfect his art.

He studied there at a night-school, painting in water colors from nude models and arrangements of drapery, but not taking lessons from any regular instructor. He never applied himself much to figure-painting, however. He sold his paintings chiefly to American travellers, and when the Revolution broke out in 1848, he returned to Sorrento, where his second child, Mrs. Leonora Scott, was born. His first child was born the year previous, in Rome, but afterwards died. In 1851, he returned to New York and Fishkill, but not meeting with such good appreciation there as he had in Italy, he went to Europe again in the autumn of 1853, and resided in Paris. One cause of this may have been the unfriendliness of his brother-in-law, who was a leading art critic in New York City, and who disliked Cranch on account of his wife, and never neglected an opportunity of disparaging his work.

One of his early landscapes is now before me. I think it must have been painted anterior to his sojourn in Rome, owing to the coldness of the coloring. It represents a scene on the Hudson near Fishkill, with some cattle in the foreground, and a rather bold-looking mountain on the opposite side of the river. The clouds above the mountain are light and fleecy; the foliage soft and graceful; the cattle also are fine, but the effect is like a chilly spring day when one requires a winter overcoat. An allegorical piece, illustrating Heine's fir-tree dreaming of the palm, has a much pleasanter effect, although it represents a wintry scene.

His art improved greatly in Paris, and he also wrote a number of short poems which his friend, James Russell Lowell, published in the ***Atlantic Monthly***. In 1856 George L. Stearns sent him an order for a painting, which Cranch executed the following year, and wrote Mr. Stearns this explanation concerning it, in a very interesting letter dated Paris, March 18, 1857:

"Your picture is done and is quite a favorite with those who have seen it. In fact, I think so well of it that I shall probably send it to the Exposition, which opens soon. After that it shall be sent to you. It is an oak and a sunset--a warm and low-toned picture--and I am sure you will like it."

This landscape represents two vigorous oak trees by the bank of a river, with a sunset seen through the branches, and reflected in the water. The scene is remarkably like a similar one on Concord River, about two hundred yards below the spot where Hawthorne and Channing discovered the body of the schoolmistress who drowned herself, as Hawthorne supposed, from lack of sympathy. It seems as if the original sketch must have been made at that point. It is of a deep rich coloring, smoothly and delicately finished,--a painting that no one has yet been able to find fault with. Rev. Samuel Longfellow, who knew almost every picture in the galleries of Europe, considered it equal to a Ruysdael, and he liked it better than a Ruysdael.

In the letter above referred to Cranch also writes:

"Since your letter (a long time ago) I have written you a good many epistles (in a kind of invisible ink of my invention) which probably you have never received.

"The truth is, I am a distinguished case of total depravity in the matter of correspondence. Letters ought to flow from one as easily and spontaneously as spoken words. But then one must write all the time and report life continuously, as one does in speech. A letter does nothing but give some little detached morsel of one's life--and we say to ourselves what is the use of holding up to a friend three thousand miles off such unsatisfactory statements, such dribblings and droppings? 'Write what is uppermost,' says one at your elbow. Ah, if we could only say what is uppermost; as I sit down for instance to write (say this letter) I am caught into a sort of whirl of thoughts, in which it is impossible to say exactly what is foremost and what is hindmost. Then if I only attempt to narrate events, where am I to begin--so you see (I am theorizing about letters) a letter must be a sort of epitome of a friend's being and life or else nothing. Applying the theory to myself, finding myself unable to shut my genie in a box and carry him on my shoulders, I simply go and state that there is such a box with a genie supposed to be in it, lying at the custom-house, and here is the roughest sort of sketch of it," etc.

This is characteristic of the man. He lived largely in an atmosphere of poetic pleasantry, which served as an alleviation to his cares and as an attraction to his friends.

Cranch did not always succeed so well. He never became a mannerist, but there was too much similarity in his subjects, and the treatment too often bordered on the commonplace. Tintoretto said: "Colors can be bought at the paint-shop, but good designs are only obtained by sleepless nights and much reflection." It is doubtful if Cranch ever laid awake over his work, either in poetry or painting. He had a dreamy, phlegmatic disposition, which seemed to carry him through life without much effort of the will. He once confessed that when he was a boy he would never fire a gun for fear it might kick him over, and when he was at Hampton beach in 1875 he was in the habit of going out to sketch at a certain hour with prosaic regularity. He did not seem to be on the watch, as an artist should, for rare effects of light and scenery, and he talked of art with very little enthusiasm. Yet he lived the true life of his profession, enjoying his work, contented with little praise, and without envy of those who were more fortunate. What is called ***odium artisticum*** was unknown to him.

He was an unpretending, courteous American gentleman. His disposition was perfect, and no one could remember having seen him out of temper. His pleasant flow of wit and humor, together with his varied accomplishments, made him a very brilliant man in society, and he counted among his friends the finest *literati* in Rome, London, and the United States. He knew Thackeray as he knew Curtis and

Lowell, and was once dining with him in a London chop-house, when Thackeray said: "Have you read the last number of The Newcombs?--if not, I will read it to you." Accordingly he gave the waiter a shilling to obtain the document, and read it aloud to Cranch and a friend who was with him.[6]

Cranch could never understand this, for it was the last thing he would have done himself without an invitation; but he enjoyed the reading, and often referred to it.

When he returned to America in 1863 he went to live on Staten Island in order to be near George William Curtis, who cared for him as Damon did for Pythias, and who served to counteract the ill-omened influence of Cranch's brother-in-law. The Century Club purchased one of his pictures, an allegorical subject, which I believe still hangs in their halls. From 1873 to 1877 Lowell would seem to have frequented Cranch's house in preference to any other in Cambridge.

When Cranch first went to live there he occupied a small but sunny and otherwise desirable house on the westerly side of Appian Way,--a name that amused him mightily,--but in 1876 he purchased the house on the southwestern corner of Ellery and Harvard Streets. Having arranged his household goods there he sent one of his own paintings as a present to Emerson in order to renew their early acquaintance. Emerson responded to it by a characteristic note, in which he said that his son and daughter, who were both good artists, had expressed their approval of his present. He then referred to the danger which arises from a multiplicity of talents, and said: "I well recollect how you made the frogs vocal in the ponds back of Sleepy Hollow."

Cranch did not feel that this was very complimentary, but a few days later there came an invitation for Mr. and Mrs. Cranch to spend the day at Concord. Emerson met them at the railway station with his carryall. He had on an old cylinder hat which had evidently seen good service, and yet became him remarkably. He was interested to hear what George William Curtis thought about politics, and to find that it agreed closely with the opinion of his friend, Judge Hoar. The Cranchs had a delightful visit.

Cranch's baritone voice was like his poem, the "Riddle," deep, rich and sonorous. He might have earned a larger income with it, perhaps, than he did by writing

---

6   Both mentioned in Hawthorne's Notebook.

and painting. He sang comic songs in a manner peculiarly his own,--as if the words were enclosed in a parenthesis,--as much as to say, "I do not approve of this, but I sing it just the same," and this made the performance all the more amusing. He sang Bret Harte's "Jim" in a very effective manner, and he often sang the epitaph on Shakespeare's tomb,

"Good friend, for Jesus sake forbeare,"

as a recitative, both in English and Italian,--In questa tomba. He seemed to bring out a hidden force in his singing, which was not apparent on ordinary occasions. His reading of poetry was also fine, but he depended in it rather too much on his voice, too little on the meaning of the verse. It was not equal to Celia Thaxter's reading.

The same types of physiognomy continually reappear among artists. William M. Hunt looked like Horace Vernet, and Cranch in his old age resembled the Louvre portrait of Tintoretto, although his features were not so strong. He used to say in jest that he was descended from Lucas Cranach, but that the second vowel had dropped out. He cared as little for the fashions as poets and artists commonly do, but there was no dandy in Boston who appeared so well in a full dress suit.

In 1873 the Velasquez method of painting was in full vogue at Boston. Cranch did not believe in imitations, or in adopting the latest style from Paris, and he set himself against the popular hue-and-cry somewhat to his personal disadvantage. Charles Perkins and the other art scholars who founded the Art Museum in Copley Square were all on Cranch's side, but that did not seem to help him with the public. "They cannot bend the bow of Ulysses," said Cranch in some disgust. He preferred Murillo to Velasquez, and once had quite an argument with William Hunt on the subject in Doll & Richards's picture-store. Hunt asserted that there was no essential difference between a sketch and a finished picture,--he might have said there was no difference between a boy and a man,--that all the artist needed was to express himself, and that it was immaterial in what way he did so. Cranch thought afterwards, though unfortunately it did not occur to him at the moment, that the test of such a theory would be its application to sculpture. He wondered what Raphael would have thought of it.

It was quite a grief to Cranch that his own daughter, who inherited his talent, should have deserted him at this juncture, and gone over to the opposition. She filled his house with rough, heavily-shaded studies of still-life, flowers, and faces of her friends; but of all Hunt's pupils, Miss Cranch, Miss Knowlton, and Miss Lamb were the only ones who achieved artistic distinction in their special work.

It was in order to withdraw her from this Walpurgis art-dance that Cranch undertook his last journey to Paris in his seventieth year. There the young lady quickly dropped her Boston method, and, acquiring a more conservative handling, became an excellent portrait painter; too soon, however, obliged to relinquish her art on account of ill-health.

Cranch's landscapes now adorn the walls of private houses; very largely the houses of his numerous friends. He did not paint in the fashion of the time, but like Millet followed a fashion of his own; and I do not know of any of his pictures in public collections, although there are many that deserve the honor. The best landscape of his that I have seen was painted just before his last visit to Paris. It represents a low- toned sunset like the "Two Oaks"; an autumnal scene on a narrow river, with maples here and there upon its banks. The sky is covered by a dull gray cloud, but in the west the sun shines through a low opening and gives promise of a better day. The peculiar liquid effect of the setting sun is wonderfully rendered, and the rich browns and russets of the foliage lead up, as it were, like a flight of steps to this final glory, --a restful and impressive scene. This landscape is not painted in the smooth manner of the "Two Oaks," but with soft, flakelike touches which slightly remind one of Murillo. Its coloring has the peculiarity that artificial light wholly changes its character, whereas Cranch's paintings, previous to 1875, appear much the same by electric light that they do in daytime. It is called the "Home of the Wood Duck."

Between 1870 and 1880 he published a number of poems in the **Atlantic Monthly** as well as a longer piece called "Satan," for which it was said by a certain wit that he received the devil's pay. His two books for young folks, "The Last of the Huggermuggers" and "Kobboltozo," ought not to be overlooked, for the illustrations in them are the only remains we have of his rare pencil drawings, as good, if not better, than Thackeray's drawings.

It is likely that the parents read these stories with more pleasure than their children; for they not only contain a deal of fine wit, but there is a moral allegory running through them both. An American vessel is wrecked on a strange island, and the sailors who have escaped death are astonished at the gigantic proportions of the sand and the sea-shells, and of the bushes by the shore. Presently the Huggermuggers appear, and the American mariners in terror run to hide themselves; but they soon find that these giants are the kindliest of human beings. There are also dwarfs on the island, larger than ordinary men, but small compared with the Huggermuggers. They are disagreeable, envious creatures, who wish to ruin the giants in order to have the island more entirely to themselves. Having accomplished this in a somewhat mysterious manner, they attempted to improve their own stature by eating a certain shell-fish which had been the favorite food of the giants; but the shell-fish had also disappeared with the Huggermuggers, and after searching for it a long time they finally summoned the Mer-King, the genius of the sea, who raised his head above the water in a secluded cove and spoke these verses:

> "Not in the Ocean deep and clear,
> Not on the Land so broad and fair,
> Not in the regions of boundless Air,
> Not in the Fire's burning sphere--
> 'Tis not here--'tis not there:
> Ye may seek it everywhere.
> He that is a dwarf in spirit
> Never shall the isle inherit.
> Hearts that grow 'mid daily cares
> Come to greatness unawares;
> Noble souls alone may know
> How the giants live and grow."

This is an allegory, but of very general application; and it has more especially a political application. Cranch may have intended it to illustrate the life of Alexander Hamilton.

Cranch was not a giant himself, but he knew how to distinguish true greatness from the spurious commodity. Emerson considered his varied accomplishments his worst enemy; but that depends on how you choose to look at it. It is probable enough that if Cranch had followed out a single pursuit to its perfection, and if he had not lived so many years in Europe, he would have been a more celebrated man; but Cranch did not care for celebrity. He was content to live and to let live. Men of great force, like Macaulay and Emerson, who impress their personality on the times in which they live, communicate evil as well as good; but Cranch had no desire to influence his fellow men, and for this reason his influence was of a purer quality. It was like the art of Albert Durer. No one could conceive of Cranch's injuring anybody; and if all men were like him there would be no more wars, no need of revolutions. Force, however, is necessary to combat the evil that is already established.

He died at his house on Ellery Street January 20, 1890, as gently and peacefully as he had lived. There is an excellent portrait of him by Duveneck in the rooms of the University Club, at Boston; but the sketch of his life, by George William Curtis, was refused on the ground that he was an Emersonian. The same objection might have been raised against Lowell, or Curtis himself with equally good reason.

T. G. APPLETON.

Thomas G. Appleton, universally known as "Tom" Appleton, was a notable figure during the middle of the last century not only in Boston and Cambridge, but in Paris, Rome, Florence, and other European cities. He was descended from one of the oldest and wealthiest families of Boston, and graduated from Harvard in 1831, together with Wendell Phillips and George Lothrop Motley. He was not distinguished in college for his scholarship, but rather as a wit, a ***bon vivant***, and a good fellow. Yet his companions looked upon him as a strong character and much above the average in intellect. After taking his degree of Bachelor of Arts he went through the Law School, and attempted to practise that profession in Boston. At the end of the first year, happening to meet Wendell Phillips on the sidewalk, the latter inquired if he had any clients. He had not; neither had Phillips, and they both agreed that waiting for fortune in the legal profession was wearisome business. They were both well adapted to it, and the only reason for their ill success would seem to have been that they belonged to wealthy and rather aristocratic families, amongst whom there is little litigation.

At the same time Sumner was laying the foundation by hard study for his future distinction as a legal authority, and Motley was discussing Goethe and Kant with the youthful Bismarck in Berlin. Wendell Phillips soon gave up his profession to become an orator in the anti-slavery cause; and Tom Appleton went to Rome and took lessons in oil painting.

Nothing can be more superficial than to presume that young men who write verses or study painting think themselves geniuses. A man may have a genius for mechanics; and in most instances men and women are attracted to the arts from the elevating character of the occupation. It is not likely that Tom Appleton considered himself a genius, for although he had plenty of self-confidence, his opinion of himself was always a modest one. He painted the portraits of some of his friends, but he never fairly made a profession of it. However, he learned the mechanism of pictorial art in this way, and soon became one of the best connoisseurs of his time.

His finest enjoyment was to meet with some person, especially a stranger, with whom he could discuss the celebrated works in the galleries of Europe. He soon became known as a man who had something to say, and who knew how to say it. He told the Italian picture-dealers to cheat him as much as they could, and he gave amusing accounts of their various attempts to do this. He knew more than they did.

After this time he lived as much in Europe as he did in America. Before 1860 he had crossed the Atlantic nearly forty times. The marriage of his sister to Henry W. Longfellow was of great advantage to him, for through Longfellow he made the acquaintance of many celebrated persons whom he would not otherwise have known, and being always equal to such occasions he retained their respect and good will. One might also say, "What could Longfellow have done without *him*?" His conversation was never forced, and the wit, for which he became as much distinguished in social life as Lowell or Holmes, was never premeditated, often making its appearance on unexpected occasions to refresh his hearers with its sparkle and originality.

In the "Autocrat of the Breakfast Table" Doctor Holmes quotes this saying by the "wittiest of men," that "good Americans, when they die, go to Paris." Now this wittiest of men was Tom Appleton, as many of us knew at that time. He said of Leonardo da Vinci's "Last Supper" that it probably had faded out from being stared at by sightseers, and that the same thing might have happened to the Sistine Madonna if it had not been put under glass,--these being the two most popular paintings in Europe. His fund of anecdotes was inexhaustible.

Earlier in life he was occasionally given to practical jokes. A woman who kept a thread and needle store in Boston was supposed to have committed murder, and was tried for it but acquitted. One day, as Appleton was going by her place of business with a friend he said: "Come in here with me; I want to see how that woman looks." Then surveying the premises, as if he wished to find something to purchase, he asked her if she had any "galluses" for sale,--gallus being a shop-boy's term at the time for suspenders.

When the Art Museum in Boston was first built its odd appearance attracted very general attention, and some one asked Tom Appleton what he thought of it. "Well," he said, "I have heard that architecture is a kind of frozen music, and if so I should call the Art Museum frozen 'Yankee Doodle.'"

Thomas G. Appleton was no dilettante; his interest in the subject was serious and abiding. He did not wear his art as he did his gloves, nor did he turn it into an intellectual abstraction. There was nothing he disliked more than the kind of pretension which tries to make a knowledge of art a vehicle for self-importance. "Who," he said, "ought not to feel humble before a painting of Titian's or Correggio's? It is only when we feel so that we can appreciate a great work of art." He believed that an important moral lesson could be inculcated by a picture as well as by a poem,--even by a realistic Dutch painting. "Women worship the Venus of Milo now," he said, "just as they did in ancient Greece, and it is good for them, too." He respected William Morris Hunt as the best American painter of his time, but thought he would be a better painter if he were not so proud. Pride leads to arrogance, and arrogance is blinding.

After he came into possession of his inheritance he showed that he could make a good use of money. One of his first acts was to purchase a set of engravings in the Vatican, valued at ten thousand dollars, for the Boston Public Library. "I was not such a fool as to pay that sum for it, though," he remarked to Rev. Samuel Longfellow. He visited the studios of struggling artists in Rome and Boston, gave them advice and encouragement,--made purchases himself, sometimes, and advised his friends to purchase when he found a painting that was really excellent. He also purchased some valuable old paintings to adorn his house on Commonwealth Avenue.

He placed two of these at one time on free exhibition at Doll's picture- store, and going into the rooms where they hung, I found Tom Appleton explaining their merits to a group of remarkably pretty school-girls.

At the same moment, another gentleman who knew Mr. Appleton entered, and said, "Ah! a Palma Vecio, Mr. Appleton; how delightful! It is a Palma, is it not?"

"That," replied Mr. Appleton, "is probably a Palma; but what do you say to this, which I consider a much better picture?" The gentleman did not know; but it looked like Venetian coloring.

"Quite right," said Mr. Appleton; "I bought it at the sale of a private collection in Rome, and it was catalogued as a Tintoretto, but I said, 'No, Bassano;' and it is the best Bassano I ever saw. The Italians call it 'Il Coconotte.'"

Mr. Appleton had no intention of palming off doubtful paintings on his friends or the public; but in regard to "Il Coconotte" he was confident of its true value, and rightly so. The painting, so called from a head in the group covered very thinly with hair, was the pride of his collection and one of the best of Bassano's works. The other painting looked to me like a Palma, and I have always supposed that it was one.

After this Mr. Appleton branched off on to an interesting anecdote concerning an Italian cicerone, and finally left his audience as well entertained as if they had been to the theatre.

In 1871 he published a volume of poems for private circulation, in which there were a number of excellent pieces, and especially two which deserve a place in any choice collection of American poetry. One is called the "Whip of the Sky" and relates to a subject which Mr. Appleton often dwelt upon,--the unnecessary haste and restlessness of American life, and is given here for the wider circulation which it amply deserves:

THE WHIP OF THE SKY.

   Weary with travel, charmed with home,
     The youth salutes New England's air;
   Nor notes, within the azure dome,
     A vigilant, menacing figure there,
      Whose thonged hand swings
      A whip which sings:
   "Step, step, step," sings the whip of the sky:
   "Hurry up, move along, you can if you try!"

   Remembering Como's languid side,
     Where, pulsing from the citron deep,
   The nightingale's aerial tide

Floats through the day, repose and sleep,
  Reclined in groves,--
  A voice reproves.
"Step, step, step," cracks the whip of the sky:
"Hurry up, jump along, rest when you die!"

Slave of electric will, which strips
  From him the bliss of easeful hours;
And bids, as from a tyrant's lips,
  Rest, quiet, fly, as useless flowers,
    He wings his heart
    To make him smart.
"Step, step, step," snaps the whip of the sky:
"Hurry up, race along, rest when you die!"

He maddens in the breathless race,
  Nor misses station, power or pelf;
And only loses in the chase
  The hunted lord of all,--himself.
    His gain is loss,
    His treasure dross.
"Step, step, step," mocks the whip of the sky,
"Hurry up, limp along, rest when you die!"

With care he burthens all his soul;
  Heaped ingots curve his willing back;
Submissive to that fierce control,
  He needs at last the sky-whip's crack,
    Till at the grave,
    No more a slave,--
"Rest, rest, rest," sighs the whip of the sky:
"Hurry not, haste no more, rest when you die!"

Celia Thaxter, the finest of poetic readers, read this to me one September morning at the Isles of Shoals, and at the conclusion she remarked: "If that could only be read every year in our public schools it might do the American people some good."

As compared with this, the sonnet on Pompeii has the effect of a strong complementary color,--for instance, like orange against dark blue. It echoes the pathetic reverie that we feel on beholding the monuments of the mighty past. It contains not the pathos of yesterday, nor of a hundred years ago, but as Emerson says, "of the time out of mind."

POMPEII.

> The silence there was what most haunted me.
> Long, speechless streets, whose stepping-stones invite
> Feet which shall never come; to left and right
> Gay colonnades and courts,--beyond, the glee,
> Heartless, of that forgetful Pagan sea.
> O'er roofless homes and waiting streets, the light
> Lies with a pathos sorrowfuler than night.
> Fancy forbids this doom of Life with Death
> Wedded; and with a wand restores the Life.
> The jostling throngs swarm, animate, beneath
> The open shops, and all the tropic strife
> Of voices, Roman, Greek, Barbarian, mix. The wreath
> Indolent hangs on far Vesuvius's crest;
> And beyond the glowing town, and guiltless sea, sweet rest.

Tom Appleton was greatly interested in the performances of the spiritualists, trance mediums, and other persons pretending to supernatural powers. How far he believed in this occult science can now only be conjectured, but he was not a man to be easily played upon. He thought at least that there was more in it than was dreamed of by philosophers. When the Longfellow party was at Florence in April, 1869, Prince George of Hanover, recently driven from his kingdom by Bismarck, called to see the poet, and finding that he had gone out, was entertained by Mr.

Appleton with some remarkable stories of hypnotic and spiritualistic performances. The prince, who was a most amiable looking young German, was evidently very much interested.

Deafness came upon Mr. Appleton in the last years of his life, though not so as to prevent his enjoying the society of those who had clear voices and who spoke distinctly. When one of his friends suggested that the trouble might be wax in his ears, he shook his head sadly and said: "Oh no: not **wax**, but **wane**."

He was finally taken ill while all alone in New York City, and the Longfellows were telegraphed for. When one of his relatives came to him he spoke of his malady in a stoically humorous manner; and his last words were when he was dying: "How interesting this all is!" A man never left this world with a more perfect faith in immortality!

DOCTOR HOLMES

I have often been inside the old Holmes house in Cambridge. It served as a boarding-house during our college days, but afterwards Professor James B. Thayer rented it for a term of years, until it was finally swept away like chaff by President Eliot's broom of reform. The popular notion that it was a quaint-looking old mansion of the eighteenth century, which seems to have been encouraged by Doctor Holmes himself, is a misconception. It was a two-and-a-half story, low-studied house, such as were built at the beginning of the last century, with a roof at an angle of forty-five degrees and a two-story ell on the right side of the front door. Doctor Holmes says:

"Gambrel, gambrel; let me beg   You will look at a horse's hinder leg.   First great angle above the hoof,-- That is the gambrel; hence gambrel roof."

Now, any one who looks carefully at the picture of the old Holmes house, in Morse's biography of the Doctor, will perceive that this was not the style of roof which the house had,--at least, in its later years.

Doctor Holmes graduated at Harvard in 1829 at the age of twenty. His class has been a celebrated one in Boston, and there were certainly some good men in it,-- especially Benjamin Pierce and James Freeman Clarke,-- but I think it was Doctor Holmes's class-poems that gave it its chief celebrity, which, after all, means that it was a good deal talked about. In one of these he said:

"No wonder the tutor can't sleep in his bed   With two twenty-niners over his head."

He was said to have composed twenty-nine poems for his class, and then declared that he had reached the proper limit,--that it would not be prudent to go beyond the magical number. It was not a dissipated class, but one with a good deal of life in it, much given to late hours and jokes, practical and unpractical. The Doctor himself is mysteriously silent concerning his college course, and so are his bi-ographers; but we may surmise that it was not very different in general tenor from Lowell's; although his Yankee shrewdness would seem to have preserved him from serious catastrophes.

In the "Autocrat of the Breakfast Table" Doctor Holmes mentions an early ac-quaintance with Margaret Fuller, which is not referred to by Mr. Morse, but must have arisen either at Mrs. Prentiss's Boston school or at the Cambridgeport school which young Oliver afterwards attended. Even at that age he recognized Marga-ret's intellectual gifts, and he was not a little emulous of her; for he fancied that he "had also drawn a small prize in the great literary lottery." He looked into one of her compositions, which was lying on the teacher's desk, and felt quite crest-fallen by discovering a word in it which he did not know the meaning of. This word was *trite*; and it may he suspected that a good many use it without being aware of its proper significance.

Margaret Fuller rose to celebrity with the spontaneity of true genius, and left her name high upon the natural bridge of American literature. Holmes did not come before the public until years after her death; and then perhaps it might not have happened but for James Russell Lowell and the *Atlantic*. He was a bright man, and possessed a peculiar mental quality of his own; but as we think of him now we can hardly call him a genius. He would evidently have liked in his youth to have made a profession of literature; but his verse lacked the charm and universality which made Longfellow popular so readily; nor did he possess the daring spirit of innovation with which Emerson startled and convinced his contemporaries. He first tried the law, and as that did not suit his taste he fell into medicine, but evi-dently without any natural bent or inclination for the profession. He was fond of the university, and when, after a temporary professorship at Dartmouth he was appointed lecturer on anatomy at the Harvard Medical-School, his friends realized that he had found his right position.

Lecturing on anatomy is a routine, but by no means a sinecure. It requires a clearness and accuracy of statement which might be compared to the work of an optician. Some idea of it can be derived from the fact that there may be eight or ten points to a human bone, each of which has a name of eight or ten syllables,-- only to be acquired by the hardest study. Doctor Holmes's lecturing manner was incisive and sometimes pungent, like his conversation, but always good-humored and well calculated to make an impression even on the most lymphatic temperaments. While it may be said that others might have done it as well, it is doubtful if he could have been excelled in his own specialty. His ready fund of wit often served to revive the drooping spirits of his audience, and many of his jests have become a kind of legendary lore at the Medical-School. Most of them, however, were of a too anatomical character to be reproduced in print.

So the years rolled over Doctor Holmes's head; living quietly, working steadily, and accumulating a store of proverbial wisdom by the way. In June, 1840, he married Amelia Lee Jackson, of Boston, an alliance which brought him into relationship with half the families on Beacon Street, and which may have exercised a determining influence on the future course of his life. Doctor Holmes was always liberally inclined, and ready to welcome such social and political improvements as time might bring; but he never joined any of the liberal or reformatory movements of his time. Certain old friends of Emerson affirmed, when Holmes published his biography of the Concord sage in 1885, that no one else was so much given to jesting as Emerson in his younger days. This may have been true; but it is also undeniable that Emerson himself had changed much during that time, and that the socialistic Emerson of 1840 was largely a different person from the author of "Society and Solitude." Holmes had already composed one of the fairest tributes to Emerson's intellectual quality that has yet been written.

"He seems a winged Franklin, heavenly wise,
Born to unlock the secrets of the skies."

Emerson began his course in direct apposition to the conventional world; but he was the great magnet of the age, and the world could not help being attracted by him. It modified its course, and Emerson also modified his, so that the final reconciliation might take place. Meanwhile Doctor Holmes pursued the even tenor of his way. Concord does not appear to have been attractive to him. He had a brother, John Holmes, who was reputed by his friends to be as witty as the "Autocrat" himself, but who lived a quiet, inconspicuous life. John was an intimate friend of Hon. E. R. Hoar and often went to Concord to visit him; but I never heard of the Doctor being seen there, though it may have happened before my time. He does not speak over-much of Emerson in his letters, and does not mention Hawthorne, Thoreau or Alcott, so far as we know, at all. They do not appear to have attracted his attention.

We are indebted to Lowell for all that Doctor Holmes has given us. The Doctor was forty-eight when the *Atlantic Monthly* appeared before the public, and according to his own confession he had long since given up hope of a literary life. We hardly know another instance like it; but so much the better for him. He had no immature efforts of early life to regret; and when the cask once was tapped, the old wine came forth with a fine bouquet. When Phillips & Sampson consulted Lowell in regard to the editorship of the *Atlantic,* he said at once: "We must get something from Oliver Wendell Holmes." He was Lowell's great discovery and proved to be his best card,--a clear, shining light, and not an *ignis fatuus.*

When the "Autocrat of the Breakfast Table" first appeared few were in the secret of its authorship and everybody asked: "Who is this new luminary?" It was exactly what the more intelligent public wanted, and Holmes jumped at once into the position in literature which he has held ever since. Readers were delighted with his wit, surprised at his originality and impressed by his proverbial wisdom. It was the advent of a sound, healthy intelligence, not unlike that of President Lincoln, which could deal with common-place subjects in a significant and characteristic manner. The landlady's daughter, the schoolmistress, little Boston, and the young man called John, are as real and tangible as the *dramatis personae* in one of Moliere's plays. They seem more real to us than many of the distinguished men and women whom we read of in the newspapers.

Doctor Holmes is the American Sterne. He did not seek a vehicle for his wit in the oddities and mishaps of English middle-class domestic life, but in the contrasts and incongruities of a Boston boarding-house. He informs us at the outset that he much prefers a family with an ancestry-- one that has had a judge or a governor in it, with old family portraits, old books and claw-footed furniture; but if Doctor Holmes had depended on such society for his material he would hardly have interested the public whom he addressed. One of Goethe's critics complained that the class of persons he had introduced in "Wilhelm Meister" did not belong to good society; and to this the "aristocratic" poet replied: "I have often been in society called good, from which I have not been able to obtain an idea for the shortest poem."

So it is always: the interesting person is the one who struggles. After the struggle is over, and prosperity commences, the moral ends,--young Corey and his bride go off to Mexico. The lives of families are represented by those of its prominent individuals. The ambitious son of an old and wealthy family makes a new departure from former precedents, thus creating a fresh struggle for himself, and becomes an orator, like Wendell Philips, or a scientist, like Darwin.

In the "Autocrat" we recognize the dingy wall-paper of the dining-room, the well-worn furniture, the cracked water-pitcher, and the slight aroma of previous repasts; but we soon forget this unattractive background, for the scene is full of genuine human life. The men and women who congregate there appear for what they really are. They wear no mental masks and other disguises like the people we meet at fashionable entertainments; and each acts himself or herself. Boarding-houses, sanitariums, and sea voyages are the places to study human nature. When a man is half seasick the old original Adam shows forth in him through all the wrappings of education, social restraint, imitation and attempts at self-improvement, with which he has covered it over for so many years. Once on a Cunard steamship I heard an architect from San Francisco tell the story of the hoop-snake, which takes its tail in its teeth and rolls over the prairies at a speed equal to any express train. He evidently believed the story himself, and as I looked round on the company I saw that they all believed it, too, excepting Captain Martyn, who gave me a sly look from the corner of his eye. "Rocked in the cradle of the deep," they had become like children again, and were ready to credit anything that was told in a confident manner. But Doctor Holmes's digressions are infectious.

The "Autocrat of the Breakfast Table" is an irregular panorama of human life without either a definite beginning or end,--unless the autocrat's offering himself to the schoolmistress (an incident which only took place on paper) can be considered so; but it is by no means a patchwork. He talks of horse-racing, the Millerites, elm trees, Doctor Johnson, the composition of poetry and much else; but these subjects are introduced and treated with an adroitness that amounts to consummate art. He is always at the boarding-house, and if his remarks sometimes shoot over the heads of his auditors, this is only because he intends that they should. The first ten or fifteen pages of the "Autocrat" are written in such a cold, formal and pedantic manner that the wonder is that Lowell should have published it. After that the style suddenly changes and the Doctor becomes himself. It is like a convention call which ends in a sympathetic conversation.

Doctor Holmes's humor permeates every sentence that he wrote. Even in his most serious moods we meet with it in a peculiar phrase, or the use of some exceptional word.

Now and then his wit is very brilliant, lighting up its surroundings like the sudden appearance of a meteor. The essence of humor consists in a contrast which places the object or person compared at a disadvantage. If the contrast is a dignified one we have high comedy; but if the reverse, low comedy. Some of Holmes's comparisons make the reader laugh out aloud. He says that a tedious preacher or lecturer, with an alert listener in the audience, resembles a crow followed by a king-bird,--a spectacle which of itself is enough to make one smile; and as for an elevated comparison, what could be more so, unless we were to seek one in the moon. There is a threefold wit in it; but the full force of this can only be appreciated in the original text.

Nature commonly sets her own stamp on the face of a humorist. The long pointed nose of Cervantes is indicative of immeasurable fun, and there have been many similar noses on the faces of less distinguished wits. Doctor Holmes ridiculed phrenology as an attempt to estimate the money in a safe by the knobs on the outside, but he evidently was a believer in physiognomy, and he exemplified this in his own case. His face had a comical expression from boyhood; its profile reminded one of those prehistoric images which Di Cesnola brought from Cyprus. As if he were conscious of this he asserted his dignity in a more decided manner than a man usually does who is confident of the respect of those about him. Thus he acquired a style of his own, different from that of any other person in Boston. He was not a man to be treated with disrespect or undue familiarity.

A medical student named Holyoke once had occasion to call on him, and as soon as he had introduced himself Doctor Holmes said: "There, me friend, stand there and let me take an observation of you." He then fetched an old book from his library which contained a portrait of Holyoke's grandfather, who had also been a physician. He compared the two faces, saying: "Forehead much the same; nose not so full; mouth rather more feminine; chin not quite so strong; but on the whole a very good likeness, and I have no doubt you will make an excellent doctor." After Holyoke had explained his business Doctor Holmes finally said: "I liked your grandfather, and shall always be glad to see you here."

Oliver Wendell Holmes, Jr., was class poet of 1861, an honor which pleased his father very much. Immediately after graduating he went to the war, and came near losing his life at the battle of Antietam. A rifle- ball passed through both lungs, and narrowly missed his heart. Alexander Hamilton died of exactly such a wound in seven hours; and yet in three days Captain Holmes was able to write to his father. The Doctor started at once for the seat of war, and met with quite a series of small adventures which he afterwards described in a felicitous article in the *Atlantic,* called "My Hunt after the Captain." His friend, Dr. Henry P. Bowditch, lost his son in the same battle, and when they met at the railway depot Holmes said: "I would give my house to have your fortune like mine."

In a letter to Motley dated February 3, 1862, he says:

"I was at a dinner at Parker's the other day where Governor Andrew and Emerson, and various unknown dingy-linened friends of progress met to hear Mr. Conway, the not unfamous Unitarian minister of Washington,-- Virginia-born, with seventeen secesh cousins, fathers, and other relatives,--tell of his late experience at the seat of Government. He is an out-and-out immediate emancipationist,--believes that is the only way to break the strength of the South; that the black man is the life of the South; that they dread work above all things, and cling to the slave as the drudge that makes life tolerable to them. I do not know if his opinion is worth much."

This was a meeting of the Bird Club which Doctor Holmes attended and the dingy-linened friends of progress were such men as Dr. Samuel G. Howe, Governor Washburn, Governor Claflin, Dr. Estes Howe, and Frank B. Sanborn. It has always been a trick of fashionable society, a trick as old as the age of Pericles, to disparage liberalism by accusing it of vulgarity; but we regret to find Doctor Holmes falling into line in this particular. He always speaks of Sumner in his letters with something like a slur--not to Motley, for Motley was Sumner's friend, but to others who might be more sympathetic. This did not, however, prevent him from going to Sumner in 1868 to ask a favor for his second son, who wanted to be private secretary to the Senator and learn something of foreign affairs. Sumner granted the request, although he must have been aware that the Doctor was not over-friendly to him; but it proved an unfortunate circumstance for Edward J. Holmes, who contracted malaria in Washington, and this finally resulted in an early death.

Why is it that members of the medical profession should take an exceptional interest in poisonous reptiles? Professor Reichert and Dr. S. Weir Mitchell spent a large portion of their leisure hours for several years in experimenting with the virus of rattlesnakes, and of the Gila monster, without, however, quite exhausting the subject. Doctor Holmes kept a rattlesnake in a cage for a pet, and was accustomed to stir it up with an ox-goad. A New York doctor lost his life by fooling with a poisonous snake, and another in Liverpool frightened a whole congregation of scientists with two torpid rattlesnakes which suddenly came to life on the president's table. Does it arise from their custom of dealing with deadly poisons, or is it because they officiate as the high priests of mortality?

Doctor Holmes's "Elsie Venner" was one of the offshoots of this peculiar medical interest, and when we think of it in that light the story seems natural enough. The idea of a snaky woman is as old as the fable of Medusa. I read the novel when I was fifteen, and it made as decided an impression on me as "Ivanhoe" or "Pickwick." I remember especially a proverbial saying of the old doctor who serves as the presiding genius of the plot: he knew "the kind of people who are never sick but what they are going to die, and the other kind who never know they are sick until they are dead." If Doctor Holmes had taken this as his text, and written a novel on those lines, he might have created a work of far-reaching importance. He appears to have known very little concerning poisonous reptiles; had never heard of the terrible fer-de-lance, which infests the cane-swamps of Brazil--a snake ten feet in length which strikes without warning and straight as a fencer's thrust. But "Elsie Venner" and Holmes's second novel, "The Guardian Angel," are, to use Lowell's expression on a different subject:

> "As full of wit, gumption and good Yankee sense,
> As there are mosses on an old stone fence."

In the autumn of 1865 some Harvard students, radically inclined, obtained possession of a religious society in the college called the Christian Union, revolutionized it and changed its name to the Liberal Fraternity. They then invited Emerson, Henry James, Sr., Doctor Holmes, and Colonel Higginson to deliver lectures in Cambridge under their auspices. This was a pretty bold stroke, but Holmes evidently liked it. He said to the committee that waited upon him: "What is your rank and file? How deep do you go down into the class?" He also promised to lecture, and that he did not was more the fault of the students than his own. He was by no means a radical in religious matters, but he hated small sectarian differences-- the substitution of dogma for true religious feeling. In his poem at the grand Harvard celebration in 1886 he made a special point of this principle:

> "For nothing burns with such amazing speed
> As the dry sticks of a religious creed."

Creeds are necessary, however, and an enlightened education teaches us not to value them above their true worth.

In 1867 Doctor Holmes published a volume of poetry which was generally well received, but was criticised in the **Nation** with needless and unmerciful severity. Rev. Edward Everett Hale and other friends of his had already been attacked in the same periodical, and the Doctor thought he knew the man who did it; but whether he was right in his conjecture cannot be affirmed. There can be no doubt that these diatribes were written by a Harvard professor who owned a large interest in the **Nation**, and who was obliged to go to Europe the following year in order to escape the odium of an imprudent speech at a public dinner. In this critique Holmes's poetry was summed up under the heading of "versified misfortunes"; and Holmes himself wrote to Mrs. Stowe that the object of the writer was evidently "to injure at any rate, and to wound if possible."

It was certainly contemptible to treat a man like Doctor Holmes in this manner,--one so universally kind to others, and whose work was always, at least, above mediocrity. He behaved in a dignified manner in regard to it, and he made no attempt at self-justification, although the wound was evidently long in healing. What recourse has a man who places himself before the public against the envenomed shafts of an invisible adversary? Of this at least we may be satisfied, that whatever is extravagant and overwrought always brings its own reaction in due course; and

Doctor Holmes's reputation does not appear to have suffered permanently from this attack. The general public, especially the republic of womankind, forms its own opinion, and pays slight attention to literary criticisms of that description.

Holmes's poetry rarely rises to eloquence, but neither does it descend to sentimentality. It resembles the man's own life, in which there were no bold endeavors, great feats, or desperate struggles; but it was a life so judicious, healthful and highly intellectual that we cannot help admiring it. "Dorothy Q." is perhaps the best of his short poems, as it is the most widely known. The name itself is slightly humorous, but it is a perfect work of art, and the line,

"Soft and low is a maiden's 'Yes,'"

has the beautiful hush of a sanctuary in it. A finer verse could not be written. Also for a comic piece nothing equal to "The Wonderful One-hoss Shay" has appeared since Burns's "Tam O'Shanter." It is based on a logical illusion which brings it down to recent times, and the gravity with which the story is narrated makes its impossibility all the more amusing. The building of the chaise is described with a practical accuracy of detail, and yet with a poetical turn to every verse:

"The hubs of logs from the 'Settler's ellum',--
Last of its timber,--they couldn't sell 'em;
Never an axe had seen their chips,
And the wedges flew from between their lips,
Their blunt ends frizzled like celery-tips";

I believe that even cultivated readers have found more real satisfaction in the "One-Hoss Shay" than in many a more celebrated lyric.

Doctor Holmes lived amid a comparatively narrow circle of friends and acquaintances. He attended the Saturday Club, but Lowell appears to have been the only member of it with whom he was on confidential terms. He was rarely seen or heard of in Longfellow's house. In the winter of 1878 he met Mrs. L. Maria Child for the first time at the Chestnut Street Club. It appears that she did not catch his name when he was introduced to her, and stranger still did not recognize his face.

When the Doctor inquired concerning her literary occupation she replied that she considered herself too old to drive a quill any longer, and then fortunately added: "Now, there is Doctor Holmes, I think he shows his customary good judgment in retiring from the literary field in proper season." What the Doctor thought of this is unknown, but he still continued to write.

At the age of seventy his *alma mater* conferred on Doctor Holmes an LL.D., and this was followed soon afterwards by Oxford and Cambridge, in England; but why was it not given ten or fifteen years earlier, when Holmes was in his prime? Then it might have been a service and a satisfaction to him; but when a man is seventy such tributes have small value for him. There had been an *Atlantic* breakfast for Doctor Holmes in Boston, and a Holmes breakfast in New York. He was in the public eye, and by honoring him the University honored itself. So Harvard conferred an LL.D. on General Winfield Scott just before the fatal battle of Bull Run,-- instead of after his brilliant Mexican campaign. If the degree was not conferred on Holmes for his literary work, what reason could be assigned for it; and if he deserved it on that account, Emerson and Hawthorne certainly deserved it much more. Let us be thankful that no such mischief was contemplated. If honorary degrees are to be given in order to attract attention to a university, or worse still, for the purpose of obtaining legacies, they had better be abolished altogether.

During his last visit to England Doctor Holmes was the guest of F. Max Muller at Oxford, and years afterwards Professor Muller wrote to an American correspondent concerning him and others:

"Froude was a dear friend of mine, related to my wife; so was Kingsley-- dear soul. Renan used to fetch books for me when we first met at the Bibliothique Royale. Emerson stayed at my house on his last visit here. But the best of all my American friends was Wendell Holmes. When he left us he said, 'I have talked to thousands of people--you are the only one with whom I have had a conversation.' We had talked about [Greek: ta megisthta]--the world as the logos, as the thought of God. What a pure soul his was--a real Serene Highness."

This is trancendentalism from the fountainhead; and here Doctor Holmes may fairly be said to have avenged himself on the *Nation's* excoriating critic.

FRANK W. BIRD, AND THE BIRD CLUB.

It is less than four miles from Harvard Square to Boston City Hall, a building rather exceptional for its fine architecture among public edifices, but the change in 1865 was like the change from one sphere of human thought and activity to another. In Boston politics was everything, and literature, art, philosophy nothing, or next to nothing. There was mercantile life, of course, and care-worn merchants anxiously waiting about the gold-board; but there were no tally-ho coaches; there was no golf or polo, and very little yachting. Fashionable society was also at a low ebb, and as Wendell Phillips remarked in 1866, the only parties were boys' and girls' dancing-parties. A large proportion of the finest young men in the city had, like the Lowells, shed their blood for the Republic. The young people danced, but their elders looked grave.

At this time the political centre of Massachusetts and, to a certain extent of New England, was the Bird Club, which met every Saturday afternoon at Young's Hotel to dine and discuss the affairs of the nation. Its membership counted both Senators, the Governor, a number of ex- Governors and four or five members of Congress. They were a strong team when they were all harnessed together.

Francis William Bird, the original organizer of the club, was born in Dedham, October 22, 1809, and the only remarkable fact concerning his ancestry would seem to be that his great-grandmother was a Hawthorne, of the same family as Nathaniel Hawthorne; but there was no trace of that strongly-marked lineage in his composition. As a boy he was quick at mathematics, but not much of a student, so that he was full eighteen years of age before he entered Brown University. His college course also left him in a depleted physical condition, and it was several years later when he commenced the actual labor of life. His father had intended him for the law; but this did not agree with his health, and his physician advised a more active employment. Accordingly we find him in 1835 engaged in the manufacture of paper at East Walpole, an occupation in which he continued until 1892,--always suffering from dyspepsia, but always equal to whatever occasion demanded of him. He was a tall, thin, wiry-looking man, with a determined expression, but of kind and friendly manners.

He must have been a skilful man of business, for all the great financial storms of the half century, in which he lived and worked, rolled over him without causing him any serious embarrassment. His note was always good, and his word was as good as his note. He always seemed to have money enough for what he wanted to do. In prosperous times he spent generously, although habitually practising a kind of stoical severity in regard to his private affairs. He considered luxury the bane of wealth, and continually admonished his children to avoid it. He was an old-fashioned Puritan with liberal and progressive ideas.

After his marriage in 1843 to Miss Abigail Frances Newell, of Boston, he built a commodious house in a fine grove of chestnuts on a hill-side at East Walpole; and there he brought up his children like Greeks and Amazons. Chestnut woods are commonly infested with hornets, but he directed us boys not to molest them, for he wished them to learn that hornets would not sting unless they were interfered with; an excellent principle in human nature. Mrs. Bird resembled her husband so closely in face and figure, that they might have been mistaken for brother and sister. She was an excellent New England woman of the old style, and well adapted to make her husband comfortable and happy.

The connection between manufacturing and politics is a direct and natural one. A man who employs thirty or forty workmen, and treats them fairly, can easily obtain an election to the Legislature without exercising any direct influence over them; but Frank Bird's workmen felt that he had a personal interest in each one of them. He never was troubled with strikes. When hard times came his employees submitted to a reduction of wages without murmuring, and when business was good they shared again in the general prosperity. As a consequence Mr. Bird could go to the Legislature as often as he desired; and when he changed from the Republican to the Democratic party, in 1872, they still continued to vote for him, until at the age of seventy-one he finally retired from public life.

On one election day he is said to have called his men together, and to have told them: "You will have two hours this afternoon to cast your votes in. The mill will close at 4 o'clock, and I expect every man to vote as I do. Now I am going to vote just as I please, and I hope you will all do the same; but if any one of my men does not vote just as he wants to, and I find it out, I will discharge him to-morrow." One can imagine Abraham Lincoln making a speech like this, on a similar occasion.

Frank W. Bird, like J. B. Sargent, of New Haven, was a rare instance of an American manufacturer who believed in free-trade. This was one reason why he joined the Democratic party in 1872. He considered that protection encouraged sleazy and fraudulent work, and placed honest manufacturers at a disadvantage; though he obtained these ideas rather from reading English magazines than from any serious study of his own. He was naturally much more of a Democrat than a Whig, or Federalist, but he opposed the doctrine of State Rights, declaring that it was much more responsible for the Civil War than the anti-slavery agitation was.

The same political exigency which roused James Russell Lowell also brought Francis William Bird before the public. In company with Charles Francis Adams he attended the Buffalo convention, in 1848, and helped to nominate Martin Van Buren for the Presidency. He was, however, doing more effective work by assisting Elizur Wright in publishing the *Chronotype* (the most vigorous of all the anti-slavery papers), both with money and writing; and in a written argument there were few who could equal him. He appears to have been the only person at that time who gave Elizur Wright much support and encouragement.

In 1850 Bird was elected to the State Legislature and worked vigorously for the election of Sumner the ensuing winter. His chief associates during the past two years had been Charles Francis Adams, the most distinguished of American diplomats since Benjamin Franklin, John A. Andrew, then a struggling lawyer, and Henry L. Pierce, afterwards Mayor of Boston. Now a greater name was added to them; for Sumner was not only an eloquent orator, perhaps second to Webster, but he had a worldwide reputation as a legal authority.

Adams, however, failed to recognize that like his grandfather he was living in a revolutionary epoch, and after the Kansas struggle commenced he became continually more conservative--if that is the word for it--and finally in his Congressional speech in the winter of 1861 he made the fatal statement that personally he would be "in favor of permitting the Southern States to secede," although he could not see that there was any legal right for it. This acted as a divider between him and his former associates, until in 1876 he found himself again in the same party with Frank W. Bird.

During the administration of Governor Banks, that is, between 1857 and 1860, Bird served on the Governor's council, although generally in opposition to Banks himself. He went as a delegate to the Chicago Convention of 1860, where he voted at first for Seward, and afterwards for Lincoln. From that time forward, until 1880, he was always to be found at the State House, and devoted so much time to public affairs that it is a wonder his business of paper manufacturing did not suffer from it. Yet he always seemed to have plenty of time, and was never so much absorbed in what he was doing but that he could give a cordial greeting to any of his numerous friends. His face would beam with pleasure at the sight of an old acquaintance, and I have known him to dash across the street like a school-boy in order to intercept a former member of the Legislature who was passing by on the other side. Such a man has a good heart.

Frank Bird's abilities fitted him for higher positions than he ever occupied; but he was so serviceable in the Legislature that all his friends felt that he ought to remain there. He was inexorable in his demand for honest government, and when he rose to speak all the guilty consciences in the house began to tremble. He was the terror of the lobbyist, and of the legislative log-roller. This made him many enemies, but he expected it and knew how to meet them. He was especially feared while Andrew was Governor, for every one knew that he had consulted with Andrew before making his motion. He was the Governor's man of business.

He came to know the character of every politician in the State,--what his opinions were, and how far he could be depended on. In this way he also became of great service to Sumner and Wilson, who wished to know what was taking place behind their backs while they were absent at Washington. Sumner did not trouble himself much as to public opinion, but this was of great importance to Wilson, who depended on politics for his daily bread. Both, however, wanted to know the condition of affairs in their own State, and they found that Frank Bird's information was always trustworthy,--for he had no ulterior object of his own.

Thus he acquired much greater influence in public affairs than most of the members of Congress. When Mr. Baldwin, who represented his district, retired in

1868, Frank Bird became a candidate for the National Legislature, but he suffered from the disadvantage of living at the small end of the district, and the prize was carried off by George F. Hoar, afterwards United States Senator; but going to Congress in the seventies was not what it had been in the fifties and sixties, when the halls of the Capitol resounded with the most impressive oratory of the nineteenth century.

Frank Bird did not pretend to be an orator. His speeches were frank, methodical and directly to the point; and very effective with those who could be influenced by reason, without appeals to personal prejudice. He hated flattery in all its forms, and honestly confessed that the temptation of public speakers to cajole their audiences was the one great demon of a democratic government. He liked Wendell Phillips on account of the manly way in which he fought against his audiences, and strove to bring them round to his own opinion.

He was as single-minded as Emerson or Lincoln. In November, 1862, Emerson said to me: "I came from Springfield the other day in the train with your father's friend, Frank Bird, and I like him very much. I often see his name signed to newspaper letters, and in future I shall always read them." Strangely enough, a few days later I was dining with Mr. Bird and he referred to the same incident. When I informed him that Emerson had also spoken of it he seemed very much pleased.

If any one paid him a compliment or expressed gratitude for some act of kindness, he would hesitate and become silent for a moment, as if he were reflecting whether he deserved it or not; and then would go on to some other subject.

His acts of kindness were almost numberless. He assisted those whom others would not assist; and if he suspected that a small office-holder was being tyrannized over, he would take no rest until he had satisfied himself of the truth of the case. In February, 1870, he learned that a high official in the Boston Post-office, who was supported in his position by the Governor of the State, was taking advantage of this to levy a blackmail on his subordinates, compelling them to pay him a commission in order to retain their places. Frank Bird was furious with honest indignation. He said: "I will go to Washington and have that man turned out if I have to see Grant himself for it"; and so he did.

One evening at Walpole a poor woman came to him in distress, because her only son had been induced to enlist in the Navy, and was already on board a man-of-war at the Boston Navy-yard. Mr. Bird knew the youth, and was aware that he was very slightly feeble-minded. The vessel would sail in three days, and there was no time to be lost. He telegraphed the facts as briefly as possible to Senator Wilson, and in twenty-four hours received an order to have the widow's son discharged. Then he would not trust the order to the commandant, who might have delayed its execution, but sent it to an agent of his own in the Navy-yard, who saw that the thing was done.

Frank Bird's most distinguished achievement in politics was the nomination of Andrew for Governor in 1860. Governor Banks was not favorable to Andrew and his friends, and used what influence he possessed for the benefit of Henry L. Dawes. An organization for the nomination of Dawes had already been secretly formed before Frank Bird was acquainted with Banks's retirement from the field. Bird and Henry L. Pierce were at Plymouth when they first heard of it, about the middle of July, and they immediately returned to Boston, started a bureau, opened a subscription- list, and with the cooperation of the Bird Club carried the movement through. It would have made a marked difference in public affairs during the War for the Union if Dawes had been Governor instead of Andrew.[7]

Frank Bird had this peculiarity, that the more kindly he felt to those who were unfortunate in life, the more antagonistic he seemed to those who were exceptionally prosperous. He appeared to have a sort of spite against handsome men and women, as if nature had been over-partial to them in comparison with others. He was not a pedantic moralist, but at the same time rather exacting in his requirements of others, as he was of himself.

The Bird Club was evolved out of the conditions of its times, like a natural growth. Its nucleus was formed in the campaign of 1848, when Bird, Andrew, Henry L. Pierce, and William S. Robinson fell into the habit of dining together and discussing public affairs every Saturday afternoon. It was not long before they were joined by Elizur Wright and Henry Wilson. Sumner came to dine with them, when he was not in Washington, and Dr. S. G. Howe came with him. The Kansas excitement brought in George L. Stearns and Frank B. Sanborn,--one the president and the other the secretary of the Kansas Aid Society. In 1860 the club had from thirty to forty members, and during the whole course of its existence it had more than

7 Dawes was an excellent man in his way, but during eighteen years in the United States Senate he never made an important speech.

sixty members; but it never had any regular organization. A member could bring a friend with him, and if the friend was liked, Mr. Bird would invite him to come again. No vote ever appears to have been taken. Mr. Bird sat at the head of the table, and if he was late or absent his place would be supplied by George L. Stearns. At his right hand sat Governor Andrew, and either Sumner or Stearns on his left. Doctor Howe and Wilson sat next to them, and were balanced on the opposite side by Sanborn, Governor Washburn, and two or three members of Congress. However, there was no systematic arrangement of the guests at this feast, although the more important members of the club naturally clustered about Mr. Bird.

N. P. Banks never appeared there, either as Governor or General; and from this it was argued that he was ambitious to become Senator; or it may have been owing to his differences with Bird, while the latter was on the Governor's Council. In this way the Bird Club became the test of a man's political opinion, and prominent politicians who absented themselves from it were looked upon with more or less distrust.

The discussions at the club were frank, manly, and unreserved. Members who talked from the point were likely to be corrected without ceremony, and sometimes received pretty hard knocks. On one occasion General B. F. Butler, who had come into the club soon after his celebrated contraband- of-war order, was complaining that the New York Republicans had nominated General Francis C. Barlow for Secretary of State, and that General Barlow had not been long enough in the Republican party to deserve it, when Robinson replied to him that Barlow had been a Republican longer than some of those present, and Frank Bird remarked that he was as good a Republican as any that were going. Butler looked as if he had swallowed a pill.

William S. Robinson was at once the wit and scribe of the club, and the only newswriter that was permitted to come to the table. He enjoyed the advantage of confidential talk and authentic information, which no other writer of that time possessed, and his letters to the Springfield *Republican*, extending over a period of fifteen years, come next in value to the authentic documents of that important period. They possessed the rare merit of a keen impartiality, and though sometimes rather sharp, were never far from the mark. He not only criticised Grant and the political bosses of that time, but his personal friends, Sumner, Wilson, and Frank

Bird himself.

In 1872 Emerson said to a member of the club: "I do not like William Robinson. His hand is against every man"; but it is doubtful if Robinson ever published so hard a criticism of any person, and certainly none so unjust. Emerson without being aware of it was strongly influenced by a cabal for the overthrow of Robinson, in which General Butler took a leading hand. Robinson was clerk of the State Senate, and could not afford to lose his position; afterwards, when he did lose it, he fell sick and died. He preferred truth-telling and poverty to a compromising prosperity, and left no one to fill his place.

Frank B. Sanborn was for a time editor of the Boston ***Commonwealth***, and afterwards of the Springfield ***Republican***; but he was better known as the efficient Secretary of the Board of State Charities, a position to which he was appointed by Governor Andrew, and from which he was unjustly removed by Governor Ames, twenty years later. He was an indefatigable worker, and during that time there was not an almshouse or other institution, public or private, in the State for the benefit of the unfortunate portion of mankind where he was not either feared or respected- -a man whose active principle was the conscientious performance of duty. He was also noted for his fidelity to his friends. He cared for the family of John Brown and watched over their interests as if they had been his own family; he made a home for the poet Channing in his old age, and was equally devoted to the Alcotts and others, who could not altogether help themselves. He was himself a charitable institution.

Henry Wilson is also worth a passing notice, for the strange resemblance of his life to President Lincoln's, if for no other reason. His name was originally Colbath, and he was reputed to have been born under a barbery- bush in one of the green lanes of New Hampshire. The name is an exceptional one, and the family would seem to have been of the same roving Bedouin-like sort as that of Lincoln's ancestors. He began life as a shoemaker, was wholly self-educated, and changed his name to escape from his early associations. He would seem to have absorbed all the virtue in his family for several generations. No sooner had he entered into politics than he was recognized to have a master hand. He rose rapidly to the highest position in the gift of his State, and finally to be Vice-President. If his health had not given way in 1873 he might even have become President in the place of Hayes; for he was a person whom every man felt that he could trust. His loyalty to Sumner bordered on veneration, and was the finest trait in his character. There was no pretense in Henry Wilson's patriotism; everyone felt that he would have died for his country.

In 1870 General Butler disappeared from the club, to the great relief of Sumner and his immediate friends. He had already shown the cloven foot by attacking the financial credit of the government; and the question was, what would he do next? He had found the club an obstacle to his further advancement in politics, and when in the autumn campaign Wendell Phillips made a series of attacks on the character of the club, and especially on Bird himself, the hand of Butler was immediately recognized in it, and his plans for the future were easily calculated. It is probable that Phillips supposed he was doing the public a service in this, but the methods he pursued were not much to his credit. Phillips learned that the president of the Hartford and Erie Railroad had recently given Mr. Bird an Alderney bull-calf, and as he could not find anything else against Bird's character he made the most of this. He spoke of it as of the nature of a legislative bribe, and in an oration delivered in the Boston Music Hall he called it "a thousand dollars in blood."

"Who," he asked of his audience, "would think of exchanging a *bird* for a bull!"

This was unfortunate for the calf, which lost its life in consequence; but it was not worth more than ten dollars, and the contrast between the respective reputations of General Butler and Mr. Bird made Wendell Phillips appear in rather a ridiculous light.

The following year, 1871, as the Bird Club expected, General Butler made a strong fight for the gubernatorial nomination, and the club opposed him in a solid body. Sanborn at this time was editing the Springfield ***Republican***, and he exposed Butler's past political course in an unsparing manner. Butler made speeches in all the cities and larger towns of the State, and when he came to Springfield he singled out Sanborn, whom he recognized in the audience, for a direct personal attack. Sanborn rose to reply to him, and the contrast between the two men was like that between Lincoln and Douglas; Sanborn six feet four inches in height, and Butler much shorter, but very thick-set. The altercation became a warm one, and Butler must have been very angry, for he grew red in the face and danced about the platform as if the boards were hot under his feet. The audience greeted both speakers with applause and hisses.

It was a decided advantage for General Butler that there were three other candidates in the field; but both Sumner and Wilson brought their influence to bear against him, and this, with Sanborn's telling editorials, would seem to have decided his defeat; for when the final struggle came at the Worcester Convention the vote was a very close one and a small matter might have changed it in his favor.

The difference between Sumner and the administration, in 1872, on the San Domingo question accomplished what Phillips and Butler were unable to effect. Frank Bird and Sumner's more independent friends left the club, which was then dining at Young's Hotel, and seceded to the Parker House, where Sumner joined them not long afterwards. Senator Wilson and the more deep-rooted Republicans formed a new organization called the Massachusetts Club, which still existed in the year 1900.

The great days of the Bird Club were over. With the death of Sumner, in 1874, its political importance came to an end, and although its members continued to meet for five or six years longer, it ceased to attract public attention.

At the age of eighty Frank W. Bird still directed the financial affairs of his paper business, but he looked back on his life as a "wretched failure." No matter how much he accomplished, it seemed to him as nothing compared with what he had wished to do. Would there were more such failures!

SUMNER.

Charles Pickney Sumner, the father of Charles Sumner, was a man of an essentially veracious nature. He was high sheriff of Suffolk County, Massachusetts, and when there was a criminal to be executed he always performed the office himself. Once when some one inquired why he did not delegate such a disagreeable task to one of his deputies, he is said to have replied, "Simply because it is disagreeable." It was this elevated sense of moral responsibility which formed the keynote of his son's character.

Charles Sumner's mother was Miss Relief Jacobs, a name in which we distinguish at once a mixture of the Hebrew and the Puritan. She belonged in fact to a Christianized Jewish family, but how long since her ancestors became Christianized remains in doubt. Yet it is easy to recognize the Hebrew element in Sumner's nature; the inflexibility of purpose, the absolute self-devotion, and even the prophetic forecast. Sumner was an old Hebrew prophet in the guise of an American statesman. True to his mother's name, he was at once a Puritan and an Israelite in whom there was no guile; for he was wholly exempt from covetousness and other meaner qualities of the Hebrew nature. In such respects Jews and Yankees are much alike. Either they are generous and high-minded, or they are not.

Charles was rather a peculiar boy, as great men are apt to be in their youth. He cared little for boyish games, and still less for the bright eyes of the girls. He had remarkably long arms and legs, which were too often in the way of his comrades, and from which he derived the nickname at the Latin-School of "gawky Sumner"; and it may be well to notice here that there is no better sign for future superiority than for a lad to be ridiculed in this manner; while the wags who invent such *sobriquets* usually come to no good end.[8] There is sufficient evidence, however, that Sumner

---

8   More than one such has died the death of an inebriate.

was well liked both at school and at college.

He had his revenge on declamation day, for whereas others stumbled through their pieces, he seemed perfectly at home on the platform; his awkwardness disappeared and his performance gave plain indications of the future orator. Wendell Phillips was in the class after him, and they both were excellent speakers.

Sumner's early life was not like that of Lincoln, neither was he obliged to split rails for a living; but it was a life of good stoical training nevertheless. Sheriff Sumner had eight children living at one time, and with the natural desire to give them as good an education as his own, he could not afford to spend much on external elegances. It was not until Charles had become a distinguished lawyer that his mother dispensed with the iron forks and spoons on her dinner table; and this gives a fair idea of their domestic economy. We learn from Pierce's biography that his college expenses did not exceed two hundred dollars a year; and this included everything.

He entered at Harvard in the class of 1830; a year after Doctor Holmes and a year before Wendell Phillips. Much more is known concerning his college life than that of other distinguished men of that time, and it is highly interesting to recognize the mature man foreshadowed in the youth of eighteen. He was a good scholar in everything but mathematics; yet, at the same time, he cared little for rank. He was an enthusiastic reader, and sometimes neglected his studies for a book in which he was more deeply interested. He also liked to converse about the books he read, and in this way acquired a reputation for loquacity which never left him as long as he lived. It was sometimes troublesome to his friends, but it was of great advantage to him as a public speaker. He lived a quiet, sober, industrious life in college, attracting comparatively little attention from either his instructors or his fellow students. Yet, he showed the independence of his character by attending a cattle-show at Brighton, a proceeding for which he would have been suspended if it had been discovered by the college faculty. There were many foolish, monkish restrictions at Harvard in those days, and among them it was not considered decorous for a student to wear a colored vest. He might wear a white vest, but not a buff or a figured one. Sumner preferred a buff vest, and insisted on wearing it. When he was reprimanded for doing so he defended his course vigorously, and exposed the absurdity of the regulation in such plain terms that the faculty concluded to let him alone for the future.[9] He was exceedingly fond of the Greek and Latin authors, and quoted from them in his letters at this time, as he did afterwards in his speeches. His college course was not a brilliant one like Everett's and Phillips's, but seems to have been based on a more solid ground-work.

It was in the Law-School that Sumner first distinguished himself. Judge Story, who had left the United States Supreme Bench to become a Harvard professor, was the chief luminary of the school and the finest instructor in law of his time. He soon discovered in Sumner a pupil after his own heart, and in spite of the disparity of their ages they became intimate friends. This is the more significant because Phillips was also in the same class, and the more brilliant scholar of the two; but Judge Story soon discovered that Phillips was studying as a means to an end, while Sumner's interest in the law was like that of a great artist who works from the pure love of his subject.

William W. Story, who was a boy at this time, records the fact that Sumner was always pleasant and kind to children.

At the age of twenty-four Charles Sumner was himself appointed an instructor at the Law-School; and during the two following years he edited the reports of Judge Story's decisions in the United States Circuit Courts.

It is evident from James Russell Lowell's "Fable for Critics" that the personalities of his contemporaries troubled him: he could not see over their heads. In 1837 Sumner went to Europe and we find from his letters to Judge Story, George S. Hillard, and others, that he had already obtained a vantage ground from which the civilized world lay before him, as all New England does from the top of Mount Washington. He goes into a French law court, and analyzes the procedure of French justice in a letter which has the value of an historical document. He noticed that Napoleon was still spoken of as *l'Empereur*, although there was a king in France,--a fact pregnant with future consequences. He remained in Paris until he was a complete master of the French language, and attended one hundred and fifty lectures at the university and elsewhere. He enjoyed the grand opera and the acting in French theatres; nor did he neglect to study Italian art. He was making a whole man of himself; and it seemed as if an unconscious instinct was guiding him to his destiny.

Fortunate was the old Sheriff to have such a son; but Charles Sumner was also

---

9   In 1860 he still continued to wear a buff vest in summer weather.

fortunate to have had a father who was willing to save and economize for his benefit. Otherwise he might have been a sheriff himself.

Judge Story's letters of introduction opened the doors wide to him in England. In the course of ten months he became acquainted with almost every distinguished person in the United Kingdom. He never asked for introductions, and he never presented himself without one. He was handed from one mansion to another all the way from London to the Scotch Highlands. Only twenty-seven years of age, he was treated on an equality by men ten to fifteen years his senior; and he proved himself equal to their expectations. No American except Lowell has ever made such a favorable impression in England as Sumner; but this happened in Sumner's youth, while Lowell in his earlier visits attracted little attention.

It is perfectly true that if he had been the son of an English sheriff this would not have happened; but he encountered the same obstacles in Boston society that he would have done under similar conditions in Great Britain. The doors of Wentworth House and Strachan Park were open to him, but those of Beacon Street were closed,--and perhaps it was better for him on the whole that they were.

Sumner's letters from Europe are at least as interesting as those written by any other American. Such breadth of vision is not often united with clearness and accuracy of detail. All his letters ought to be published in a volume by themselves. Sumner returned to America the following year and settled himself quietly and soberly to his work as a lawyer. He was not a success, however, as a practitioner in the courts, unless he could plead before a bench of judges. In the Common Pleas an ordinary pettifogger would often take a case away from him. He could not, if he would, have practised those seductive arts by which Rufus Choate drew the jury into his net, in spite of their deliberate intentions to the contrary. Yet, Sumner's reputation steadily improved, so that when Longfellow came to live in Cambridge he found Sumner delivering lectures at the Harvard Law-School, where he might have remained the rest of his life, if he had been satisfied with a merely routine employment, and the fortunes of the republic had not decided differently.

The attraction between Sumner and Longfellow was immediate and permanent. It was owing more perhaps to the essential purity of their natures, than to mutual sympathy in regard to art and literature; although Longfellow held Sumner's literary judgment in such respect that he rarely published a new poem without first subjecting his work to Sumner's criticism.

Those who admired Sumner at this time, for his fine moral and intellectual qualities, had no adequate conception of the far nobler quality which lay concealed in the depths of his nature. Charles Sumner was a hero,--one to whom life was nothing in comparison with his duty.

It was in the anti-Irish riot of June, 1837, that he first gave evidence of this. Nothing was more hateful to him than race prejudice, and what might be called international malignity, which he believed was the most frequent cause of war.

As soon as Sumner was notified of the disturbance, he hastened to the scene of action, seized on a prominent position, and attempted to address the insurgents; but his pacific words only excited them to greater fury. They charged on him and his little group of supporters, knocked him down and trampled on him. Dr. S. G. Howe, who stood near by, a born fighter, protected Sumner's prostrate body, and finally carried him to a place of safety, although twice his own size. Sumner took his mishap very coolly, and, as soon as he could talk freely, addressed his friends on the evils resulting from race prejudice.

This incident may have led Sumner to the choice of a subject for his Fourth of July oration in 1845. The title of this address was "The True Grandeur of Nations," but its real object was one which Sumner always had at heart, and never relinquished the hope of,--namely, the establishment of an international tribunal, which should possess jurisdiction over the differences and quarrels between nations, and so bring warfare forever to an end. The plan is an impracticable one, because the decisions of a court only have validity if it is able to enforce them, and how could the decisions of an international tribunal have value in case the parties concerned declined to accept them? It would only result in waging war in order to prevent war. Yet, of all the Fourth of July orations that were delivered in the nineteenth century, Sumner's and Webster's are the only two that have survived; and the "True Grandeur of Nations" has recently been published by the London Peace Society as an argument in favor of their philanthropic movement.

Sumner was now in the prime of manhood, and a rarely handsome man. He had an heroic figure, six feet two inches in height, and well proportioned in all respects. His features, too large and heavy in his youth, had become strong and regular, and although he had not acquired that leonine look of reserved power with which he confronted the United States Senate, his expression was frank and fear-less. As L. Maria Child, who heard him frequently, said, he seemed to be as much in his place on the platform as a statue on its pedestal. His gestures had not the natural grace of Phillips's or the more studied elegance of Everett, but he atoned for these deficiencies by the manly earnestness of his delivery. He made an impression on the highly cultivated men and women who composed his audience which they always remembered.

The question has often been raised by the older abolitionists, "Why did not Sumner take an earlier interest in the anti-slavery struggle?" The answer is twofold. That he did not join the Free-soilers in 1844 was most probably owing to the influ-ence of Judge Story, who had already marked Sumner out for the Supreme Bench, and wished him to concentrate his energies in that direction. His friends, too, at this time--Hillard, Felton, Liebe, and even Longfellow--were either opposed to intro-ducing the slavery question into politics or practically indifferent to it.

On the other hand, Sumner never could agree with Garrison's position on this question. He held the Constitution in too great respect to admit that it was an agree-ment with death and a government with the devil. He believed that the founders of the Constitution were opposed to slavery, and that the expression, "persons held to labor," was good evidence of this. One of his finest orations in the Senate was intended to prove this point. Furthermore he perceived the futility of Garrison's idea--and this was afterwards disproved by the war--that if it were not for the Na-tional Government the slaves would rise in rebellion and so obtain their freedom. He always asserted that slavery would be abolished under the Constitution or not at all. Like Abraham Lincoln he waited for his time to come.

Charles Sumner was the reply that Massachusetts made to the Fugitive Slave Law, and a telling reply it was. Unlike his legal contemporaries he recognized the law as a revolutionary act which, unless it was successfully opposed, would strike a death-blow at American freedom. He saw that it could only be met by counter-rev-olution, and he prepared his mind for the consequences. It was only at such a time that so uncompromising a statesman as Sumner could have entered into political life; for the possibility of compromise had passed away with the suspension of the writ of ***habeas corpus***, and Sumner's policy of "no compromise" was the one which brought the slavery question to a successful issue. For fifteen years in Congress he held to that policy as faithfully as a planet to its course, and those who differed with him were left in the rear.

Sumner's first difference was with his conservative friends, and especially with his law-partner, George S. Hillard, a brilliant man in his way, and for an introductory address without a rival in Boston. Hillard was at heart as anti-slavery as Sumner, and his wife had even assisted fugitive slaves, but he was swathed in the bands of fashionable society, and he lacked the courage to break loose from them. He adhered to the Whigs and was relegated to private life. They parted without acrimony, and Sumner never failed to do his former friend a service when he found an opportunity.

His difference with Felton was of a more serious kind. Emerson, perhaps, judged Felton too severely,--a man of ardent temperament who was always in danger of saying more than he intended.

Sumner's election to the Senate was a chance in ten thousand. It is well known that at first he declined to be a candidate. He did not think he was fitted for the position, and when Caleb Gushing urged him to court the favor of fortune he said: "I will not leave my chair to become United States Senator." Whatever vanity there might be in the man, he was entirely free from the ambition for power and place.

There were several prominent public men at the time who would have given all they owned for the position, but they were set aside for the man who did not want it,--the bold jurist who dared to set himself against the veteran statesmen of his country. It reads like a Bible-tale, or the story of Cincinnatus taken from his plow to become dictator.

The gates of his *alma mater* were now closed to Sumner, not only during his life but even long after that. Such is the fate of revolutionary characters, that they tear asunder old and familiar bonds in order to contract new ties. In Washington he found a broader and more vigorous life, if less cultivated, and the Free-soil leaders with whom he now came in contact in his own State were much more akin to his own nature than Story, and Felton, and Hillard. Sumner was never popular in Washington, as he had been among the English liberals and Cambridge men of letters; but he was respected on all sides for his fearlessness, his ability, and the veracity of his statements. His previous life now proved a great advantage to him in most respects, but he had become accustomed to dealing and conversing with a certain class of men, and this made it difficult for him to assimilate himself to a wholly different class. Sumner's ardent temperament required constant self-control in this new and trying position; and a man who continually reflects beforehand on his own actions acquires an appearance of greater reserve than a person of really cold nature.

Seward had thus far been the leader of the Free-soil and Republican parties, not only before the country at large but in the Senate. It was soon found, however, that Sumner was not only a more effective speaker, but possessed greater resources for debate. Judge Story had noticed long before that facts were so carefully and systematically arranged in Sumner's mind that whatever spring was touched he could always respond to the subject with a full and exact statement. He was like a librarian who could lay his hand on the book he wanted without having to look for it in the catalogue,--and this upon a scale which seems almost incredible. Webster possessed the same faculty, but united it with a sense of artistic beauty which Sumner could not equal.

Sumner, however, was the best orator in Congress at this time, as well as the best legal authority. On all constitutional questions it was felt that he had Judge Story's support behind him. His oration on "Freedom National, Slavery Sectional," was a revelation, not only to the opposition, but to his own party. From that time forth, he became the spokesman of his party on all the more important questions.

It frequently happens that the essential character of a government changes while its form remains the same. In 1801 France was nominally a Republic, but its administration was Imperial. In 1853 the United States ceased to be a democracy and became an oligarchy, governed by thirty thousand slave-holders,--until the people reconquered their rights on the field of battle. Accustomed to despotic power in their own States for more than two generations, and justifying themselves always by divine right, the slave-holders possessed all the self-confidence, pretension, and arrogance of the old French nobility. They were a self-deluded class of men, of all classes the most difficult to deal with, and Sumner was the Mirabeau who faced them at Washington and who pricked the bubble of their Olympian pretensions by a most pitiless exposure of their true character.

Those men had come to believe that the ownership of slaves was equivalent to a patent of nobility, and they were encouraged in this monarchical illusion by the nobility of Europe. In Disraeli's "Lothair" an English duke is made to say: "I consider an American with large estates in the South a genuine aristocrat." The pretension was ridiculous, and the only way to combat it was to make it appear so. Sumner characterized Butler, of South Carolina, and Douglas, of Illinois, who was their northern man of business, as the Don Quixote and Sancho Panza of an antiquated cause. The satire hit its mark only too exactly; and two days later Sumner was assaulted for it in an assassin-like manner,--struck on the head from behind while writing at his desk, and left senseless on the floor. Sumner was considered too low in the social scale for the customary challenge to a duel, and there was no court in Washington that would take cognizance of the outrage.

The following day, when Wilson made the most eloquent speech of his life in an indignant rebuke to Butler and Brooks, Butler started from his seat to attack him, but was held back by his friends. They might as well have allowed him to go, for Wilson was a man of enormous strength and could easily have handled any Southerner upon the floor.

In "The Crime against Kansas" there are two or three sentences which Sumner afterwards expunged, and this shows that he regretted having said them; but it is the greatest of his orations, and Webster's reply to Hayne is the only Congressional address with which it can be compared. One is in fact the sequence of the other; Webster's is the flower, and Sumner's the fruit; the former directed against the active principle of sedition, and the latter against its consequences; and both were directed against South Carolina, where the war originated. Sumner's speech has not the finely sculptured character of Webster's, but its architectural structure is grand and impressive. His Baconian division of the various excuses that were made for the Kansas outrages into "the apology *tyrannical*, the apology *imbecile*, the apology *absurd*, and the apology *infamous*," was original and pertinent.

Preston S. Brooks only lived about six months after his assault on Sumner, and some of the abolitionists thought he died of a guilty conscience. Both in feature and expression he bore a decided likeness to J. Wilkes Booth, the assassin of President Lincoln. It might have proved the death of Sumner, but for the devotion of his Boston physician, Dr. Marshall S. Perry, who went to him without waiting to be telegraphed for. It was also fortunate for him that his brother George, a very intelligent man, happened to be in America instead of Europe, where he lived the greater part of his life. The assault on Sumner strengthened the Republican party, and secured his re-election to the Senate; but it produced nervous irritation of the brain and spinal cord, a disorder which can only be cured under favorable conditions, and even then is likely to return if the patient is exposed to a severe mental strain. Sumner's cure by Dr. Brown-Sequard was considered a remarkable one, and has a place in the history of medicine. The effect of bromide and ergot was then unknown, and the doctor made such good use of his cauterizing- iron that on one occasion, at least, Sumner declared that he could not endure it any longer. Neither could he tell positively whether it was this treatment or the baths which he afterwards took at Aix-les-Bains that finally cured him. His own calm temperament and firmness of mind may have contributed to this as much as Dr. Brown-Sequard.

When Sumner returned to Boston, early in 1860, all his friends went to Dr. S. G. Howe to know if he was really cured, and Howe said: "He is a well man, but he will never be able to make another two hours' speech." Yet Sumner trained himself and tested his strength so carefully that in the following spring he delivered his oration on the barbarism of slavery, more than an hour in length, before the Senate; and in 1863 he made a speech three hours in length, a herculean effort that has never been equalled, except by Hamilton's address before the Constitutional Convention of 1787.

I remember Sumner in the summer of 1860 walking under my father's grape trellis, when the vines were in blossom, with his arms above his head, and saying: "This is like the south of France." To think of Europe, its art, history, and scenery, was his relaxation from the cares and excitement of politics; but there were many who did not understand this, and looked upon it as an affectation. Sumner in his least serious moments was often self-conscious, but never affected. He talked of himself as an innocent child talks. On all occasions he was thoroughly real and sincere, and he would sometimes be as much abashed by a genuine compliment as a maiden of seventeen.

At the same time Sumner was so great a man that it was simply impossible to disguise it, and he made no attempt to do this. The principle that all men are created equal did not apply in his case. To realize this it was only necessary to see him and Senator Wilson together. Wilson was also a man of exceptional ability, and yet a stranger, who did not know him by sight, might have conversed with him on a railway train without suspecting that he was a member of the United States Senate; but this could not have happened in Sumner's case. Every one stared at him as he walked the streets; and he could not help becoming conscious of this. That there were moments when he seemed to reflect with satisfaction on his past life his best friends could not deny; but the vanity that is born of a frivolous spirit was not in him. He was more like a Homeric hero than a Sir Philip Sidney, and considering the work he had to do it was better on the whole that he should be so.

He carried the impracticable theory of social equality to an extent beyond that of most Americans, and yet he was frequently complained of for his reserve and aristocratic manners. The range of his acquaintance was the widest of any man of his time. It extended from Lord Brougham to J. B. Smith, the mulatto caterer of Boston, who, like many of his race, was a person of gentlemanly deportment, and was always treated by Sumner as a valued friend. As the champion of the colored race in the Senate this was diplomatically necessary; but to the rank and file of his own party he was less gracious. He had not grown up among them, but had entered politics at the top, so that even their faces were unfamiliar to him. The representatives of Massachusetts, who voted for him at the State House, were sometimes chagrined at the coldness of his recognition,--a coldness that did not arise from lack of sympathy, but from ignorance of the individual. Before Sumner could treat a stranger in a friendly manner, he wished to know what sort of a person he had to deal with. There is a kind of insincerity in universal cordiality,--like that of the candidate who is seeking to obtain votes.

A recent writer, who complains of Sumner's lack of graciousness, would do well to ask his conscience what the reason for it was. If he will drop the three last letters of his own name the solution will be apparent to him.

The more Sumner became absorbed in public affairs the less he seemed to be suited to general society,--or general society to him. He was always ready to talk on those subjects that interested him, but in general conversation, in the pleasant give-and-take of wit and anecdote, he did not feel so much at home as he had in his Cambridge days. His thoughts were too serious, and the tendency of his mind was argumentative.

Every man is to a certain extent the victim of his occupation; and the formalities of the Senate were ever tightening their grasp on Sumner's mode of life. One afternoon, as he was leaving Dr. Howe's garden at South Boston, the doctor's youngest daughter ran out from the house, and called to him, "Good-bye, Mr. Sumner." His back was already turned, but he faced about like an officer on parade, and said with formal gravity: "Good evening, child," so that Mrs. Howe could not avoid laughing at him. Yet Sumner was fond of children in his youth. L. Maria Child heard of this incident and made good use of it in one of her story-books.

The grand fact in Sumner's character, however, rests beyond dispute that he never aspired to the Presidency. That lingering Washington malady which victimized Clay, Webster, Calhoun, Seward, Chase, Sherman, and Blaine, and made them appear almost like sinners in torment, never attacked Sumner. He had accepted office as a patriotic duty, and, like Washington, he was ready to resign it whenever his work would be done.

Sumner's speech on the barbarism of slavery, timed as it was to meet the Baltimore convention, was evidently intended to drive a wedge into the split between the Northern and Southern Democrats, but it also must have encouraged the secession movement. Sumner, however, can hardly be blamed for this, after the indignity he had suffered. That a high member of the Government could have been assaulted with impunity in open day indicated a condition of affairs in the United States not unlike that of France at the time when Count Toliendal was judicially murdered by Louis XV. Washington City was an oligarchical despotism.

A dark cloud hung over the Republic during the winter of 1860-'61. The impending danger was that war would break out before Lincoln could be inaugurated. Such secrecy was observed by the Republican leaders that even Horace Greeley could not fathom their intentions. Late in December John A. Andrew and George L. Stearns went to Washington to survey the ground for themselves, and the latter wrote to William Robinson, "The watchword is, ***keep quiet***." He probably obtained this from Sumner, and it gives the key to the whole situation.

It demolishes Von Hoist's finely-spun melodramatic theory in regard to that period of our history, in which he finally compares the condition of the United States to a drowning man who sees lurid flames before his eyes. In the Republican and Union parties there were all shades of compromise sentiment,--from those who were ready to sacrifice anything in order to prevent secession, to Abraham Lincoln, who was only willing to surrender the barren and unpopulated State of New Mexico to the slaveholders.[10] But Sumner, Wade, Trumbull, Wilson, and King stood together like a rocky coast against which the successive waves of compromise dashed without effect. Von Hoist was notified of this fact years before the last volume of his history was published, but he disregarded it evidently because it interfered with his favorite theory.

The last of January, however, a report was circulated in Boston that Sumner had joined the compromisers for the sake of consistency with the peace principles which he had advocated in his Fourth of July oration. Boston newspapers made the most of this, although it did not seem likely to Sumner's friends, and George L. Stearns finally wrote to him for permission to make a denial of it. Sumner first replied to him by telegraph saying: "I am against sending commissioners to treat of surrender by the North. Stand firm." Then he wrote him this memorable letter.

WASHINGTON, 3d Feb., '61.

My Dear Sir:

There are but few who stand rooted, like the oak, against a storm. This is the nature of man. Let us be patient.

My special trust is this: ***No possible compromise or concession will be of the least avail.*** Events are hastening which will supersede all such things. This will save us. But I like to see Mass. in this breaking up of the Union ever true. God keep her from playing the part of Judas or--of Peter! You may all bend or cry pardon--I will not. Here I am, and I mean to stand firm to the last. God bless you!

Ever yours,

CHARLES SUMNER.

---

10   A not unreasonable proposition.

The handwriting of this letter is magnificent. Sumner had a strongly character-istic hand with something of artistic grace in it, too; but in this instance his writing seems like the external expression of the mood he was in when he wrote the letter.

The question may be asked, Why then did not Sumner rise in the Senate and make one of his telling speeches against compromise during that long, wearisome session? I think the answer will be found in the watchword: "Keep quiet!" He perfectly understood the game that Seward was playing and he was too wise to interfere with it. Seward was the cat and compromise was the mouse. Whatever mistakes he may have afterwards made, Seward at this time showed a master hand. He encouraged compromise, but he must have been aware that the proposed constitutional amendment, which would forever have prevented legislation against slavery, would not have been confirmed by the Northern States. He could easily count the legislatures that would reject it. It finally passed through Congress on the last night of this session by a single vote, and was ratified by only three States!

As soon as Lincoln was inaugurated there was no more talk of compromise, and Seward was firmness itself. He declined to receive the disunion commissioners;[11] he compelled the Secretary of War to reinforce Fort Pickens; he overhauled General Scott, who proved an impediment to vigorous military operations. These facts tell their own tale.

After Seward and Chase had left the Senate Sumner was *facile princeps*. Trumbull was a vigorous orator and a rough-rider in debate, but he did not possess the store of legal knowledge and the vast fund of general information which Sumner could draw from. One has to read the fourth volume of Pierce's biography to realize the dimensions of Sumner's work during the period from 1861 to 1869. Military affairs he never interfered with, but he was Chairman of the Committee on Foreign Affairs, the most important in the Senate, and in the direction of home politics he was second to none. No other voice was heard so often in the legislative halls at Washington, and none heard with more respect. A list of the bills that he introduced and carried through would fill a long column.

The test of statesmanship is to change from the opposition to the leadership in a Government,--from critical to constructive politics. Carl Schurz was a fine orator

11   At the same time he coquetted with them unofficially.

and an effective speaker on the minority side, but he commenced life as a revolutionist and always remained one. If he had once attempted to introduce legislation, he would have shown his weakness, exactly where Sumner proved his strength. Froude says that to be great in politics "is to recognize a popular movement, and to have the courage and address to lead it"; but three times Sumner planted his standard away in advance of his party, and stood by it alone until his followers came up to him.

He was always in advance of his party, but conspicuously so in regard to the abolition of slavery, the exposure of Andrew Johnson's perfidy, and the reconstruction of the rebellious States. We might add the annexation of San Domingo as a fourth; for I believe there are few thinking persons at present who do not feel grateful to him for having saved the country from that uncomfortable acquisition.

The bill to abolish slavery in the District of Columbia was introduced by Wilson. Sumner did not like to be always proposing anti-slavery measures himself, and he wished Wilson to have the honor of it. Wilson would not, of course, have introduced the measure without consulting his colleague.

Lincoln evidently desired to enjoy the sole honor of issuing the Emancipation Proclamation of 1862, and he deserved to have it; but Sumner thought it might safely have been done after the battles of Fort Donaldson and Shiloh, and the victories of Foote and Farragut on the Mississippi, six months before it was issued; and he urged to have it done at that time. Whether his judgment was correct in this, it is impossible to decide.

Early in July, 1862, he introduced a bill in the Senate for the organization of the "contrabands" and other negroes into regiments,--a policy suggested by Hamilton in 1780,--and no one can read President Lincoln's Message to Congress in December, 1864, without recognizing that it was only with the assistance of negro troops that the Union was finally preserved.

In spite of the continued differences between Sumner and Seward on American questions they worked together like one man in regard to foreign politics. Sumner's experience in Europe and his knowledge of public men there was much more extensive than Seward's, and in this line he was of invaluable assistance to the Secretary of State.

Lowell could make a holiday of six years at the Court of St. James, but during the war it was a serious matter to be Minister to England. In the summer of 1863 affairs there had reached a climax. The **Alabama** and **Florida** were scaring all American ships from the ocean, and five ironclad rams, built for the confederate government, were nearly ready to put to sea from English ports. If this should happen it seemed likely that they would succeed in raising the blockade. As a final resort Lincoln and Seward sent word to Adams to threaten the British Government with war unless the rams were detained.

Meanwhile it was necessary to brace up the American people to meet the possible emergency. On September 10 Sumner addressed an audience of three thousand persons in Cooper Institute, New York, for three hours on the foreign relations of the United States; and there were few who left the hall before it was finished. He arraigned the British Government for its inconsistency, its violation of international law, and its disregard of the rights of navigators. It was not only a heroic effort, but a self- sacrificing one; for Sumner knew that it would separate him forever from the larger number of his English friends.

At the same time Minister Adams had an equally difficult task before him. War with England seemed to be imminent. He held a long consultation with Benjamin Moran, the Secretary of Legation, and they finally concluded to see if an opinion could be obtained on the confederate rams from an English legal authority. They went to Sir Robert Colyer, one of the lords of the admiralty, and asked him if he was willing to give them an opinion. He replied that he considered the law above politics, and that he wished to do what was right. After investigating the subject Colyer made a written statement to the effect that the United States was wholly justified in demanding detention of the rams. Adams then placed this opinion together with Lincoln's notification before the British Cabinet, but the papers were returned to him with a refusal of compliance. "There is nothing now," said Adams to Moran, "but for us to pack up and go home"; but Moran replied, "Let us wait a little; while there is life there is hope"; and the same evening Adams was notified that Her Majesty's Government still had the subject under consideration. The rams proved a dead loss.

When Benjamin Moran related this incident to the Philadelphia Hock Club after his return, he added: "We owe it to our Irish-American citizens as much as to the monitors that we did not suffer from English interference."

Seward, and also Chase, wished to issue letters of reprisal to privateers to go in search of the *Alabama*, but Sumner opposed this in an able speech on the importance of maintaining a high standard of procedure for the good reputation of the country; and he carried his point.

Sumner's greatest parliamentary feat was occasioned by Trumbull's introduction of a bill for the reconstruction of Louisiana in the winter of 1864. There were only ten thousand loyal white voters in the State; and nothing could be more imprudent or prejudicial than such a hasty attempt at reorganization of the rebellious South, before the war was fairly ended. It was like a man building an annex to one side of his house while the other side was on fire; yet it was known to be supported by Seward, and, as was alleged, also by Lincoln. It was thrust upon Congress at the last moment, evidently in order to prevent an extended debate, and Sumner turned this to his own advantage. For two days and nights his voice resounded through the Senate chamber, until, with the assistance of his faithful allies, Wade and Wilson, he succeeded in preventing the bill from being brought to a vote. It was an extreme instance of human endurance, without parallel before or since, and may possibly have shortened Sumner's life. Five weeks later President Lincoln, in his last speech, made the significant proposition of universal amnesty combined with universal suffrage. Would that he could have lived to see the completion of his work!

Something may be said here of Sumner's influence with Mrs. Lincoln. If Don Piatt is to be trusted, Mrs. Lincoln came to Washington with a strong feeling of antipathy towards Seward and "those eastern abolitionists." She was born in a slave state and had remained pro- slavery,--a fact which did not trouble her husband because he did not allow it to trouble him. Fifteen months in Washington brought a decided change in her opinions, and Sumner would seem to have been instrumental in this conversion. It is well known that she preferred his society to that of others. She had studied French somewhat, and he encouraged her to talk it with him,--which was looked upon, of course, as an affectation on both sides.

At the time of General McClellan's removal, October, 1862, Mrs. Lincoln was at the Parker House in Boston. Sumner called on her in the forenoon, and she said at once: "I suppose you have heard the news, and that you are glad of it. So am I. Mr. Lincoln told me he expected to remove him before I left Washington."

Sumner resembled Charles XII. of Sweden in this: there is no evidence that he ever was in love. His devotion to the law in early life, surrounded as he was by interesting friends, may have been antagonistic to matrimony. The woman he ought to have married was the noble daughter of his old friend, Cornelius Felton, whom he often met, but whose worth he never recognized. The marriage which he contracted late in life was not based on enduring principles, and soon came to a grievous end. It was more like the marriages that princes make than a true republican courtship. Sumner apparently wanted a handsome wife to preside at his dinner parties in Washington, but he chose her from among his opponents instead of from among his friends.

Since there has been much foolish talk upon this subject, it may be well to state here that the true difficulty between Mr. and Mrs. Sumner was owing to the company which he invited to his house. She only wished to entertain fashionable people, but a large proportion of Sumner's friends could not be included within these narrow limits. As Senator from Massachusetts that would not do for him at all. This is the explanation that was given by Mrs. Sumner's brother, and it is without doubt the correct one; but women in such cases are apt to allege something different from the true reason.

Sumner's most signal triumph happened on the occasion of President Johnson's first Message to Congress in January, 1865. He rose from his seat and characterized it as a "whitewashing document." That day he stood alone, yet within six weeks every Republican Senator was at his side.

Sumner knew how to be silent as well as to talk. On one occasion he was making a speech in the Senate when he suddenly heard Schuyler Colfax behind him saying, "This is all very good, Sumner, but here I have the Appropriation bills from the House, and the Democrats know nothing about them." Sumner instantly resumed his seat, and the bills were acted on without serious opposition. He would sometimes sit through a dinner at the Bird Club without saying very much, but if he once started on a subject that interested him there was no limit to it.

Sumner's speech on the "Alabama claims" was considered a failure because the administration did not afterwards support him; and it is true that no government would submit to a demand for adventitious damages so long as it could prevent this; but it was a far-reaching exposure of an unprincipled foreign policy, and this speech formed the groundwork for the Treaty of Washington and the Geneva arbitration.

It was a more important case than the settlement of the Northeastern boundary.

Sumner died the death of a hero. The administration of General Grant might well be called the recoil of the cannon: it was the reactionary effect of a great military movement on civil affairs. Sumner alone withstood the shock of it, and he fought against it for four years like a veteran on his last line of defence, feeling victory was no longer possible. Many of his friends found the current too strong for them; his own party deserted him; even the Legislature of his own State turned against him in a senseless and irrational manner. Still his spirit was unconquerable, and he continued to face the storm as long as life was in him. It was a magnificent spectacle.

It was the last battlefield of a veteran warrior, and although Sumner retired from it with a mortal wound, he had the satisfaction of winning a glorious victory. No end could have been more appropriate to such a life. ***Dulce et decorum est pro patria mori.***

Since Richard Coeur de Leon forgave Bertram de Gordon, who caused his death, there has never been a more magnanimous man than Charles Sumner. Once when L. Maria Child was anathematizing Preston S. Brooks in his presence, he said: "You should not blame him. It was slavery and not Brooks that struck me. If Brooks had been born and brought up in New England, he would no more have done the thing he did than Caleb Cushing would have done it,"--Cushing always being his type of a pro-slavery Yankee.

In 1871 Charles W. Slack, the editor of the Boston ***Commonwealth***, for whom Sumner had obtained a lucrative office, turned against his benefactor in order to save his position. When I spoke of this to Sumner, he said: "Well, it is human nature. Slack is growing old, and if he keeps his office for the next six years, he will have a competency. I have no doubt he feels grateful to me, and regrets the course he is taking." At the same time, he spoke sadly.

Sumner resembled Lord Chatham more closely than any statesman of the nineteenth century. He carried his measures through by pure force of argument and clearness of foresight. From 1854 to 1874 it was his policy that prevailed in the councils of the nation. He succeeded where others failed.

He defeated Franklin Pierce, Seward, Trumbull, Andrew Johnson, Hamilton Fish, and even Lincoln, on the extradition of Mason and Slidell. He tied Johnson down, so that he could only move his tongue.

In considering Sumner's oratory, we should bear in mind what Coleridge said to Allston, the painter,--"never judge a work of art by its defects." His sentences have not the classic purity of Webster's, and his delivery lacked the ease and elegance of Phillips and Everett. His style was often too florid and his Latin quotations, though excellent in themselves, were not suited to the taste of his audiences. But Sumner was always strong and effective, and that is, after all, the main point. Like Webster he possessed a logical mind, and the profound earnestness of his nature gave an equally profound conviction to his words. Besides this, Sumner possessed the heroic element, as Patrick Henry and James Otis possessed it. After Webster's death there was no American speaker who could hold an audience like him.

Matthew Arnold, in his better days, said that Burke's oratory was too rich and overloaded. This is true, but it is equally true that Burke is the only orator of the eighteenth century that still continues to be read. He had a faulty delivery and an ungainly figure, but if he emptied the benches in the House of Commons he secured a larger audience in coming generations. The material of his speeches is of such a vital quality that it possesses a value wholly apart from the time and occasion of its delivery.

Much the same is true of Sumner, who would have had decidedly the advantage of Burke so far as personal impressiveness is concerned. His Phi Beta Kappa address of 1845 is so rich in material that it is even more interesting to read now than when it was first delivered, and his remarks on Allston in that oration might be considered to advantage by every art critic in the country. It should always be remembered that a speech, like a play, is written not to be read, but to be acted; and those discourses which read so finely in the newspapers are not commonly the ones that sounded the best when they were delivered.

Great men create great antagonisms. The antagonism which Lincoln excited was concentrated in Booth's pistol shot, and the Montagues and Capulets became reconciled over his bier; but the antagonism against Sumner still continues to smoke and smoulder like the embers of a dying conflagration.

CHEVALIER HOWE.

The finest modern statue in Berlin is that of General Ziethen, the great Hussar commander in the Seven Years' War.[12] He stands leaning on his sabre in a dreamy, nonchalant attitude, as if he were in the centre of indifference and life had little interest for him. Yet there never was a man more ready for action, or more quick to seize upon and solve the *nodus* of any new emergency. The Prussian anecdote-books are full of his exploits and hairbreadth escapes, a number of which are represented around the base of the statue. He combined the intelligence of the skilful general with the physical dexterity of an acrobat.

Very much such a man was Samuel Gridley Howe, born in Boston November 10, 1801, whom Whittier has taken as the archetype of an American hero in his tune.

If a transient guest at the Bird Club should have seen Doctor Howe sitting at the table with his indifferent, nonchalant air, head leaning slightly forward and his grayish-black hair almost falling into his eyes, he would never have imagined that he was the man who had fought the Turks hand-to-hand like Cervantes and Sir John Smith; who had been imprisoned in a Prussian dungeon; who had risked his life in the July Revolution at Paris; and who had taken the lead in an equally important philanthropic revolution in his own country.

Next to Sumner he is the most distinguished member of the club, even more so than Andrew and Wilson; a man with a most enviable record. He does not talk much where many are gathered together, but if he hears an imprudent statement, especially an unjust estimate of character, his eyes flash out from beneath the bushy brows, and he makes a correction which just hits the nail on the head. He is fond of his own home and is with difficulty enticed away from it. Once in awhile he will

12   Von Schlater's statue of the Great Elector is of course a more magnificent work of art.

dash out to Cambridge on horseback to see Longfellow, but the lion-huntresses of Boston spread their nets in vain for him. He will not even go to the dinner parties for which Mrs. Howe is in constant demand, but prefers to spend the evening with his children, helping them about their school lessons, and listening to the stories of their everyday experiences.

There never was a more modest, unostentatious hero; and no one has recorded his hairbreadth escapes and daring adventures, for those who witnessed them never told the tale, nor would Doctor Howe willingly speak of them himself. He was of too active a temperament to be much of a scholar in his youth, although in after life he went through with whatever he undertook in a thorough and conscientious manner. He went to Brown University, and appears to have lived much the same kind of life there which Lowell did at Harvard,--full of good spirits, admired by his classmates, as well as by the young ladies of Providence, and exceptionally fond of practical jokes; always getting into small difficulties and getting out of them again with equal facility. He was so amiable and warm-hearted that nobody could help loving him; and so it continued to the end of his life.

He could not himself explain exactly why he joined the Greek Revolution. He had suffered himself while at school from the tyranny of older boys, and this strengthened the sense of right and justice that had been implanted in his nature. He had not the romantic disposition of Byron; neither could he have gone from a desire to win the laurels of Miltiades, for he never indicated the least desire for ce-lebrity. It seems more likely that his adventurous disposition urged him to it, as one man takes to science and another to art.

It was certainly a daring adventure to enlist as a volunteer against the Turks. Byron might expect that whatever advantage wealth and reputation can obtain for an individual he could always count upon; but what chances would young Howe have in disaster or defeat? I never heard that Byron did much fighting, though he spent his fortune freely in the cause; and Doctor Howe, as it happened, was not called upon to fight in line of battle, though he was engaged in some pretty hot skirmishes and risked himself freely.

He went to Greece in the summer of 1824 and remained till after the battle of Navarino in 1827. Greece was saved, but the land was a desert and its people starving. Doctor Howe returned to America to raise funds and beg provisions for liberated Hellas, in which he was remarkably successful; but we find also that he published a history of the Greek Revolution, the second edition of which is dated 1828. For this he must have collected the materials before leaving Greece; but as it contains an account of the sea-fight of Navarino, it must have been finished after his return to America. The book was hastily written, and hastily published. To judge from appearances it was hurried through the press without being revised either by its author or a competent proofreader; but it is a vigorous, spirited narrative, and the best chronicle of that period in English. Would there were more such histories, even if the writing be not always grammatical. Doctor Howe does not sentimentalize over the ruins of Sparta or Plato's Academy, but he describes Greece as he found it, and its inhabitants as he knew them. He possesses what so many historians lack, and that is the graphic faculty. He writes in a better style than either Motley or Bancroft. His book ought to be revised and reprinted.

We quote from it this clearsighted description of the preparation for a Graeco-Turkish sea-fight:

"Soon the proud fleet of the Capitan Pashaw was seen coming down toward Samos, and the Greek vessels advanced to meet it. And here one cannot but pause a moment to compare the two parties, and wonder at the contrast between them. On one side bore down a long line of lofty ships whose very size and weight seemed to give them a slow and stately motion; completely furnished at every point for war; their decks crowded with splendidly armed soldiers, and their sides chequered with double and triple-rows of huge cannon that it seemed could belch forth a mass of iron which nothing could resist. On the other side came flying along the waves a squadron of light brigs and schooners, beautifully modelled, with sails of snowy white, and with fancifully painted sides, showing but a single row of tiny cannon. There seemed no possibility of a contest; one fleet had only to sail upon the other, and by its very weight, bear the vessels under water without firing a gun.

"But the feelings which animated them were very different. The Turks were clumsy sailors; they felt ill at ease and as if in a new element; but above all, they felt a dread of Greek fire-ships, which made them imagine every vessel that approached them to be one. The Greeks were at home on the waves,--active and fearless mariners, they knew that they could run around a Turkish frigate and not be injured; they knew the dread their enemies had of fire-ships, and they had their favorite, the daring Kanaris, with them."

*　　　*　　　*　　　*　　　*

The heroic deeds of the modern Greeks fully equalled those of the ancients; and the death of Marco Bozzaris was celebrated in all the languages of western Europe. William Muller, the German poet, composed a volume of fine lyrics upon the incidents of the Greek Revolution; so that after his death the Greek Government sent a shipload of marble to Germany for the construction of his monument.

One day Doctor Howe, with a small party of followers, was anchored in a yawl off the Corinthian coast, when a Turk crept down to the shore and commenced firing at them from behind a large tree. After he had done this twice, the doctor calculated where he would appear the third time, and firing at the right moment brought him down with his face to the earth. Doctor Howe often fired at Turks in action, but this was the only one that he felt sure of having killed; and he does not appear to have even communicated the fact to his own family.

After Doctor Howe's triumphant return to Greece with a cargo of provisions in 1828 he was appointed surgeon-general of the Greek navy, and finally, as a reward for all his services, he received a present of Byron's cavalry helmet,--certainly a rare trophy.[13]

Doctor Howe's mysterious imprisonment in Berlin in 1832 is the more enigmatical since Berlin has generally been the refuge of the oppressed from other European countries. The Huguenots, expelled by Louis XIV., went to Berlin in such

---

13　This helmet hung for many years on the hat tree at Dr. Howe's house in South Boston.

numbers that they are supposed by Menzel to have modified the character of its inhabitants. The Salzburg refugees were welcomed in Prussia by Frederick William I.,
who had an official hanged for embezzling funds that were intended for their benefit. In 1770 Frederick the Great gave asylum to the Jesuits who had been expelled
from every Catholic capital in Europe; and when the brothers Grimm and other
professors were banished from Cassel for their liberalism, they were received and
given positions by Frederick William IV. Why then should the Prussian government have interfered with Doctor Howe, after he had completed his philanthropic
mission to the Polish refugees? Why was he not arrested in the Polish camp when
he first arrived there?

The futile and tyrannical character of this proceeding points directly to Metternich, who at that time might fairly be styled the Tiberias of Germany. The Greek
Revolution was hateful to Metternich, and he did what he could to prevent its
success. His intrigues in England certainly delayed the independence of Greece for
two years and more. He foresaw clearly enough that its independence would be a
constant annoyance to the Austrian government,--and so it has proved down to the
present time. Metternich imagined intrigues and revolution in every direction; and
besides, there can be no doubt of the vindictiveness of his nature. The cunning of
the fox is not often combined with the supposed magnanimity of the lion.

The account of his arrest, which Doctor Howe gave George L. Stearns, differs
very slightly from that in Sanborn's biography. According to the former he persuaded the Prussian police, on the ground of decency, to remain outside his door
until he could dress himself. In this way he gained time to secrete his letters. He
tore one up and divided the small pieces in various places. While he was doing this
he noticed a bust of some king of Prussia on top of the high porcelain stove which
forms a part of the furniture of every large room in Berlin. Concluding it must be
hollow he tipped it on edge and inserted the rest of his letters within. The police
never discovered this stratagem, but they searched his room in the most painstaking
manner, collecting all the pieces of the letter he had torn up, so that they read every
word of it. Whether his letters were really of a compromising character, or he was
only afraid that they might be considered so, has never been explained.

The day after his arrest he was brought before a tribunal and asked a multitude
of questions, which he appears to have answered willingly enough; and a week or

more later the same examiners made a different set of inquiries of him, all calculated to throw light upon his former answers. Doctor Howe admitted afterwards
that if he had attempted to deceive them they would certainly have discovered the
fact. He was in prison five weeks, for which the Prussian government had the impu-
dence to charge him board; and why President Jackson did not demand an apology
and reparation for this outrage on a United States citizen is not the least mysterious
part of the affair.

A good Samaritan does not always find a good Samaritan. After his return to
Paris Doctor Howe went to England, but was taken so severely ill on the way that
he did not know what might have become of him but for an English passenger with
whom he had become acquainted and who carried him to his own house and cared
for him until he was fully recovered. This excellent man, name now forgotten, had
a charming daughter who materially assisted in Howe's convalescence, and he said
afterwards that if he had not been strongly opposed to matrimony at that time she
would probably have become his wife. He was not married until ten years later; but
he always remembered this incident as one of the pleasantest in his life.

The true hero never rests on his laurels. Doctor Howe had no sooner returned
from Europe than he set himself to work on a design he had conceived in Paris for
the instruction of the blind. Next to Doctor Morton's discovery of etherization,
there has been no undertaking equal to this for the amelioration of human misery.
He brought the best methods from Europe, and improved upon them. Beginning at
first in a small way, and with such means as he could obtain from the merchants
of Boston, he went on to great achievements. He had the most difficulty in dealing
with legislative appropriations and enactments, for as he was not acquainted with
the ruling class in Massachusetts, they consequently looked upon him with suspicion. He not only made the plan, but he carried it out; he organized the institution
at South Boston and set the machinery in motion.

The story of Laura Bridgman is a tale told in many languages. The deaf and
blind girl whom Doctor Howe taught to read and to *think* soon became as celebrated as Franklin or Webster. She was between seven and eight years old when
he first discovered her near Hanover, N. H., and for five years and a half she had
neither seen nor heard. It is possible that she could remember the external world
in a dim kind of way, and she must have learned to speak a few words before she

lost her hearing. Doctor Howe taught her the names of different objects by pasting them in raised letters on the objects about her, and he taught her to spell by means of separate blocks with the letters upon them. She then was taught to read after the usual method of instructing the blind, and communicated with her fingers after the manner of deaf mutes. Doctor Howe said in his report of the case:

"Hitherto, the process had been mechanical, and the success about as great as teaching a very knowing dog a variety of tricks. The poor child had sat in mute amazement and patiently imitated everything her teacher did; but now the truth began to flash upon her; her intellect began to work; she perceived that here was a way by which she could herself make up a sign of anything that was in her own mind, and show it to another mind, and at once her countenance lighted up with a human expression; it was no longer a dog or parrot,--it was an immortal spirit, eagerly seizing upon a new link of union with other spirits!"

Finally she was educated in the meaning of the simplest abstract terms like right and wrong, happy and sad, crooked and straight, and in this she evinced great intelligence, for she described being alone as ***all one***, and being together ***all two***,--the original meaning of alone and altogether, which few persons think of. In trying to express herself where she found some difficulty she made use of agglutinative forms of speech.[14]

The education of Laura has rare value as a psychological study; for it proves incontestably that mind is a thing in itself, and not merely a combination of material forces, as the philosophers of our time would have us believe. Laura Bridgman's mind was there, though wholly unable to express itself, and so soon as the magic key was turned, she developed as rapidly and intelligently as other girls of her age. She soon became much more intelligent than the best trained dog who has all his senses in an acute condition; and she developed a sensibility toward those about her such as Indian or Hottentot girls of the same age would not have done at all. She soon began to indicate that sense of order which is the first step on the stairway of civilization. If these qualities had not been in her they never could have come out.

Why is it that so many superior women remain unmarried, and why do men of superior intellect and exceptional character so often mate themselves with weak or narrow-minded women? That a diffident man, with a taste for playing on the flute,

---

14   Like the Aztecs, Kanackers and other primitive races.

should be captured by a virago, is not so remarkable,--that is his natural weakness; but it is also true that the worthiest man often chooses indifferently. This thing they call matrimony is in fact like diving for pearls: you bring up the oyster, but what it contains does not appear until afterward. A friend of Sumner, who imagined his wife had a beautiful nature because she was fond of wild- flowers, discovered too late that she cared more for botany than for her husband.

Chevalier Howe met with better fortune. He waited long and to good purpose. It was fitting that such a man should marry a poetess; and he found her, not in her rose-garden or some romantic sylvan retreat, but in the city of New York. Miss Julia Ward was the daughter, as she once styled herself, of the Bank of Commerce, but her mind was not bent on money or a fashionable life. She was graceful, witty and charming in the drawing-room; but there was also a serious vein in her nature which could only be satisfied by earnest thought and study. She went from one book to another through the whole range of critical scholarship, disdaining everything that was not of the best quality. She soon knew so much that the young men became afraid of her, but she cared less for their admiration than for her favorite authors. Above all, the deep religious vein in her nature, which never left her, served as a balance to her romantic disposition. Her first admirer is said to have been an eloquent preacher who came to New York while Miss Ward was in her teens.

Another man might have crossed Julia Ward's path and only have remembered her as a Sumner friend. Doctor Howe recognized the opportunity, and had no intention of letting it slip. His reputation and exceptional character attracted her; and he wooed and won her with the same courage that he fought the Greeks. Her sister married Crawford, the best sculptor of his time, whom Sumner helped to fame and fortune.

Doctor Howe's wedding journey, which included a complete tour of Europe, seems to have been the first rest that he had taken in twenty years. Such wedding journeys are frequent enough now, but it is a rare bride that finds the doors of distinguished houses opened to her husband from Edinburgh to Athens. Was it not a sufficient reward for any man's service to humanity?

For that matter Doctor Howe's lifelong work received comparatively slight recognition or reward. A few medals were sent to him from Europe,--a gold one from the King of Prussia,--and he was always looked upon in Boston as a distinguished citizen; but his vocation at the Blind Asylum withdrew him from the public eye, and the public soon forgets what happened yesterday. What a blaze of enthusiasm there was for Admiral Dewey in 1899, and how coldly his name was received as a presidential candidate one year later!

Doctor Howe was once nominated for Congress as a forlorn hope, and his name was thrice urged unavailingly for foreign appointments. He certainly deserved to be made Minister to Greece, but President Johnson looked upon him as a very "ultra man",--the real objection being no doubt that he was a friend of Sumner, and the second attempt made by Sumner himself was defeated by Hamilton Fish. Doctor Howe was fully qualified at any time to be Minister to France, and as well qualified as James Russell Lowell for the English Mission; but the appointment of such men as Lowell and Howe has proved to be a happy accident rather than according to the natural order of events. What reward did Doctor Morton ever obtain, until twenty-five years after his death his name was emblazoned in memorial hall of Boston State House! It is an old story.

Yet Doctor Howe may well be considered one of the most fortunate Americans of his time. Lack of public appreciation is the least evil that can befall a man of truly great spirit,--unless indeed it impairs the usefulness of his work, and Edward Everett, who had sympathized so cordially with Doctor Howe's efforts in behalf of the Greeks, could also have told him sympathetically that domestic happiness was fully as valuable as public honor. Fortunate is the man who has wandered much over the earth and seen great sights, only the better to appreciate the quiet and repose of his own hearth-stone! The storm and stress period of Doctor Howe's life was over, and henceforth it was to be all blue sky and smooth sailing.

Sumner expressed a kind of regret at Doctor Howe's marriage,--a regret for his own loneliness; but he found afterwards that instead of losing one friend he had made another. His visits to South Boston were as frequent as ever, and he often brought distinguished guests with him,-- English, French, and German. There was no lady in Boston whom he liked to converse with so well as Mrs. Howe; and if he met her on the street he would almost invariably stop to speak with her a few minutes. He sometimes suffered from the keen sallies of her wit, but he accepted this as part of the entertainment, and once informed her that if she were president of the Senate it would be much better for the procedure of the public business.

George Sumner also came; like his brother, a man much above the average in general ability, and considered quite equal to the Delivery of a Fourth of July oration. He was the more entertaining talker of the two, and in other respects very much like Tom Appleton,--better known on the Paris boulevards than in his native country. Instead of being witty like Appleton he was brilliantly encyclopaedic; and they both carried their statements to the verge of credibility.

Doctor Howe organized the blind asylum so that it almost ran itself without his oversight, and as always happens in such cases he was idolized by those who were under his direction. There was something exceedingly kind in his tone of voice,--a voice accustomed to command and yet much subdued. His manner towards children was particularly charming and attractive. He exemplified the lines in Emerson's "Wood-notes":

"Grave, chaste, contented though retired,
And of all other men desired,"

applied to Doctor Howe more completely than to the person for whom they were originally intended; for Thoreau's bachelor habits and isolated mode of life prevented him from being an attractive person to the generality of mankind.

It was said of James G. Blaine that he left every man he met with the impression that he was his best friend. This may have been well intended, but it has the effect of insincerity, for the thing is practically impossible. The true gentleman has always a kind manner, but he does not treat the man whom he has just been introduced to as a friend; he waits for that until he shall know him better. It is said of Americans generally that they are generous and philanthropic, but that they do not make good friends,--that their idea of friendship depends too much on association and the influence of mutual interests, instead of the underlying sense of spiritual relationship. When they cease to have mutual interests the friendship is at an end, or only continues to exist on paper. Doctor Howe was as warm-hearted as he was firm-hearted, but he never gave his full confidence to any one until he had read him through to the backbone. His friends were so fond of him that they would go any distance to see him. His idea of friendship seemed to be like that of the friends in the sacred band of Thebes, whose motto was either to avenge their comrades on the field of battle or to die with them.

He did not like a hypocritical morality, which he said too often resulted in the hypocritical sort. He complained of this in Emerson's teaching, which he thought led his readers to scrutinize themselves too closely as well as to be too censorious of others; and he respected Emerson more for his manly attitude on the Kansas question than for anything he wrote.

He always continued to be the chevalier. He was like Hawthorne's gray-haired champion, who always came to the front in a public emergency, and then disappeared, no one knew whither. When the Bond Street riot took place in 1837, there was Doctor Howe succoring the oppressed; in 1844 he joined the Conscience Whigs and was one of the foremost among them; he helped materially toward the election of Sumner in 1851, and for years afterwards was a leader in the vigilance committee organized to resist the Fugitive Slave law. He stood shoulder to shoulder with George L. Stearns in organizing resistance to the invasions of Kansas by the Missourians; and again in 1862 when Harvard University made its last desperate political effort in opposition to Lincoln's Emancipation Proclamation; but when his friends and his party came into power Howe neither asked nor hinted at any reward for his brilliant services.

Edward L. Pierce, the biographer of Sumner, was not above exhibiting his prejudices as to certain members of the Bird Club, both by what he has written and what he neglected to write. He says of the Chevalier: "Dr. Howe, who had a passion for revolutions and civil disturbances of all kinds, and had no respect for the restrictions of international law or comity, was vexed with Sumner for not promoting the intervention of the United States in behalf of the insurgent Cubans."

This reminds one of Boswell's treatment of Doctor Johnson's friends. Like John Adams and Hampden, Doctor Howe was a revolutionary character,--and so were Sumner and Lincoln,--but he was a man in all matters prudent, discreet and practical. He was as much opposed to inflammatory harangues and French socialistic notions as he was to the hide-bound conservatism against which he had battled all his life. Like Hampden and Adams his revolutionary strokes were well timed and right to the point. Experience has proved them to be effective and salutary. It was the essential merit of Sumner and his friends that they recognized the true character of the times in which they lived and adapted themselves to it. Thousands of well-educated men lived through the anti-slavery and civil war period without being aware that they were taking part in one of the great revolutionary epochs of history. That Doctor Howe and Senator Sumner differed in regard to the Cuban rebellion is a matter of small moment. Howe considered the interests of the Cubans; Sumner the interests of republicanism in Spain and in Europe generally. Both were right from their respective standpoints.

At the beginning of the war he was sixty years of age,--too old to take an active part in it. This cannot be doubted, however, that if he had been thirty years younger he would either have won distinction as a commander or have fallen on the, field of honor. The best contribution from the Howe family to the war was Julia Ward Howe's "Battle Hymn of the Republic." The war was a grand moral struggle, a conflict of historical forces; and neither Lowell, Emerson, nor Whittier expressed this so fully and with such depth of feeling as Mrs. Howe. There are occasions when woman rises superior to man, and this was one of them. It was evidently inspired by the John Brown song, that simple martial melody; but it rises above the personal and temporal into the universal and eternal. Its measure has the swing of the Greek tragic chorus, extended to embrace the wider scope of Christian faith, and its diction is of an equally classic purity and vigor. The last stanza runs:

> "In the beauty of the lily Christ was born across the sea,
> With a glory in his bosom that transfigures you and me.
> As he died to make men holy let us die to make men free;
>   As we go marching on."

This was the fine fruit of Mrs. Howe's early religious faith. It welled up in her nature from a deep undercurrent, which few would have suspected who only met her at Sam G. Ward's dinner parties and other fashionable entertainments. Yet, there was always a quiet reserve in her laughter, and her wittiest remarks were always followed by a corresponding seriousness of expression. Although she studied Spinoza, admired Emerson, and attended meetings of the Radical Club on Chestnut Street, she never separated herself from the Church, and always expressed her dissent from any opinion that seemed to show a lack of reverence.

On a certain occasion when a member of the club spoke of newspapers as likely to supersede the pulpit, Mrs. Howe replied to him: "God forbid that should happen. God forbid we should do without the pulpit. It is the old fable of the hare and the tortoise. We need the hare for light running, but the slow, steady tortoise wins the goal at last." Religious subjects, however, were not so much discussed at the Radical Club as philosophy and politics,--and in these Mrs. Howe felt herself very much at home.

On another occasion, when a member of the club said that he was prepared, like Emerson, to accept the universe, Mrs. Howe interposed with the remark that it was Margaret Fuller who accepted the universe; she "was not aware that the universe had been offered to Emerson." She said this because Margaret Fuller was a woman.

Once, when writing for the newspapers was under discussion, Mrs. Howe remarked that in that kind of composition one felt prescribed like St. Simeon Stylites by the limitations of the column.

One of the best of her witty poems describes Boston on a rainy day, and is called "Expluvior," an innocent parody on Longfellow's "Excelsior," which, by the way, ought to have been called Excelsius.

> "The butcher came a walking flood,
> Drenching the kitchen where he stood.
> 'Deucalion, is your name?' I pray.
> 'Moses,' he choked and slid away.
> ### *Expluvior*,"

is one of the most characteristic verses; but in the last stanza she wishes to construct a dam at the foot of Beacon Hill and cause a flood that would sweep the rebel sympathizers out of Boston.

The office of the Blind Asylum was formerly near the middle of Bromfield Street on the southern side. This is now historic ground. Between 1850 and 1870 some of the most important national councils were held there in Dr. Howe's private office. It was the first place that Sumner went to in the morning and the last place that Governor Andrew stopped before returning to his home at night. There Dr. Howe and George L. Stearns consulted with John Brown concerning measures for the defence of Kansas; and there Howe, Stearns, and Bird concerted plans for the election of Andrew in 1860, and for the re-election of Sumner in 1862. It was a quiet, retired spot in the midst of a hustling city, where a celebrated man could go without attracting public attention.

Chevalier Howe outlived Sumner just one year, and Wilson followed him not long after.

THE WAR GOVERNOR.

Sebago is one of the most beautiful of the New England lakes, and has been celebrated in Longfellow's verse for its curiously winding river between the upper and the lower portion, as well as for the Indian traditions connected with it. John A. Andrew's grandfather, like Hawthorne's father, lived in Salem and both families emigrated to Sebago, the former locating himself in the small town of Windham. At the time when Hawthorne was sailing his little boat on the lake, at the age of fourteen, John Andrew was in his nurse's arms,--born May 31, 1818. Like Hawthorne and Longfellow he went to Bowdoin College, but did not distinguish himself there as a scholar,--had no honors at commencement. We are still in ignorance concerning his college life, what his interests were, and how he spent his time; but Andrew never cared much for anything which had not an immediate and practical value. Greek and Latin, merely for their own sake as ancient languages, did not appeal to him; nor did the desiccated history and cramping philosophy of those days attract him more strongly. Yet he ultimately developed one of the finest of American intellects.

He was admitted to the Suffolk bar at the age of twenty-two. He had already formed decided opinions on the slavery question. The practitioner with whom he studied was precisely the opposite of Andrew,--a brilliant scholar, but formal and unsympathetic. Although a young man of fine promise he was soon excelled by his less learned but more energetic pupil. At the age of twenty-six we find Andrew presiding at a convention of Free-soilers, the same which nominated Dr. S. G. Howe for Congress. Why he did not appear in politics between 1844 and 1859 is something of a mystery, which may be explained either by his devotion to his profession or his unwillingness to make politics a profession. He was in constant communication with Charles Francis Adams, Frank W. Bird, and other leading independents, and played a part in the election of Sumner as well as at various nominating conventions; but he apparently neither sought office nor was sought for it. It may have been a modest conscientiousness of his own value, which prevented the acceptance of public honors until he was prepared to claim the best; but the fact is difficult to account for on any supposition.

Neither was his success at the bar remarkable. He never earned a large income, and died comparatively poor. There were few who cared to meet him in debate, yet his legal scholarship was not exceptional, and his political opinions may have proved an impediment to him in a city which was still devoted to Webster and Winthrop. Moreover, his kindness of heart prompted him to undertake a large number of cases for which he received little or no remuneration. As late as 1856 he was known as the poor man's lawyer rather than as a distinguished pleader. One cannot help reflecting what might have been John A. Andrew's fortune if he had been born in Ohio or Illinois. In the latter State he would have proved a most important political factor; for he was fully as able a speaker as Douglas, and he combined with this a large proportion of those estimable qualities which we all admire in Abraham Lincoln. He had not the wit of Lincoln, nor his immense fund of anecdote, which helped so much to make him popular, but the cordial manners and manly frankness of Andrew were very captivating. He would have told Douglas to his face that he was a demagogue, as Mirabeau did to Robespierre, and would have carried the audience with him. It certainly seems as if he would have risen to distinction there more rapidly than in old-fashioned, conventional Boston.

Governor Andrew was an inch shorter than the average height of man, and much resembled Professor Child in personal appearance. He was a larger man than Professor Child, and his hair was darker, but he had the same round, good-humored face, with keen penetrating eyes beneath a brow as finely sculptured as that of a Greek statue, and closely curling hair above it. He was broad-shouldered, remarkably so, and had a strong figure but not a strong constitution. His hands were soft and as white as a woman's; and though his step was quick and elastic he disliked to walk long distances, and was averse to physical exercise generally.

He also resembled Professor Child in character,--frank without bluntness; sincere both formally and intellectually,--full to the brim of moral courage. He was not only kind-hearted, but very tender-hearted, so that his lips would quiver on occasions and his eyes fill with tears,--what doctors improperly call a lachrymose nature; but in regard to a question of principle or public necessity he was as firm as Plymouth Rock. Neither did he deceive himself, as kindly persons are too apt to do, in regard to the true conditions of the case in hand. He would interrogate an applicant for assistance in as judicious a manner as he would a witness in a court room. He never degenerated into the professed philanthropist, who makes a disagreeable and pernicious habit of one of the noblest attributes of man. "A mechanical virtue," he would say, "is no virtue at all."

The impressions of youth are much stronger and more enduring than those of middle life, and I still remember Andrew as he appeared presiding at the meeting for the benefit of John Brown's wife and daughters in November, 1859. This was his first notable appearance before the public, and nothing could have been more daring or more likely to make him unpopular; and yet within twelve months he was elected Governor. His attitude and his whole appearance was resolute and intrepid. He had set his foot down, and no power on earth could induce him to withdraw it. A clergyman who had been invited to speak at the meeting had at first accepted, but being informed by some of his parishioners that the thing would not do, declined with the excuse that he had supposed there would be two sides to the question. "As if," said Andrew, "there could be two sides to the question whether John Brown's wife and daughters should be permitted to starve." Thomas Russell, Judge of the Superior Court, sat close under the platform, clapping his hands like pistol shots.

John A. Andrew's testimony before the Harper's Ferry investigating committee has a historical value which Hay and Nicolay, Wilson, and Von Holst would have done well to have taken into consideration; but the definitive history of the war period is yet to be written. There was no reason why Andrew should have been summoned. He had never met John Brown but once--at a lady's house in Boston--and had given him twenty-five dollars without knowing what was to be done with it. Jefferson Davis and the other Southern members of the committee evidently sent for him to make capital against the Republican party, but the result was different from what they anticipated. Andrew told them squarely that the Harper's Ferry invasion was the inevitable consequence of their attempt to force slavery on Kansas against the will of its inhabitants, and that the Pottawatomie massacre, whether John Brown was connected with it or not, was not so bad in its moral effect as the assault on Sumner. It was what they might expect from attempting to tyrannize over frontier farmers. It is not to be supposed that such men will be governed by the nice sense of justice of an eastern law court.

His testimony in regard to the personal magnetism of John Brown is of great value; but he also admitted that there was something about the old man which he could not quite understand,--a mental peculiarity which may have resulted from his hard, barren life, or the fixedness of his purpose.

Andrew had already been elected to the Legislature, and had taken his seat there in January, 1860. Almost in an instant he became the leader of his party in the House. Always ready to seize the right moment, he united the two essential qualities of a debater, a good set speech and a pertinent reply. Perfectly fearless and independent, he was exactly the man to guide his party through a critical period. There were few in the house who cared to interfere with him.

Andrew was chairman of the Massachusetts delegation at the Chicago Convention in May, and although he voted for Seward he was directly instrumental in the nomination of Lincoln. It is said to have been at his suggestion that the Massachusetts delegation called together the delegations of those States that defeated Fremont in 1856, and inquired of them which of the candidates would be most certain to carry their constituencies; and with one accord they all answered Lincoln. Thus Lincoln's nomination was practically assured before the voting began.

It has been repeatedly asserted that the nomination of Andrew for Governor was the result of a general popular movement; but this was simply impossible. He was chiefly known to the voters of the State at that time as the presiding officer of a John Brown meeting, and that was quite as likely to retard as to advance his interests. He had, however, become a popular leader in the Legislature, and the fact that Governor Banks was opposed to him and cast his influence in favor of a Pittsfield candidate, left a sort of political vacuum in the more populous portion of the State, which Frank W. Bird and Henry L. Pierce took advantage of to bring his name forward. Sumner and Wilson threw their weight into the scales, and Andrew was easily nominated; but he owed this to Frank W. Bird more than to any other supporter.

In the New York *Herald* of December 20, 1860, there was the following item: "Governor-elect Andrew, of Massachusetts, and George L. Stearns have gone to

Washington together, and it is said that the object of their visit is to brace up weak-kneed Republicans." This was one object of their journey, but they also went to survey the ground and see what was the true state of affairs at the Capital. Stearns wrote from Washington to the Bird Club: "The watchword here is 'Keep quiet,'" a sentence full of significance for the interpretation of the policy pursued by the Republican leaders that winter. Andrew returned with the conviction that war was imminent and could not be prevented. His celebrated order in regard to the equipment of the State militia followed immediately, and after the bombardment of Fort Sumter this was looked upon as a true prophecy. He foresaw the difficulty at Baltimore, and had already chartered steamships to convey regiments to Washington, in case there should be a general uprising in Maryland.

Both Sumner and Wilson opposed the appointment of General Butler to the command of the Massachusetts Volunteers, and preferred Caleb Gushing, who afterwards proved to be a more satisfactory member of the Republican party than Butler; but, on the whole, Andrew would seem to have acted judiciously. They were both bold, ingenious and quick-witted men, but it is doubtful if Gushing possessed the dash and intrepidity which Butler showed in dealing with the situation at Baltimore. That portion of his military career was certainly a good success, and how far he should be held responsible for the corrupt proceedings of his brother at New Orleans I do not undertake to decide.

It is likely that Governor Andrew regretted his choice three weeks later, when General Butler offered his services to the Governor of Maryland to suppress a slave insurrection which never took place, and of which there was no danger then or afterwards. A sharp correspondence followed between the Governor and the General, in which the latter nearly reached the point of insubordination. For excellent reasons this was not made public at the time, and is little known at the present day; but General Butler owed his prominence in the war wholly to Governor Andrew's appointment.

Another little-known incident was Andrew's action in regard to the meeting in memory of John Brown, which was held on December 2, 1861, by Wendell Phillips, F. B. Sanborn and others, who were mobbed exactly as Garrison was mobbed thirty years earlier. The Mayor would do nothing to protect them, and when Wendell Phillips went to seek assistance from Andrew the latter declined to interfere. It would be a serious matter to interfere with the Mayor, and he did not feel that the occasion demanded it. Moreover he considered the celebration at that time to be prejudicial to the harmony of the Union cause. Phillips was already very much irritated and left the Governor's office in no friendly mood. Andrew might have said to him: "You have been mobbed; what more do you want? There is no more desirable honor than to be mobbed in a good cause."

Governor Andrew's appointments continued to be so favorable to the Democrats that Martin F. Conway, the member of Congress from Kansas, said: "The Governor has come into power with the help of his friends, and he intends to retain it by conciliating his opponents." It certainly looked like this; but no one who knew Andrew intimately would believe that he acted from interested motives. Moreover it was wholly unnecessary to conciliate them. It is customary in Massachusetts to give the Governor three annual terms, and no more; but Andrew was re-elected four times, and it seemed as if he might have had as many terms as Caius Marius had consulships if he had only desired it.

His object evidently was to unite all classes and parties in a vigorous support of the Union cause, and he could only do this by taking a number of colonels and other commissioned officers from the Democratic ranks. For company officers there was no better recommendation to him than for a young man to be suspended, or expelled, from Harvard University. "Those turbulent fellows," he said, "always make good fighters, and," he added in a more serious tone, "some of them will not be greatly missed if they do not return." The young aristocrat who was expelled for threatening to tweak his professor's nose obtained a commission at once.

Another case of this sort was so pathetic that it deserves to be commemorated. Sumner Paine (named after Charles Sumner), the finest scholar in his class at Harvard, was suspended in June, 1863, for some trifling folly and went directly to the Governor for a commission as Lieutenant. Having an idea that the colored regiments were a particular hobby with the Governor, he asked for a place in one of them; but Andrew replied that the list was full; he could, however, give him a Lieutenancy in the Twentieth Massachusetts, which was then in pursuit of General Lee. Sumner Paine accepted this, and ten days later he was shot dead on the field of Gettysburg. Governor Andrew felt very badly; for Paine was not only a fine scholar but very handsome, and, what is rare among hard students, full of energy and good spirits.

Governor Andrew tried a number of conclusions, as Shakespeare would call them, with the National Government during the war, but the most serious difficulty of this kind resulted from Secretary Stanton's arbitrary reduction of the pay of colored soldiers from thirteen to eight dollars a month. This, of course, was a breach of contract, and Governor Andrew felt a personal responsibility in regard to it, so far as the Massachusetts regiments were concerned.

He first protested against it to the Secretary of War; but, strange to say, Stanton obtained a legal opinion in justification of his order from William Whiting, the solicitor of the War Department. Governor Andrew then appealed to President Lincoln, who referred the case to Attorney- General Bates, and Bates, after examining the question, reported adversely to Solicitor Whiting and notified President Lincoln that the Government would be liable to an action for damages. The President accordingly referred this report to Stanton, who paid no attention whatever to it.

Meanwhile the Massachusetts Legislature had passed an act to make good the deficiency of five dollars a month to the Massachusetts colored regiments, but the private soldiers, with a magnanimity that should never be forgotten, refused to accept from the State what they considered due them from the National Government. At last Governor Andrew applied to Congress for redress, declaring that if he did not live to see justice done to his soldiers in this world he would carry his appeal "before the Tribunal of Infinite Justice."

Thaddeus Stevens introduced a bill for the purpose June 4,1864, and after waiting a whole year the colored soldiers received their dues. Andrew declared in his message to Congress that this affair was a disgrace to the National Government; and I fear we shall have to agree with him.[15]

Sixty years ago Macaulay noticed the injurious effects on oratory of newspaper publication. Parliamentary speeches were written to be read rather than to be listened to. It was a peculiarity of Andrew, however, that he wrote his letters and even his messages to the Legislature as if he were making a speech. In conversation he was plain, sensible and kindly.

He made no pretensions to oratory in his public addresses, but his delivery was easy, clear, and emphatic. At times he spoke rather rapidly, but not so much so as <u>to create a confused impression. I never knew him to make an</u> ***argumentum ad***

15   At this time there were not less than five thousand officers drawing pay in the Union armies above the requisite proportion of one officer to twenty-two privates.

hominem, nor to indulge in those rhetorical tricks which even Webster and Everett were not wholly free from. He convinced his hearers as much by the fairness of his manner as by anything that he said.

The finest passage in his speeches, as we read them now, is his tribute to Lincoln's character in his address to the Legislature, following upon Lincoln's assassination. After describing him as the man who had added "martyrdom itself to his other and scarcely less emphatic claims to human veneration, gratitude and love," he continued thus: "I desire on this grave occasion to record my sincere testimony to the unaffected simplicity of his manly purpose, to the constancy with which he devoted himself to his duty, to the grand fidelity with which he subordinated himself to his country, to the clearness, robustness, and sagacity of his understanding, to his sincere love of truth, his undeviating progress in its faithful pursuit, and to the confidence which he could not fail to inspire in the singular integrity of his virtues and the conspicuously judicial quality of his intellect."

Could any closer and more comprehensive description be given of Andrew's own character; and is there another statement so appreciative in the various biographies of Lincoln?

The instances of his kindness and helpfulness were multitudinous, but have now mostly lapsed into oblivion. During his five years in office it seemed as if every distressed man, woman, and child came to the Governor for assistance. William G. Russell, who declined the position of Chief Justice, once said of him: "There was no better recommendation to Andrew's favor than for a man to have been in the State's prison, if it could only be shown that he had been there longer than he deserved."

Andrew considered the saving of a human soul more important than rescuing a human life. That he was often foiled, deceived, and disappointed in these reformatory attempts is perfectly true; but was it not better so than never to have made them? For a long time he had charge of an intemperate nephew, who even sold his overcoat to purchase drink; but the Governor never deserted the fellow and cared for him as well as he could.

This is the more significant on account of Andrew's strong argument against prohibitory legislation, which was the last important act of his life.

In February, 1864, there was a military ball at Concord for the benefit of the Thirty-second Massachusetts Regiment. Governor Andrew was present, and seeing the son of an old friend sitting in a corner and looking much neglected while his brother was dancing and having a fine time, the Governor went to him, took him by the arm and marched several times around the hall with him. He then went to Mrs. Hawthorne, inquired what her husband was writing, and explained the battle of Gettysburg to her, drawing a diagram of it on a letter which he took from his coat pocket. Years afterwards Mrs. Hawthorne spoke of this as one of the pleasantest interviews of her life.

He would come in late to dinner at the Bird Club, looking so full of force that he seemed as much like a steam-engine as a man. They usually applauded him, but he paid no attention to it. "Waiter, bring me some minced fish with carrots and beets," he would say. His fish-dinner became proverbial, but he complained that they could not serve it at fine hotels in the way our grandmothers made it. He said it did not taste the same.

His private secretary states that Governor Andrew's favorite *sans souci* was to take a drive into the country with some friend, and after he had passed the thickly settled suburbs to talk, laugh and jest as young men do on a yachting excursion,-- but his talk was always refined. There was no recreation that Professor Francis J. Child liked better than this.

Andrew's valedictory address on January 5, 1865, which was chiefly concerned with the reconstruction of the Southern States, was little understood at the time even by his friends; and in truth he did not make out his scheme as clearly as he might have done. He considered negro suffrage the first essential of reconstruction, but he did not believe in enfranchising the colored people and disfranchising the whites. He foresaw that this could only end in disaster; and he advised that the rebellious States should remain under military government until the white people of the South should rescind their acts of secession and adopt negro suffrage of their own accord. There would have been certain advantages in this over the plan that was afterwards adopted--that is, Sumner's plan--but it included the danger that the Southern States might have adopted universal suffrage and negro citizenship for the sake of Congressional representation, and afterwards have converted it into a dead letter, as it is at present. Andrew considered Lincoln's attempts at reconstruction as premature, and therefore injudicious.

For nearly twenty-five years John A. Andrew was a parishioner of Rev. James

Freeman Clarke, who preached in Indiana Place Chapel. In 1848 Rev. Mr. Clarke desired to exchange with Theodore Parker, but older members of his parish strenuously opposed it. Andrew, then only twenty-seven years old, came forward in support of his pastor, and argued the case vigorously, not because he agreed with Parker's theological opinions, but because he considered the opposition illiberal. After this both Andrew and Clarke would seem to have become gradually more conservative, for when the latter delivered a sermon or lecture in 1866 in opposition to Emerson's philosophy, the ex-Governor printed a public letter requesting him to repeat it. It is easy to trace the influence of James Freeman Clarke in Governor Andrew's religious opinions and Andrew's influence on Rev. Mr. Clarke's politics. Each was a firm believer in the other.

The movement to supersede Sumner with Andrew as United States Senator, in 1869, originated in what is called the Back Bay district. It was not because they loved Andrew there, but because they hated Sumner, who represented to their minds the loss of political power which they had enjoyed from the foundation of the Republic until his election in 1850, and have never recovered it since. Andrew's political record and his democratic manners could hardly have been to their liking.

The Boston aristocracy counted for success on the support of the Grand Army veterans, who were full of enthusiasm for Andrew; but it is not probable that the ex-Governor would have been willing to lead a movement which his best friends disapproved of, and which originated with the same class of men who tried so hard to defeat him in 1862. Moreover, they would have found a very sturdy opponent in Senator Wilson. It was Wilson who had made Sumner a Senator, and for fifteen years they had fought side by side without the shadow of a misunderstanding between them. Under such conditions men cannot help feeling a strong affection for one another. Besides this, Wilson would have been influenced by interested motives. Sumner cared nothing for the minor Government offices--the classified service--except so far as to assist occasionally some unfortunate person who had been crowded out of the regular lines; and this afforded Wilson a fine opportunity of extending his influence. If Andrew were chosen Senator in the way that was anticipated Wilson knew well enough that this patronage would have to be divided between them.

Andrew could not have replaced Sumner in the Senate. He lacked the physical strength as well as the experience, and that extensive range of legal and historical knowledge which so often disconcerted Sumner's opponents. He had a genius for the executive, and the right position for him would have been in President Grant's cabinet. That he would have been offered such a place can hardly be doubted.

But Governor Andrew's span of life was over. He might have lived longer if he had taken more physical exercise; but the great Civil War proved more fatal to the statesmen who were engaged in it than to the generals in the field. None of the great leaders of the Republican party lasted very long after this.

Andrew's friends always felt that the man was greater than his position, and that he really missed the opportunity to develop his ability to its full extent. His position was not so difficult as that of Governor Morgan, of New York, or Governor Morton, of Indiana; for he was supported by one of the wealthiest and most patriotic of the States. It was his clear insight into the political problems of his time and the fearlessness with which he attacked them that gave him such influence among his contemporaries, and made him felt as a moral force to the utmost limits of the Union. No public man has ever left a more stainless reputation, and we only regret that he was not as considerate of himself as he was of others.

THE COLORED REGIMENTS

The first colored regiment in the Civil War was organized by General Hunter at Beaufort, S. C., in May, 1862, without permission from the Government; and some said, perhaps unjustly, that he was removed from his command on that account. It was reorganized by General Saxton the following August, and accepted by the Secretary of War a short time afterwards. Rev. T. W. Higginson, who had led the attack on Boston Court House in the attempt to rescue Anthony Burns, was commissioned as its Colonel.

In August also George L. Stearns, being aware that Senator Sumner was preparing a speech to be delivered at the Republican State convention, went to his house on Hancock Street and urged that he should advocate in it the general enlistment of colored troops; but Sumner said decisively, "No, I do not consider it advisable to agitate that question until the Proclamation of Emancipation has become a fact. Then we will take another step in advance." At a town meeting held in Medford, in December, Mr. Stearns made a speech on the same subject, and was hissed for his pains by the same men who were afterwards saved from the conscription of 1863 by the negroes whom he recruited.

Lewis Hayden, the colored janitor of the State House, always claimed the credit of having suggested to Governor Andrew to organize a colored regiment of Massachusetts Volunteers. William S. Robinson, who was then Clerk of the State Senate, supported Hayden in this; but he also remarked that Representative Durfee, of New Bedford, proposed a bill in May, 1861, for the organization of a colored regiment, and that it was only defeated by six votes.

As soon as the Proclamation of Emancipation had been issued the Governor went to Washington for a personal interview with the Secretary of War, and returned with the desired permission. Mr. Stearns went with him and obtained a commission for James Montgomery, who had defended the Kansas border during Buchanan's administration, to be Colonel of another colored regiment in South Carolina. Colonel Montgomery arrived at Beaufort about the first of February.

Governor Andrew formed the skeleton of a regiment with Robert G. Shaw as Colonel, but was able to obtain few recruits. There were plenty of sturdy negroes about Boston, but they were earning higher wages than ever before, and were equally afraid of what might happen to them if they were captured by the Confederate forces. Colonel Hallowell says: "The Governor counselled with certain leading colored men of Boston. He put the question, Will your people enlist in my regiments? 'They will not,' was the reply of all but Hayden. 'We have no objection to white officers, but our self-respect demands that competent colored men shall be at least eligible to promotion.'" By the last of February less than two companies had been recruited, and the prospects of the Fifty-fourth Massachusetts did not look hopeful.

When Governor Andrew was in doubt he usually sent for Frank W. Bird and George L. Stearns, but this time Mr. Stearns was before him. To the Governor's question, "What is to done?" he replied, "If you will obtain funds from the Legislature for their transportation, I will recruit you a regiment among the black men of Ohio and Canada West. There are a great many runaways in Canada, and those are the ones who will go back and fight." "Very good," said the Governor; "go as soon as you can, and our friend Bird will take care of the appropriation bill." A handsome recruiting fund for incidental expenses had already been raised, to which Mr. Stearns was, as usual, one of the largest subscribers.

He arrived at Buffalo, New York, the next day at noon, and went to a colored barber to have his hair cut. He disclosed the object of his mission, and the barber promised to bring some of his friends together to discuss the matter that evening. The following evening Mr. Steams called a meeting of the colored residents of Buffalo, and made an address to them, urging the importance of the occasion, and the advantage it would be to their brethren in slavery and to the future of the negro race, if they were to become well-drilled and practiced soldiers. "When you have rifles in your hands," he said, "your freedom will be secure." To the objection that only white officers were being commissioned for the colored regiments he replied: "See how public opinion changes; how rapidly we move forward! Only three months ago I was hissed in a town meeting for proposing the enlistment of colored troops; and now here we are! I have no doubt that before six months a number of colored officers will be commissioned." His speech was received with applause; but when he asked, "Now who will volunteer?" there was a prolonged silence. At length a sturdy-looking fellow arose and said: "I would enlist if I felt sure that my wife and children would not suffer for it." "I will look after your family," said Mr. Stearns, "and see that they want for nothing; but it is a favor I cannot promise again." After this ten or twelve more enrolled themselves, and having provided for their maintenance until they could be transported to the camp at Readville, he went over to Niagara, on the Canada side, to see what might be effected in that vicinity.

In less than a week he was again in Buffalo arranging a recruiting bureau, with agencies in Canada and the Western States as far as St. Louis--where there were a large number of refugees who had lately been liberated by Grant's campaign at Vicksburg. Mr. Lucian B. Eaton, an old lawyer and prominent politician of the city, accepted the agency there as a work of patriotic devotion. Among Mr. Stearns's most successful agents were the Langston brothers, colored scions of a noble Virginia family,-- both excellent men and influential among their people. All his agents were required to write a letter to him every evening, giving an account of their day's work, and every week to send him an account of their expenses. Thus Mr. Stearns sat at his desk and directed their movements by telegraph as easily as pieces on a chess-board. The appropriation for transportation had already passed the Massachusetts Legislature, but where this did not suffice to meet an emergency he drew freely on his own resources.

By the last of April recruits were coming in at the rate of thirty or forty a day, and Mr. Stearns telegraphed to the Governor: "I can fill up another regiment for you in less than six weeks,"--a hint which resulted in the Massachusetts Fifty-fifth, with Norwood P. Hallowell, a gallant officer who had been wounded at Antietam, for its commander.

The Governor, however, appears to have suddenly changed his mind, for on May 7th Mr. Stearns wrote to his wife:

"Yesterday at noon I learned from Governor Andrew by telegram that he did not intend to raise another regiment. I was thunderstruck. My work for three weeks would nearly, or quite, fall to the ground. I telegraphed in reply: 'You told me to take all the men I could get without regard to regiments. Have two hundred men on the way; what shall I do with them?' The reply came simultaneously with your letter: 'Considering your telegraph and Wild's advice, another regiment may proceed, expecting it full in four weeks. Present want of troops will probably prevent my being opposed.' I replied: 'I thank God for your telegram received this morning. You shall have the men in four weeks.' Now all is right."

The Surgeon-General had detailed one Dr. Browne for duty at Buffalo to examine Mr. Stearns's recruits, and if found fit for service by him there was presumably no need of a second examination. This, however, did not suit the medical examiner at Readville, who either from ill will or from some unknown motive, insisted on rejecting every sixth man sent there from the West. Thus there was entailed on Mr. Stearns an immense expense which he had no funds to meet, and he was obliged to make a private loan of ten thousand dollars without knowing in the least how or where he was to be reimbursed.

Finally, on May 8, Mr. Stearns made a remonstrance against this abuse to Governor Andrew in a letter in which he also gave this account of himself:

"I have worked every day, Sunday included, for more than two months   and from fourteen to sixteen hours a day; I have filled the West with   my agents; I have compelled the railroads to accept lower terms of   transportation than the Government rates; I have filled a letter-book   of five hundred pages, most of it closely written."

This letter is now in the archives of the State House at Boston, and on the back of it Governor Andrew has written:

"This letter is respy. referred to Surgeon-General Dole with the request that he would confer with Surgeon Stone and Lieutenant-Colonel Hallowell. It is surprising, and not fair nor fit, that a man trying as Mr. Stearns is, to serve the country at a risk, should suffer thus by such disagreement of opinion.

"JOHN A. ANDREW."

Shortly after this Mr. Stearns returned to Boston for a brief visit, and was met in the street by a philanthropic lady, Mrs. E. D. Cheney, who asked: "Where have you been all this time, Mr. Stearns? I supposed you were going to help us organize the colored regiment? You will be glad to know that it is doing well. We have nearly a thousand men." Mr. Stearns made no reply, but bowed and passed on. This is the more surprising, as Mrs. Cheney was president of a society of ladies who had presented the Fifty-fourth Regiment with a flag; but the fault would seem to have been more that of others than her own. At the celebration which took place on the departure of the regiment for South Carolina, however, Wendell Phillips said: "We owe it chiefly to a private citizen, to George L. Stearns, of Medford, that these heroic men are mustered into the service,"--a statement which astonished a good many.[16]

The Governors of the Western States had never considered their colored population as of any importance, but now, when it was being drained off to fill up the quota of Massachusetts troops they began to think differently. The Governor of Ohio advised Governor Andrew that no more recruiting could be permitted in his State unless the recruits were assigned to the Ohio quota. Andrew replied that the Governor of Ohio was at liberty to recruit colored regiments of his own; but the Massachusetts Fifty-fifth, having now a complement, it was decided not to continue the business any further, and Mr. Stearns's labors at Buffalo were thus brought to an end about the middle of June. He had recruited fully one- half of the Fifty-fourth, and nearly the whole of the Fifty-fifth regiments.

He now conceived the idea of making his recruiting bureau serviceable by placing it in the hands of the Government. He therefore went to Washington and meeting his friend, Mr. Fred Law Olmstead, at Willard's Hotel, the latter offered to go with him to the War Department and introduce him to Secretary Stanton. They found Stanton fully alive to the occasion, and in reply to Mr. Stearns's offer he said:

"I have heard of your recruiting bureau, and I think you would be the best man to run the machine you have constructed. I will make you an Assistant Adjutant-General with the rank of Major, and I will give you authority to recruit colored regiments all over the country."

16   The statement made by Governor Andrew's private secretary concerning the colored regiments in his memoir of the Governor would seem to have been intentionally misleading.

Stearns thanked him, and replied that there was nothing which he had so much at heart as enlisting the black men on a large scale; for no people could be said to be secure in their freedom unless they were also soldiers; but his wife was unwell, and had suffered much from his absence already, and he did not feel that he ought to accept the offer without her consent. In answer to the question how funds for recruiting were to be obtained without any appropriation by Congress, Mr. Stanton said they could be supplied from the Secret Service fund.

When Mr. Stearns and Mr. Olmstead were alone on the street again, the latter said: "Mr. Stearns, go to your room and sleep if you can."

Having returned to Boston, to arrange his affairs for a prolonged absence, and having obtained his wife's consent, Mr. Stearns ordered his recruiting bureau to report at Philadelphia, where he soon after followed it.

The battle of Gettysburg had stirred Philadelphia to its foundations, and its citizens were prepared to welcome anything that promised a vigorous prosecution of the war. Major Stearns was at once enrolled among the members of the Union League Club, the parent of all the union leagues in the country, and was invited to the meetings of various other clubs and fashionable entertainments. A recruiting committee was formed from among the most prominent men in the city. Camp William Penn, while the colored regiment was being drilled, became a fashionable resort, and fine equipages filled the road thither every after-noon. By the middle of July the first regiment was nearly full.

Fine weather does not often last more than a few weeks at a time, and in the midst of these festivities suddenly came Secretary Stanton's order reducing the pay of colored soldiers from thirteen to eight dollars a month. This was a breach of contract and the men had a right to their discharge if they wished it; but that, of course, was not permitted them. Such an action could only be excused on the ground of extreme necessity. The Massachusetts Legislature promptly voted to pay the deficiency to the Fifty-fourth and Fifty-fifth regiments; but the one at Philadelphia was in organization, and Mr. Stearns found himself in the position of a man who has made promises which he is unable to fulfil.

Hon. William D. Kelley and two other gentlemen of the committee went with Major Stearns to Washington to see Stanton, and endeavored to persuade him to revoke the order. Kelley was one of the most persistent debaters who ever sat in

Congress, and he argued the question with the Secretary of War for more than an hour,--to the great disgust of the latter,--but Stanton was as firm as Napoleon ever was. Major Stearns never had another pleasant interview with him.

The Secretary's argument was that some white regiments had complained of being placed on an equality with negroes, and that it interfered with recruiting white soldiers. There was doubtless some reason in this; but the same result might have been obtained by a smaller reduction.

The next morning some one remarked to Major Stearns that it was exceedingly hot weather, even for Washington, and his reply was: "Yes, but the fever within is worse than the heat without." He talked of resigning; but finally said, decisively, "I will go and consult with Olmstead."

He found Mr. Olmstead friendly and sympathetic. He spoke of Secretary Stanton in no complimentary terms, but he advised Mr. Stearns to continue with his work, and endure all that he could for the good of the cause,-- not to be worried by evils for which he was in no way responsible. Mr. Stearns returned to Willard's with a more cheerful countenance.

In the afternoon Judge Kelley came in with the news of the repulse of the Fifty-fourth Massachusetts regiment at Fort Wagner and the death of Colonel Shaw.

There was a colored regiment in process of formation at Baltimore, and another was supposed to be organizing at Fortress Monroe.

Both were nominally under Mr. Stearns's supervision, and he inspected the former on his return trip to Philadelphia, and sent his son to investigate and report on the latter. Not the trace of a colored regiment could be discovered at Fortress Monroe, but there were scores of Union officers lounging and smoking on the piazza of the Hygeia Hotel. Mr. Stearns thought that business economy had better begin by reducing the number of officers rather than the pay of the soldiers. On July 28 Major Stearns wrote from Baltimore:

"I am still perplexed as to the mode in which I can best carry out the   work intrusted to me. It is so difficult to adjust my mode of rapid   working to the slow routine of the Department that I sometimes almost   despair of the task and want to abandon it."

No private business could succeed if carried on after the manner of the National Government at that time, and this was not the fault of Lincoln's administration at all, but of the whole course of Jackson democracy from 1829 to 1861. The clerks in the various departments did not hold their positions from the heads of those departments, but from outside politicians who had no connection with the Government business, and as a consequence they were saucy and insubordinate. They found it to their interest to delay and obstruct the procedure of business in order to give the impression that they were overworked, and in that way make their positions more secure and if possible of greater importance.

Major Stearns had found himself continually embarrassed in his Government service from lack of sufficient funds, and the continual delay in having his accounts audited. The auditors of the War Department repeatedly took exception to expenditures that were absolutely necessary, and he was obliged to advance large sums from his own capital in order to provide the current expenses of his agents. In this emergency he returned to Boston and held a conference with Mr. John M. Forbes and other friends; and they all agreed that he ought to be better supported in the work of recruiting than he had been. A subscription was immediately set on foot, and in a few days a recruiting fund of about thirty thousand dollars was raised and placed in charge of Mr. R. P. Hallowell.

On September 1, Secretary Stanton transferred Major Stearns to Nashville, where he could obtain recruits in large numbers, not only from Tennessee but from the adjoining States. Fugitives flocked to his standard from Alabama, Mississippi, and Kentucky. For the succeeding five months he organized colored regiments so rapidly that it was with difficulty the General commanding at Nashville could supply the necessary quota of officers for them. His letter-writing alone rarely came to less than twenty pages a day, and besides this he was obliged to attend personally to innumerable details which were constantly interfering with more important affairs. Serious questions concerning the rights and legal position of the freedmen were continually arising, and these required a cool head and a clear understanding for their solution.

Edward J. Bartlett, of Concord, who was one of his staff in Nashville, stated afterwards that he never saw a man who could despatch so much business in a day as George L. Stearns. He says:

"I shall never forget the fine appearance of the first regiment we

sent off. They were all picked men, and felt a just pride in wearing
the blue. As fast as we obtained enough recruits they were formed
into regiments, officered and sent to the front. When men became
scarce in the city we made trips into the country, often going beyond
the Union picket line, and generally reaping a harvest of slaves.
These expeditions brought an element of danger into our lives, for
our forage parties were fired into by the enemy more than once, but we
always succeeded in bringing back our men with us. The black regiments
did valuable service for the Union, leaving their dead on many a
southern battle-field. Mr. Stearns was a noble man, courteous, with
great executive ability, and grandly fitted for the work he was
engaged in."

At this time Major Stearns's friend, General Wilde, was recruiting a colored
brigade in North Carolina, and General Ullman was organizing colored regiments
in Louisiana.

Major Stearns's labors were brought to a close in February, 1864, by the eccentric conduct of Secretary Stanton,--the reason for which has never been explained.
He obtained leave of absence to return to Boston at Christmas time, and after a
brief visit to his family went to Washington and called upon the Secretary of War,
who declined to see him three days in succession. On the evening of the fourth
day he met Mr. Stanton at an evening party and Stanton said to him in his roughest manner: "Major Stearns, why are you not in Tennessee?" This was a breach of
official etiquette on the part of the Secretary of War and Major Stearns sent in his
resignation at once. His reason for doing so, however, was not so much on account
of this personal slight as from the conclusion that he had accomplished all that was
essential to be done in this line. His chief assistant at Nashville, Capt. R. D. Muzzey,
was an able man and perfectly competent to run the machine which Mr. Stearns
had constructed.

The importance of his work cannot readily be measured. It was no longer easy
to obtain white volunteers. With a population ten millions less than that of France,
the Northern States were maintaining an army much larger than the one which
accompanied Napoleon to Moscow. General Thomas's right wing, at the battle of

Nashville, was formed almost entirely of colored regiments. They were ordered to make a feint attack on the enemy, so as to withdraw attention from the flanking movement of his veterans on the left; but when the charge had once begun their officers were unable to keep them in check--the feint was changed into a real attack and contributed largely to the most decisive victory of the whole war.

In his last annual Message President Lincoln congratulated Congress on the success of the Government's policy in raising negro regiments, and on the efficiency of the troops organized in this way. It seems very doubtful if the war could have been brought to a successful termination without them.

In 1898 the Legislature of Massachusetts, at the instance of the veterans of the Fifty-fourth and Fifty-fifth regiments, voted to have a memorial tablet for the public services of George Luther Stearns set up in the Doric Hall of Boston State House, and the act was approved by Governor Walcott, who sent the quill with which he signed it to Major Stearns's widow.

EMERSON'S TRIBUTE TO GEORGE L. STEARNS.

Delivered in the First Parish Church of Medford on the Sunday following Major Stearns's death, April 9, 1867.

"We do not know how to prize good men until they depart. High virtue has such an air of nature and necessity that to thank its possessor would be to praise the water for flowing or the fire for warming us. But, on the instant of their death, we wonder at our past insensibility, when we see how impossible it is to replace them. There will be other good men, but not these again. And the painful surprise which the last week brought us, in the tidings of the death of Mr. Stearns, opened all eyes to the just consideration of the singular merits of the citizen, the neighbor, the friend, the father, and the husband, whom this assembly mourns. We recall the all but exclusive devotion of this excellent man during the last twelve years to public and patriotic interests. Known until that time in no very wide circle as a man of skill and perseverance in his business; of pure life; of retiring and affectionate habits; happy in his domestic relations,--his extreme interest in the national politics, then growing more anxious year by year, engaged him to scan the fortunes of freedom with keener attention. He was an early laborer in the resistance to slavery. This brought him into sympathy with the people of Kansas. As early as 1855 the Emigrant Aid Society was formed; and in 1856 he organized the Massachusetts State Kansas Committee, by means of which a large amount of money was obtained for the 'free-State men,' at times of the greatest need. He was the more engaged to this cause by making in 1857 the acquaintance of Captain John Brown, who was not only an extraordinary man, but one who had a rare magnetism for men of character, and attached some of the best and noblest to him, on very short acquaintance, by lasting ties. Mr. Stearns made himself at once necessary to Captain Brown as one who respected his inspirations, and had the magnanimity to trust him entirely, and to arm his hands with all needed help.

"For the relief of Kansas, in 1856-57, his own contributions were the largest and the first. He never asked any one to give so much as he himself gave, and his interest was so manifestly pure and sincere that he easily obtained eager offerings in quarters where other petitioners failed. He did not hesitate to become the banker of his clients, and to furnish them money and arms in advance of the subscriptions which he obtained. His first donations were only entering wedges of his later; and, unlike other benefactors, he did not give money to excuse his entire preoccupation in his own pursuits, but as an earnest of the dedication of his heart and hand to the interests of the sufferers,--a pledge kept until the success he wrought and prayed for was consummated. In 1862, on the President's first or preliminary Proclamation of Emancipation, he took the first steps for organizing the Freedman's Bureau,--a department which has since grown to great proportions. In 1863, he began to recruit colored soldiers in Buffalo; then at Philadelphia and Nashville. But these were only parts of his work. He passed his time in incessant consultations with all men whom he could reach, to suggest and urge the measures needed for the hour. And there are few men of real or supposed influence, North or South, with whom he has not at some time communicated. Every important patriotic measure in this region has had his sympathy, and of many he has been the prime mover. He gave to each his strong support, but uniformly shunned to appear in public. For himself or his friends he asked no reward: for himself, he asked only to do the hard work. His transparent singleness of purpose, his freedom from all by-ends, his plain good sense, courage, adherence, and his romantic generosity disarmed first or last all gainsayers. His examination before the United States Senate Committee on the Harper's Ferry Invasion, in January, 1860, as reported in the public documents, is a chapter well worth reading, as a shining example of the manner in which a truth- speaker baffles all statecraft, and extorts at last a reluctant homage from the bitterest adversaries.

"I have heard, what must be true, that he had great executive skill, a clear method, and a just attention to all the details of the task in hand. Plainly he was no boaster or pretender, but a man for up-hill work, a soldier to bide the brunt; a man whom disasters, which dishearten other men, only stimulated to new courage and endeavor.

"I have heard something of his quick temper: that he was indignant at this or that man's behavior, but never that his anger outlasted for a moment the mischief done or threatened to the good cause, or ever stood in the way of his hearty co-operation with the offenders, when they returned to the path of public duty. I look upon him as a type of the American republican. A man of the people, in strictly private life, girt with family ties; an active and intelligent manufacturer and merchant, enlightened enough to see a citizen's interest in the public affairs, and virtuous enough to obey to the uttermost the truth he saw,--he became, in the most natural manner, an indispensable power in the State. Without such vital support as he, and such as he, brought to the government, where would that government be! When one remembers his incessant service; his journeys and residences in many States; the societies he worked with; the councils in which he sat; the wide correspondence, presently enlarged by printed circulars, then by newspapers established wholly or partly at his own cost; the useful suggestions; the celerity with which his purpose took form; and his immovable convictions,--I think this single will was worth to the cause ten thousand ordinary partisans, well-disposed enough, but of feebler and interrupted action.

"These interests, which he passionately adopted, inevitably led him into personal communication with patriotic persons holding the same views,-- with two Presidents, with members of Congress, with officers of the government and of the army, and with leading people everywhere. He had been always a man of simple tastes, and through all his years devoted to the growing details of his prospering manufactory. But this sudden association now with the leaders of parties and persons of pronounced power and influence in the nation, and the broad hospitality which brought them about his board at his own house, or in New York, or in Washington, never altered one feature of his face, one trait in his manners. There he sat in the council, a simple, resolute Republican, an enthusiast only in his love of freedom and the good of men; with no pride of opinion, and with this distinction, that, if he could not bring his associates to adopt his measure, he accepted with entire sweetness the next best measure which could secure their assent. But these public benefits were purchased at a severe cost. For a year or two, the most affectionate and domestic of men became almost a stranger in his beautiful home. And it was too plain that the excessive toil and anxieties into which his ardent spirit led him overtasked his strength and wore out prematurely his constitution. It is sad that such a life should end prematurely; but when I consider that he lived long enough to see with his own eyes the salvation of his country, to which he had given all his heart; that he did not know an idle day; was never called to suffer under the decays and loss of his powers, or to see that others were waiting for his place and privilege, but lived while he lived, and beheld his work prosper for the joy and benefit of all mankind,--I count him happy among men.

"Almost I am ready to say to these mourners, Be not too proud in your grief, when you remember that there is not a town in the remote State of Kansas that will not weep with you as at the loss of its founder; not a Southern State in which the freedmen will not learn to-day from their preachers that one of their most efficient benefactors has departed, and will cover his memory with benedictions; and that, after all his efforts to serve men without appearing to do so, there is hardly a man in this country worth knowing who does not hold his name in exceptional honor. And there is to my mind somewhat so absolute in the action of a good man, that we do not, in thinking of him, so much as make any question of the future. For the Spirit of the Universe seems to say: 'He has done well; is not that saying all?'"

This monograph was printed in the ***Boston Commonwealth***, April 20, 1867, and has never been republished. It is exceptional in Emerson's writings as the account of a man with whom he was personally and intimately acquainted.

ELIZUR WRIGHT

The influence of Ohio in the United States of America during the past half century may be compared to that of Virginia during the first forty years of the Republic. All of our Presidents, elected as such since 1860, have come from Ohio, or adjacent territory. Cleveland came from beyond the Alleghenies, and Lincoln was born on the southern side of the Ohio River. General Grant and General Sherman came from Ohio; and so did Salmon P. Chase, and John Brown, of Harper's Perry celebrity. Chase gave the country the inestimable blessing of a national currency; and even the Virginians admitted that John Brown was a very remarkable person.

The fathers of these men conquered the wilderness and brought up their sons to a sturdy, vigorous manliness, which resembles the colonial culture of Franklin, Adams, and Washington.

Sitting in the same school-house with John Brown, in 1816, was a boy named Elizur Wright who, like Brown, came from Connecticut, and to whom the people of this country are also somewhat under obligation. Every widow and orphan in the United States who receives the benefit of a life- insurance policy owes a blessing to Elizur Wright, who was the first to establish life insurance in America on a strong foundation, and whose reports on that subject, made during his long term as Insurance Commissioner for Massachusetts, have formed a sort of constitution by which the policy of all life-insurance companies is still guided. His name deserves a place beside those of Horace Mann and William Lloyd Garrison.

Apart from this, his biography is one of the most interesting, one of the most picturesque, when compared with those of the many brilliant men of his time. His grandfather was a sea captain, and his father, who was also named Elizur, was a farmer in Canaan, Connecticut. His mother's name was Clarissa Richards, and he was born on the twelfth of February, 1804. In the spring of 1810 the family moved to Talmage, Ohio, making the journey in a two-horse carriage with an ox-team to transport their household goods. Their progress was necessarily slow, and it was nearly six weeks before they reached Talmage, as it was generally necessary to camp at night by the way-side. This romantic journey, the building of their log- cabin, the clearing of the forest, and above all his solitary watches in the maple-orchard (where he might perhaps be attacked by wolves), made a deep poetic impression on young Elizur, and furnished him with a store of pleasant memories in after life.

They lived at first in a log-cabin, and afterwards his father built a square frame-house with a piazza and veranda in front, which is still standing. The school where Elizur, Jr., met John Brown was at a long distance for a boy to walk. He does not appear to have made friends with John, remarkably alike as they were in veracity, earnestness, and adherence to principle; but John was somewhat the elder, and two or three years among boys counts for more than ten among grown people. In later life, however, Mr. Wright told an interesting anecdote of young Brown, which runs as follows:

John was the best-behaved boy in the school, and for this reason the teacher selected him to occupy a vacant place beside the girls. Some other boys were jealous of this, and after calling Brown a milk-sop, attacked him with snowballs. John proved himself as good a fighter then as he did afterwards at Black Jack. He made two or three snow-balls, rushed in at close quarters, and fought with such energy that he finally drove all the boys before him.

Elizur Wright may have taken note of this affair, and it served him when he entered Yale College in 1822. He had never heard of hazing, and when the Sophomores came to his room to tease him, he received them with true Western cordiality. He found out his mistake quickly enough, and at the first insult he rose in wrath and ordered them out with such furious looks that they concluded it was best to go.

He helped to support himself during his college course not only by teaching in winter, but by making fires, waiting on table, and ringing the recitation bell. In spite of these menial services, he was popular in his class and had a number of aristocratic friends,--among them Philip Van Rensselaer. He was one of the best scholars in his class,--first in mathematics, and so fluent in Greek that to the end of his life he could read it with ease.

He did not wait for graduation. In May, 1826, the Groton Academy suddenly wanted a teacher, and Elizur Wright was invited to take the position. The college faculty sent him his degree a month later,--which they might not have done if they had known how little he cared for it. In his school at Groton was a pretty, dark-eyed girl named Susan Clark, who, for two years previously, had been at school with Margaret Fuller and was very well acquainted with her. Elizur Wright became interested in Miss Clark, and three years later they were married.

One day, while he was living at Groton, Mr. Wright went by the Boston stage to Fitchburg, and on his return held a long conversation with a fellow-passenger, a tall, slender young man with aquiline features, who gave his name as Ralph Waldo Emerson. Mr. Wright found him an exceedingly interesting gentleman, but of so fragile an appearance that it seemed impossible that he should live many years.

From this time the paths of these two young scholars diverged. Emerson became an idealist and an ethical reformer. Elizur Wright became a realist and a political reformer. Realism seems to belong to the soil of Ohio.

Ill health came next in turn, a natural consequence of his severe life at Yale College. He was obliged to leave his school, and for an occupation he circulated tracts for the American Congregational Society, making a stipulation, however, which was characteristic of him, that he should not distribute any that ran contrary to his convictions. In this itinerant fashion he became sufficiently recuperated at the end of a year to marry Miss Clark, September 13, 1829, and accept the professorship of mathematics at Western Reserve College, at Hudson, Ohio. There he remained till 1833, strengthening himself in the repose of matrimony for the conflict that lay before him,--a conflict that every justice-loving man feels that he will have to face at one time or another.

This probably came sooner than he expected. Some anti-slavery tracts, circulated by Garrison, reached Western Reserve College and set the place in a ferment. Elizur Wright became the champion of the anti-slavery movement, not only in the town of Hudson but throughout the State. What Garrison was in New England he became in the West. In the spring of 1833 he resigned his professorship and spent the next five months delivering lectures on the slavery question. In December of the same year the first national anti-slavery convention met in Philadelphia, and

Elizur Wright was unanimously chosen secretary of it. After that he went to New York to edit a newspaper, the *Anti-Slavery Reporter*, remaining until 1839. During the pro-slavery riot in New York he was attacked on the sidewalk by two men with knives, but instantly rescued by some teamsters who were passing. When he reached his home in Brooklyn he found a note from the Mayor advising him to leave the city for some days; to which he replied advising the Mayor to stop the New York ferry-boats. Meanwhile, as Mrs. Wright was too ill to be removed, he purchased an axe and prepared to defend his house to the last extremity. The Mayor, however, adopted his advice, and by this excellent stratagem Brooklyn was saved from the fury of the mob. In 1837 he moved to Dorchester, Massachusetts, to prosecute a similar work in Boston.

Nothing is more remarkable in Mr. Wright's life than his perfect self- poise and peace of mind during such a long period of external agitation. It is doubtful, in spite of his highly nervous temperament, if he ever lost a night's sleep. When he was editing the *Chronotype*, and waiting for the telegraphic news to arrive, he would sometimes lie down on a pile of newspapers and go to sleep in less than half a minute. For mental relaxation he studied the higher mathematics and wrote poetry-- much of it very good. His faith in Divine Providence was absolute. He had the soul of a hero.

During his first years in Boston, Elizur Wright translated La Fontaine's Fables into English verse,--one of the best metrical versions of a foreign poet,--and it is much to be regretted that the book is out of print. It did not sell, of course, and Elizur Wright, determined that neither he nor the publisher should lose money on it, undertook to sell it himself. In carrying out this plan he met with some curious experiences. He called on Professor Ticknor, who received him kindly, spoke well of his translation, offered to dispose of a number of copies, but--advised him to keep clear of the slavery question.

He went to Washington with the twofold object of selling his book and talking emancipation to our national legislators; and he succeeded in both attempts, for there were few men who liked to argue with Elizur Wright. His brain was a storehouse of facts and his analysis of them equally keen and cutting. One Congressman, a very gentlemanly Virginian, said to him: "Mr. Wright, I wish you could go across the Potomac and look over my district. I think you will find that African slavery is not half as bad as it is represented." Elizur Wright went and returned with the emphatic reply: "I find it much worse than I expected." Having disposed of more than half of his edition in this manner, in the spring of 1842 he went to England, and with the kind assistance of Browning and Pringle succeeded in placing the rest of his books there to his satisfaction. Having a great admiration for Wordsworth's poetry, he made a long journey to see that celebrated author, but only to be affronted by Wordsworth's saying that America would be a good place if there were only a few gentlemen in it. With Carlyle he had, as might have been expected, a furious argument on the slavery question, and "King Thomas," as Dr. Holmes calls him, encountered for once a head as hard as his own. The Brownings, Robert and Elizabeth, received him with true English hospitality. More experienced than Wordsworth in the great world, they recognized Elizur Wright to be what he was,--a man of intellect and rare integrity. Mr. Wright always spoke of Browning as one of the most satisfactory men with whom he had ever conversed.

In 1840, as is well known, the anti-slavery movement became divided into those who still believed in the efficacy of "moral suasion" and those who considered that the time had come for introducing the question into practical politics. The Texas question made the latter course inevitable, and Elizur Wright concluded that moral suasion had done its work. As he expressed it, in a letter to Mrs. Maria Chapman: "Garrison has already left his enemies thrice dead behind him." He was a delegate to the convention of April 1, 1840, which nominated James G. Birney for the Presidency, and took an active share in the Free-soil movement of 1844,-- a movement which produced exactly the opposite effect from that which was intended; for the defeat of Henry Clay opened the door for the Mexican war and the annexation of a much larger territory than Texas. If Clay had been elected, the history of the United States must have been different from what it has proved.

How Elizur Wright supported his family during this long period of philanthropy will always be a mystery, but support them he did. He had no regular salary like Garrison, but, in an emergency, he could turn his hand to almost anything, and earn money by odd jobs. Fortunately, he had a wife who was not afraid of any kind of house-work. He purchased his clothes of a tailor named Curtis, who kept a sailors' clothing store on North Street, and his mode of living otherwise was not less economical.

That his children suffered by their father's philanthropy must be admitted, but it is a general rule that the families of public benefactors also contribute largely to the general good. His eldest daughters inherited their father's intellect, and as they grew up cheerfully assisted him in various ways.

When the Mexican war began there was great indignation over it in New England, and Lowell wrote his most spirited verses in opposition to it. Elizur Wright took advantage of the storm to establish a newspaper, the *Chronotype*, in opposition to the Government policy. He began this enterprise almost without help, but soon obtained assistance from leading Free-soilers like John A. Andrew, Dr. S. G. Howe, and especially Frank W. Bird, the most disinterested of politicians, who gave several thousand dollars in support of the *Chronotype*. The object of the paper, stated in Mr. Wright's own words, was "To examine everything that is new and some things that are old, without fear or favor; to promote good nature, good neighborhood, and good government; to advocate a just distribution of the proper reward, whether material or immaterial, both of honest labor and rascally violence, cunning and idleness; last, but not least, to get an honest living." In 1848 he had a list of six thousand subscribers; and his incisive pen was greatly feared. The *Post*, which was the Government organ in Boston, attacked him once, but met with such a crushing rejoinder that its editor concluded not to try that game again. His capacity for brain labor was wonderful. He could work fourteen hours a day, and did not seem to need recreation at all.

In the campaign of 1844 Elizur Wright made a number of speeches for the Free-soil candidate in various New England cities. One morning he was returning from a celebration at Nashua, when at the Lowell station Daniel Webster entered the train with two or three friends, and turned over the seat next to Mr. Wright. A newsboy followed Webster, and they all purchased papers. Elizur Wright purchased a Whig paper, and seeing a statement in it concerning the Free-soil candidate which he believed from internal evidence to be untrue, he said quite loud: "Well! this is the finest roorback I have met with." Webster inquired what it was, and, after looking at the statement, pronounced it genuine. A short argument ensued, which closed with Webster's proposing to bet forty pounds that the allegation was true. "I am not a betting man," replied Wright, "but since the honor of my candidate is at stake, I accept your wager." Webster then gave him his card, and Wright returned it by writing his name on a piece of the newspaper.

Elizur Wright no sooner reached his office than he found letters and documents there disproving the Whig statement *in toto*, and later in the day he carried them over to Mr. Webster, who had an office in what was then Niles's Block. Mr. Webster looked carefully through them, congratulated Mr. Wright on his good fortune, and handed him two hundred- dollar bills. Peter Harvey, who was in Webster's office at the time, afterwards stopped Elizur Wright on the sidewalk and said to him: "Mr. Wright, you could have afforded to lose that wager much better than Webster could."

It is remarkable how all the different interests in this man's life-- mathematics, philanthropy, journalism, and the translation of La Fontaine--united together like so many different currents to further the grand achievement of his life. While in England he had taken notice of the life-insurance companies there, which were in a more advanced stage than those in America. They interested him as a mathematical study, and also from the humanitarian point of view. He purchased "David Jones on Annuities," and the best works on life insurance. These he read with the same ardor with which young ladies devour an exciting novel, and without the least expectation that they might ever bring dollars and cents to him; until one day in the spring of 1852 an insurance solicitor placed an advertising booklet in his hand as he was entering the office of the *Chronotype*.

Elizur Wright looked it over and perceived quickly enough that no company could undertake to do what this one pretended to and remain solvent. The booklet served him for an editorial, and before one o'clock the next day agents from every life company in Boston were collected in his office. They supposed at first that it was an attempt at blackmail, but soon discovered that Elizur Wright knew more about the subject than any of them. Neither threats nor persuasions had any effect on this uncompromising backwoodsman. Only on one condition would Mr. Wright retract his statements,--that the companies should reform their circulars and place their affairs in a more sound condition. The consequence of this was an invitation from the presidents of several of the companies for Mr. Wright to call at their offices and discuss the subject with them.

The situation was this, and Mr. Wright saw it clearly: the presidents of the companies were excellent men,--as honorable and trustworthy as the presidents of our best national banks,--and they knew how to organize and conduct their companies in all business matters, but of life insurance as a science they knew as little as they knew of Greek. In those days there was a prejudice against college graduates which prevented their obtaining the highest mercantile positions, and it is doubtful if there was any person connected with the life-insurance companies who could solve a problem in the higher mathematics. The consequence of this was that it placed the presidents quite at the mercy of their own accountants. Recent events have proved with what facility the teller of a bank can abstract twenty or thirty thousand dollars without its appearing in the accounts. Temptations and opportunities of this sort must have been much greater in life-insurance companies, as they were formerly conducted, than it is now in banks. Money may have been stolen without its having been discovered.

Besides this, the temptations of the companies to continually over-bid one another for public favor was another evil which, sooner or later, would lead some of them into bankruptcy. This danger could only be averted by placing their rates of insurance on a scientific basis, which should be the same and unalterable for all companies.

The charters of the companies had been drafted in the interest of the management, without much consideration for the rights or advantages of those who were insured. There were no laws on the statute book which would practically prevent directors of life-insurance companies from doing as they pleased with the immense trust properties in their possession. After two or three interviews with Elizur Wright the presidents of the companies came to the conclusion that he was exactly the man that they wanted, and they commissioned him to draw up a revised set of tables and rates which could serve them for a uniform standard. This work occupied him and two of his daughters for a full year, for which he was compensated with the paltry sum of two thousand dollars. The time was fast approaching, however, when Elizur Wright would be in a position to dictate his own terms to the insurance companies.

It was now that the Bird Club, the most distinguished political club of its time, became gradually formed out of the leading elements of the Free-soil party. At one time this club counted among its members two Senators, three Governors, and a number of Congressmen, and it was a power in the land. Elizur Wright's services as editor of the **Chronotype** gave him an early entrance to it; and having life insurance on the brain, as it were, other members of the club soon became interested in the subject as a political question. In this way Mr. Wright was soon able to effect legislation. Sumner, Wilson, Andrew, and Bird gave him an almost unqualified support. In 1858 he was appointed Insurance Commissioner for Massachusetts, a position which he held until 1866. As Commissioner he formulated the principal legislation on life insurance; and his reports, which have been published in a volume, are the best treatise in English on the practical application of life- insurance principles.

In 1852 he resigned the editorship of the **Chronotype**, and from that time till 1858 he was occupied with life-insurance work, the editing of a paper called the **Railroad Times**, and making a number of mechanical inventions, most important of which was a calculating machine, enough in itself to give a man distinction.

This machine was simply a Gunther rule thirty feet in length wrapped on a cylinder and turned by a crank. Gunther's rule is a measure on which logarithms are represented by spaces, so that by adding and subtracting spaces on this cylinder Mr. Wright could perform the longest sums in multiplication and division in two or three minutes of time.

Not only did the Massachusetts insurance companies come under Mr. Wright's surveillance, but the New York Life, the Connecticut Mutual, and the Mutual Benefit of New Jersey, all large and powerful companies, were obliged to conform to his regulations, for their Boston offices were too lucrative to be surrendered. About this time Gladstone caused an overhauling of the English life-insurance companies, and a number which proved to be unsound were obliged to surrender their charters. Among these latter were two companies which held offices in Boston, and whose character had already been exposed by Elizur Wright.

In 1850, when he became Commissioner, Mr. Wright sent to their agents for a statement of their financial standing, and not receiving a reply requested them to leave the State. Finding that the matter could not be evaded, they at length forwarded two reports signed by two actuaries, both Fellows of the Royal Society, which were not of a satisfactory character, so that Mr. Wright insisted on his previous order. The agents then applied for support to Prof. Benjamin Pierce, the distinguished mathematician of Harvard University, and one of the most aggressively pro-slavery men about Boston. He probably looked upon Elizur Wright as a vulgar fanatic, and supposing that a Fellow of the Royal Society must necessarily be an honorable man, came forward in support of Messrs. Neisen and Woolhouse without sufficiently investigating the question at issue; and the result was a controversy between Elizur Wright and himself in which he was finally beaten off the field.

The statements of both Neisen and Woolhouse was proved to be fraudulent, and the two English companies were expelled from the State.

Mr. Wright's insurance reports brought him such celebrity that all the companies wished to have his name connected with them. His son, Walter C. Wright, became actuary of the New England Life, and his daughter, Miss Jane Wright, was made actuary of the Mutual Union Company. Mr. Wright and his eldest son, John, set up a business for calculating the value of insurance policies, in which the logarithm machine helped them to obtain a large income. With his first ten thousand dollars Mr. Wright purchased a large house and a tract of land in Middlesex Fells, where his family still resides.

In 1865 the office of Life Insurance Commissioner was filched from him by a trade politician who knew as much of the subject as fresh college graduates do of the practical affairs of life. Mr. Wright always regretted this, for he felt that his work was not yet complete; and it is a fact that American life insurance, with its good and bad features, still remains almost exactly as he left it.

It was only after Elizur Wright had ceased to be Commissioner that he discovered a serious error in the calculation of the companies, which may be explained in the following manner:

In the beginning, nearly all the insurance policies were made payable at death, with annual premiums; but the introduction of endowment policies, payable at a certain age, effected a peculiar change in their affairs, of which the managers of the companies were not sensible. Elizur Wright perceived that there were two distinct elements in the endowment policies which placed them at a disadvantage with ordinary life policies, and he called this combination "savings-bank life insurance." An endowment policy, being payable at a fixed date, required a larger premium than one which ran on indefinitely and by customary usage, and the agent who negotiated the policy received the same percentage for commission that he would on an ordinary-life policy; that is, he received a much larger commission in proportion. This evil was increased in cases where endowment policies were paid for, as often happened, in five or ten instalments; and where they were paid for in a single instalment the agent received four or five times what he was properly entitled to.

The same principle was observed by the companies in the distribution of their surplus, so that the holders of endowment policies were practically mulcted at both ends of the line.

In his reports as Insurance Commissioner Elizur Wright had recommended this class of policies as a salutary provision against poverty in old age, and he felt under obligations to the public to correct this injustice,[17] but the insurance agents had also advocated them for evident reasons and were naturally opposed to any project of reform. The managers of the companies also treated the subject coldly, for the discrimination against endowments enabled them to accumulate a larger reserve which made them appear to better advantage before the general public. The numerous agents and solicitors formed a solid body of opposition and raised a chorus against Elizur Wright like that which the robins make when you pick your own cherries. This class of persons when they are actuated by a common impulse make a formidable impression.

Mr. Wright, after arguing his case with the insurance companies for nearly a year without effect, appealed to the public through the newspapers. This, however, had unexpected consequences. Mr. Wright's letters produced the impression, which he did not intend at all, that the insurance companies were unsound, and policy-holders rushed to the offices to make inquiries. Many surrendered their policies.

In this emergency the officers of the companies went to the editors and explained to them that their business would be ruined if Mr. Wright was permitted to continue his attacks on them. They then made Mr. Wright what may have been intended for a magnanimous offer, though he did not look on it in that light,-- namely, an offer of ten thousand dollars a year, if he would retire from the actuary business and not molest them any longer.[18] Elizur Wright refused this, as he might have declined the offer of a cigar, and appealed to the Legislature. The companies then withdrew their business from Mr. Wright and thus reduced his income from twelve thousand dollars a year to about three thousand; but this troubled him no

17   On a policy of ten thousand dollars, it would amount to an appreciable sum.

18   These events took place thirty years ago and have no relation to the present condition and practice of American insurance companies.

more than it would have Diogenes.

In the summer of 1872 a portly gentleman called at Elizur Wright's office on State Street and introduced himself as the president of a well-known Western insurance company. As it was a pleasant day Mr. Wright invited his visitor to Pine Hill, where they could converse to better advantage than in a Boston office; but being much absorbed in his subject, while passing through Medford Centre, he neglected to order a dinner; and the consequence of this was that his portly friend was obliged to make a lunch on cold meat and potato salad. That same evening Mr. Wright's daughter twitted him on his lack of forethought, and hoped such a thing would not happen again, to which he only replied: "The kindest thing you can do for such a man is to starve him." Such was his philosophy on all occasions.

He devised a plan for combining life insurance with a savings bank, by which the laboring man could obtain a certain amount of insurance for his family (or old age) instead of interest upon his deposits. This was an admirable idea, and if he had undertaken to carry it out in the prime of life he might have succeeded in realizing it; but he was now upwards of seventy, and his friends concluded that the experiment would be a risky one, as a favorable result would depend entirely on Mr. Wright's longevity. At the same time he had another enterprise in hand, namely, to convert the Middlesex Fells, in which Pine Hill is situated, into a public park. This was greatly needed for the crowded population on the northern side of Boston, and though the plan was not carried out until after his death, he was the originator and earliest promoter of it.

Elizur Wright's most conspicuous trait was generosity. He lived for the world and not for himself. He was a man of broad views and great designs; a daring, original thinker. He respected Emerson, but preferred the philosophy of John Stuart Mill, from the study of which he became an advocate of free trade and woman suffrage.

He died November 21, 1885, in the midst of a rain-storm which lasted six days and nights. He lies interred at Mt. Hope Cemetery.

DR. W. T. G. MORTON

A distinguished American called upon Charles Darwin, and in the course of conversation asked him what he considered the most important discovery of the nineteenth century. To which Mr. Darwin replied, after a slight hesitation: "Painless surgery." He thought this more beneficial in its effects on human affairs than either the steam-engine or the telegraph. Let it also be noted that he spoke of it as an invention, rather than as a discovery.

The person to whom all scientific men now attribute the honor of this discovery, or invention, is Dr. William T. G. Morton; and, although in that matter he was not without slight assistance from others, as well as predecessors in the way of tentative experiments, yet it was Doctor Morton who first proved the possibility of applying anaesthesia to surgical operations of a capital order; and it was he who pushed his theory to a practical success. It may also be admitted that Columbus could not have discovered the Western Hemisphere without the assistance of Ferdinand and Isabella; but it was Columbus who divined the existence of the American continent, and afterwards proved his theory to be true. There is an underlying similarity between the labors and lives of Columbus and Morton, in spite of large superficial differences.

William Thomas Greene Morton was born August 19, 1819, in Charlton, Massachusetts, a small town in the Connecticut Valley. His father was a flourishing farmer and lived in an old-fashioned but commodious country house, with a large square chimney in the centre of it. William was not only a bright but a very dexterous boy, and was sent to school in the academy at Northfield, and afterwards at Leicester. It is a family tradition that he early showed an experimental tendency by brewing concoctions of various kinds for the benefit of his young companions, and that he once made his sister deathly sick in this manner. His father, finding him a more energetic boy than the average of farmers' sons, advised him to go to Boston, to seek whatever fortune he could find there.

This resulted in his obtaining employment, probably through the Charlton clergyman, in the office of a religious periodical, the ***Christian Witness***; but the situation, though a comfortable one, was not adapted to his tastes, and from some unexplained attraction to the profession, he decided to study dentistry. This he accordingly did, graduating at the Baltimore Dental College in 1842. He then engaged an office in Boston, and soon acquired a lucrative practice. He was an uncommonly handsome man, with a determined look in his eye, but also a kindly expression and pleasing manners, which may have brought him more practice than his skill in dentistry,--although that was also good.

The following year he was married to Miss Elizabeth Whitman, of Farmington, Connecticut, whose uncle, at least, had been a member of Congress,--a highly genteel family in that region. In fact, her parents objected to Doctor Morton on account of his profession, and it was only after his promise to study medicine and become a regular practitioner that they consented to the match. Accordingly, Doctor Morton in the autumn of 1844 commenced a course at the Harvard Medical-School.

Mrs. Morton was a handsome young woman, with a fair face and elegant figure. It would have been difficult to find a better looking couple anywhere in the suburbs, and with good health and strength it seemed as if fortune would certainly smile on them. Doctor Morton built a summer cottage at Wellesley, where the public library now stands, and planted a grove of trees about it; but a mere earthly paradise could not satisfy him. He was not an ambitious man, or he would not have chosen the dental profession; but the food he lived on was not of this world. He had the daring spirit, the speculative temperament, and restless energy of the born discoverer. Already he had made improvements in the manufacture of artificial teeth. He was the first, or one of the first, to recognize the importance of chemistry in connection with the practice of medicine. He had no sooner returned to Boston than he commenced the study of chemistry with Dr. Charles T. Jackson, spending from six to ten hours a week in his laboratory; and he thus became acquainted with the properties and peculiarities of most of the chemical ingredients known at that time.

Mrs. Morton soon discovered with awe and trepidation that she had married no ordinary man. That he had a real skeleton in his closet was to have been expected; but, besides this, there were rows of mysterious-looking bottles, with substances in them quite different from the medicines which were prescribed by the doctors in Farmington. He tried experiments on their black water-spaniel and nearly killed him; and even descended to fishes and insects. He would muse for hours by himself, and if she asked him what he was thinking of he gave her no explanation that she could understand. Although he was so attractive and pleasing, he did not care much for human society.[19] He was kind and good to her, and with that she was content. A more devoted wife, or faithful mother, has not been portrayed in poetry or romance.

These phenomena in Doctor Morton's early life remind one of certain processes in the budding of a flower. They indicate a tendency to some object which perhaps was not at the time wholly clear to the man himself. Impelled by the humanitarian spirit of the age, he moved forward with a clear eye and firm hand to grasp the opportunity when it arrived,--nor was it long delayed.

In considering the discovery of etherization we ought to eliminate all evidence of an ***ex parte*** character, unless it is supported circumstantially; but there is no reason why we should disbelieve Mrs. Morton's statement that her husband made experiments with sulphuric ether; that his clothes smelt of it; and that he tried to persuade laboring-men to allow him to experiment upon them with it. As Dr. J. Collins Warren says: "Anaesthesia had been the dream of many surgeons and scientists, but it had been classed with aerial navigation and other improbable inventions."[20] As long ago as 1818 Faraday had discovered the chief properties of ether, with the exception of its effect in deadening sensibility. In 1836 Dr. Morrill Wyman and Dr. Samuel Parkman had experimented with it on themselves at the Massachusetts Hospital, but without taking a sufficient quantity to produce unconsciousness. It was actually employed in 1842 by Dr. Crawford W. Long, at the University of Pennsylvania, in some minor cases of surgery, but he would seem to have lost confidence in his method and afterwards abandoned it.

In December, 1844, Horace Wells, a dentist of Hartford, had a tooth extracted by his own request while under the influence of nitrous oxide; and the following month he came to Boston, and having made his discovery known, an operation at

19   McClure's Magazine, September, 1896.
20   Anaesthesia in Surgery, 15.

the hospital was undertaken with his assistance, but the patient screamed, and it proved a failure so far as anaesthesia was concerned.

From these facts we readily draw the following conclusions: That the discovery of painless surgery was essentially a practical affair for which only a slight knowledge of chemistry was required; that it was not a discovery made at hap-hazard, but one that necessitated a skilful hand and a clear understanding of the subject; and that the supposition which has sometimes been advanced that Doctor Morton was necessarily indebted to Doctor Jackson for a knowledge of the hypnotic effect of ether is wholly gratuitous.

We will now quote directly from Doctor Warren's lecture on "The Influence of Anaesthesia on the Surgery of the Nineteenth Century," delivered before the American Surgical Association in 1897:

"Morton having acquainted himself by conversation with Mr. Metcalf and Mr. Burnett, both leading druggists, as to purity and qualities of ether, and having also conversed with Mr. Wightman, a philosophical instrument- maker, and with Doctor Jackson as to inhaling apparatus, proceeded to experiment upon himself. After inhaling the purer quality of ether from a handkerchief he awoke to find that he had been insensible for seven or eight minutes.

"The same day a stout, healthy man came to his office suffering from great pain and desiring to have a tooth extracted. Dreading the pain, ho accepted willingly Morton's proposal to use ether, and the tooth was extracted without suffering. Morton reported his success the next day to Jackson, and conversed with him as to the best methods of bringing his discovery to the attention of the medical profession and the public. Jackson pointed out that tooth-pulling was not a sufficient test, as many people claimed to have teeth pulled without pain. It was finally decided that the crucial test lay in a public demonstration in the operating theatre of a hospital in a surgical case."

There is one statement in the above to which, according to our rules of literary procedure, we feel obliged to take exception,--that is, the statement concerning the interview between Morton and Jackson after the successful administration of ether to Morton's patient. It is substantially Doctor Jackson's own statement. Doctor Morton gave a wholly different account before the Congressional Committee of 1852. He said:

"I went to Doctor Jackson, told him what I had done, and asked him to give me a certificate that ether was harmless in its effects. This he positively refused to do. I then told him I should go to the principal surgeons and have the question thoroughly tried. *I then called on Doctor Warren, who promised me an early opportunity to try the experiment, and soon after I received the invitation....*"

Now as these are both *ex parte* statements, and as there are no witnesses on either side, according to the rule we have already established, they will both have to be eliminated.[21] Doctor Morton, however, says previously that it was Doctor Hayward with whom he consulted as to the best method of bringing his discovery before the world.

In the consideration of this subject we come upon a man of rare character--rare even, in his profession. Dr. John C. Warren was the perfect type of an Anglo-Saxon surgeon. His courage and dexterity were fully equalled by his kindness and sympathy for the patient. Cool and collected in the most trying emergencies, it has been said of him that he never performed a capital operation without feeling a pain in his heart; and the evidence of this was marked upon his face, so that it is even visible in the photographs of him. He deserved to have his portrait painted by Rubens. In 1847 Dr. Mason Warren published a review of etherization, in which he makes this important statement:

"In the autumn of 1846 Dr. W. T. G. Morton, a dentist in Boston, a person of great ingenuity, patience, and pertinacity of purpose, called on me several times to show some of his inventions. At that time I introduced him to Dr. John C. Warren. Shortly after, in October, I learned from Doctor Warren that Doctor Morton had visited him and informed him that he was in possession of or had discovered a means of preventing pain, which he had proved in dental operations, and wished Doctor Warren to give him an opportunity in a surgical operation. After some questions on the subject in regard to its action and the safety of it, Doctor Warren promised that he would do so.... The operation was therefore deferred until Friday, October 16, when the ether was administered by Doctor Morton, and the operation performed by Doctor Warren."

It was eminently fitting that Dr. John C. Warren should be the one to introduce

---

21   The Congressional Committee of 1852 did not find Doctor Jackson's report of this interview trustworthy.

painless surgery to the medical profession. Next to Morton he deserves the highest credit for the revolution which it effected: a glorious revolution, fully equal to that of 1688. His quick recognition of Morton's character, and the confidence he placed in him as the man of the hour, deserve the highest commendation. Doctor Warren had invited Doctor Jackson to attend this critical experiment with sulphuric ether at the Massachusetts Hospital; but he declined with the trite excuse that he was obliged to go out of town. This has been generally interpreted by the medical profession as a lack of courage on Jackson's part to face the music, but it may also have been owing to his jealousy of Morton.

This happened October 16th, and on November 13th, Dr. C. T. Jackson wrote to M. Elie de Beaumont, a member of the French Academy, this remarkable letter:

"I request permission to communicate through your medium to the Academy of Sciences a discovery which I have made, and which I believe important for the relief of suffering humanity, as well as of great value to the surgical profession. Five or six years ago I noticed the peculiar state of insensibility into which the nervous system is thrown by the inhalation of the vapor of pure sulphuric ether, which I respired abundantly,--first by way of experiments, and afterwards when I had a severe catarrh, caused by the inhalation of chlorine gas. I have latterly made a useful application of this fact by persuading a dentist of this city to administer the vapor of ether to his patients, when about to undergo the operation of extraction of teeth. It was observed that persons suffered no pain in the operation, and that no inconvenience resulted from the administration of the vapor."

It was the opinion of Robert Rantoul and other members of the Congressional Committee that Doctor Jackson suffered from a "heated and disordered imagination," and that is the most charitable view that one can take of such a letter as this. Whatever may have been the result of Doctor Jackson's investigations with sulphuric ether, it is certain that he added nothing to the scientific knowledge of his time in that respect;[22] and if he persuaded Doctor Morton to make use of it, why was he not present to oversee his subordinate? also, why did he make a charge on his books a few days later against Doctor Morton of five hundred dollars for advice and information concerning the application of ether? It is not customary to charge subordinates for their service but to reward them. The two horns of this dilemma

---

22   Edinburgh Medical Journal, April 1, 1857.

are sharp and penetrating.

In a later memorial of the same general tenor, which Doctor Jackson forwarded to Baron Humboldt, he stated that he had applied to other dentists in Boston to make the experiment of etherization, but found them unwilling to take the risk; but the names of the dentists have never been made public, nor did any such appear afterwards to testify in Doctor Jackson's behalf.

Still more remarkable was the action of the French Academy of Arts and Sciences in these premises. The French Academy was founded by Richelieu, but abolished in the first French Revolution, with so many other enchanted phantasms. Napoleon re-established it, and gave it new life and vigor by a discriminating choice of membership; but it is a close corporation which renews itself by its own votes, and such a body of men is always in danger of becoming a mutual admiration society, and if this happens its public utility is at an end. In the present instance the action of the French Academy was illogical, unscientific, and mischievous.

Doctor Jackson's letter was brought before that august body on January 18, 1847, but previous to that time Doctor Warren had written to Doctor Velpeau, an eminent French surgeon, concerning the success of etherization at the Massachusetts Hospital, and suggesting the use of it in the hospitals at Paris; and Doctor Velpeau referred to this fact at the meeting of January 18th. The contents of this letter have never been made public; but it is incredible that Doctor Jackson's claim should have received any support from it. Nevertheless, the members of the French Academy decided to divide one of the Mouthyon prizes (of five thousand francs for great scientific discoveries) between Dr. W. T. G. Morton and Elie de Beaumont's American friend, Dr. C. T. Jackson; and they *conferred this particular favor on Dr. Jackson at his own representation, without one witness in his favor, and without making an inquiry into the circumstances of the discovery.* Could the Northfield Academy of boys and girls have acted in a more heedless or unscientific manner?

After the justice of this decision had been questioned, the French Academy promulgated a defence of their previous action, of which the essence was that the scientific theory of Doctor Jackson was as essential to the discovery of etherization as the practical skill of Doctor Morton; that is, they attempted to decide a matter of fact by an *a priori* dogmatism. Was not the instruction that Doctor Morton received from the dental college in Baltimore also essential to the discovery,--and to go behind that,--what he learned at the primary school at Churiton? When learning is divorced from reason it becomes mere pedantry or sublimated ignorance, and is more dangerous to the community than unlettered ignorance can be.

This blunder of the French Academy had evil consequences for both Morton and Jackson; for it placed the latter in a false position towards the world, and brought about a collision between them which not only lasted during their lives, but was also carried on by their friends and relatives long afterwards. It is doubtful if Jackson would have contested Morton's claim without European support.

With true dignity of character Doctor Morton declined to divide the Mouthyon prize with Doctor Jackson, and the French Academy accordingly had a large gold medal stamped in his honor, and as this did not exhaust the original donation, the remainder of the sum was expended on a highly ornamental case. The trustees of the Massachusetts Hospital partly subscribed and partly collected a thousand dollars which they presented to Doctor Morton in a handsome silver casket. The King of Sweden sent him the Cross of the Order of Wasa; and he also received the Cross of the Order of St. Vladimir from the Tsar of Russia. He was only twenty-seven years of age at this time.

The ensuing eight years of Morton's life were spent in a desperate effort for recognition--recognition of the importance of his discovery and of his own merits as the discoverer. No one can blame him for this. As events proved, it would have been far better for him if he had finished his course at the medical-school and set up his sign in the vicinity of Beacon Street; but the wisest man can but dimly foresee the future. Doctor Morton had every reason to believe that there was a fortune to be made in etherization. He consulted Rufus Choate, who advised him to obtain a patent or proprietary right in his discovery. Hon. Caleb Eddy undertook to do this for him, and being supported by a sound opinion from Daniel Webster, easily obtained it. Now, however, Morton's troubles began.

He exempted the Massachusetts Hospital from the application of his royalty, and it was only right that he should do so; but, unfortunately, it was the only large hospital where etherization was regularly practised. In order to extend its application Doctor Morton secured the services of three young physicians, practised them in the use of the gas, and paid them a thousand dollars each to go forth into the world as proselytes of his discovery; but they met everywhere with a cold reception, and were several times informed that if the Massachusetts Hospital enjoyed the use of etherization, other hospitals ought to have the same privilege; so that his enterprise proved of no immediate advantage.

The Mexican War was now at its height, and Doctor Morton offered the use of etherization to the government for a very small royalty, but his offer was declined by the Secretary of War. He soon discovered, however, that surgeons in the army and navy were making free use of it,--contrary to law and the rights of men. Individuals all over the country--dentists and surgeons--were doing the same thing; and it was more difficult to prevent this than to execute the game-laws. For such an order of affairs the decision of the French Academy was largely responsible, for if men only find a shadow of right on the side of self-interest, they are likely enough to take advantage of it.

Meanwhile Doctor Jackson, with a few friends and a large body of Homoeopaths who acted in opposition to the regulars of the Massachusetts Hospital, kept up a continual fusillade against Doctor Morton; but this did him little harm, for early in 1847 the trustees of the hospital decided, by a unanimous vote, that the honor of discovering etherization properly belonged to him.

Doctor Jackson questioned the justice of this decision, and applied for a reconsideration of the subject. Whereupon the subject was reconsidered the following year, and the same verdict rendered as before. Doctor Jackson then carried his case to the Boston Academy of Arts and Sciences, when Professor Agassiz asked him the pertinent question: "But, Doctor Jackson, did you make one little experiment?" adding drily, after receiving a negative reply: "It would have been better if you had."

It is to be regretted that Doctor Jackson should have attacked Doctor Morton's private life (which appears to have been fully as commendable as his own), and also that R. W. Emerson should have entered the lists in favor of his brother-in-law. In one of his later books Emerson designates Doctor Jackson as the discoverer of etherization. This was setting his own judgment above that of the legal and medical professions, and even above the French Academy; but Emerson had lived so long in intuitions and poetical concepts that he was not a fairly competent person to judge of a matter of fact. It is doubtful if he made use of the inductive method of reasoning during his life.

Doctor Morton sought legal advice in regard to the infringement of his patent rights; but he found that legal proceedings in such cases were very expensive, and was counselled to apply to Congress for redress and assistance. This seemed to him a good plan, for if he could exchange his rights in etherization for a hundred thousand dollars, he would be satisfied; but in the end it proved a Nessus shirt to strangle the life out of him. He soon found that Congress could not be moved by a sense of justice, but only by personal influence. He gave up his business in Boston and went to Washington with his family, but this soon exhausted his slender resources. Knowing devils informed him that if he wished to obtain a hundred thousand dollars from the government he would have to expend fifteen or twenty thousand in lobbying, but the idea of this was hateful to him, and he declined to make the requisite pledges.

The winter of 1850 and of 1851 passed without result, until finally in December of the latter year, Bissel, of Illinois, made a speech in Doctor Morton's favor, calling attention to the fact that the government had been pirating his patent, and proposing that the subject be referred to a committee. Robert Rantoul seconded the motion, and the step was taken. It was considered better for the chances of success that the proposition should come from a Western man.

This committee continued its meeting throughout the winter and made a thorough-going examination of the question before it. The frankness and plain character of Doctor Morton's testimony is much in his favor, and the description he gave of his own proceedings previous to the first operation in the Massachusetts Hospital show how hard he wrestled with his discovery,--wrestled like Jacob of old,--working half the night with an instrument-maker to devise a suitable apparatus for inhalation. Doctor Jackson and Horace Wells also presented their claims to the committee and were respectfully considered.

The report of this committee is a valuable document,--a study for young lawyers in the sifting of evidence,--and of itself a severe criticism on the judgment of the French Academy, which it considered at too great a distance to judge fairly of the circumstances attending the advent of painless surgery. The committee decided unanimously that Doctor Wells did not carry his experiments far enough to reach a decided result; that Doctor Jackson's testimony was contradictory and not much to be depended on; and that the credit of discovering painless surgery properly appertained to Dr. W. T. G. Morton. They recommended an appropriation of a hundred thousand dollars to be given to Doctor Morton in return for the free use of etherization by the surgeons of the army and navy.

A hundred thousand dollars was little enough. The British Government paid thirty thousand pounds as a gratuity for the discovery of vaccination; and more recently a poor German student made a much larger sum by the invention of a drug which has since fallen into disuse. Half a million would not have been more than Morton deserved, and a hundred thousand might have been bestowed on Wells.

Doctor Morton must have thought now that the clouds were lifting for him at last; but they soon settled down darker than ever. The committee's report was only printed towards the close of the session, and Congress, gone rabid over the Presidential election, neglected to consider it. Neither did it take further action the following winter. A year later a bill was introduced in the Senate for Doctor Morton's relief, and was ably supported by Douglas, of Illinois, and Hale, of New Hampshire. It passed the Senate by a small majority, but was defeated by the "mud-gods" of the House--defeated by men who were pilfering the national treasury in sinecures for their relatives and supporters. In the history of our government I know of nothing more disgraceful than this,--except the exculpation of Brooks for his assault on Sumner.

Doctor Morton was a ruined man. His slender means had long since been exhausted, and he had been running in debt for the past two or three years, as Hawthorne did at the old manse. Even his house at Wellesley was mortgaged. His business was gone, and his health was shattered. He felt as a man does in an earthquake. The government could not have treated him more cruelly unless it had put him to death.

It was now, as a final resort, that he went to see President Pierce, always a kindly man, except where Kansas affairs were concerned; and Pierce advised him to bring a suit for infringement of his rights against a surgeon in the navy. Doctor Morton found a lawyer who was willing to take the risk for a large share of the profits, and gained his case. His house was saved, but he returned to Wellesley poorer than when he came to Boston to seek his fortune, a youth of eighteen.

There was great indignation at the Massachusetts Hospital when the result of Doctor Morton's case before Congress was known there, and soon after his return an effort was made to raise a substantial testimonial for him. That noble-hearted physician, Dr. Henry I. Bowditch, interested himself so conspicuously in this that Doctor Morton named his youngest son for him.

A similar effort was made by the medical profession in New York city, and a sufficient sum obtained to render Doctor Morton moderately comfortable during the remainder of his earthly existence, and to educate his eldest son.

Doctor Morton's health was too much shattered for professional work now, and he resigned himself to his fate. He raised cattle at Wellesley, and imported fine cattle as a healthful out-of-door occupation. In the autumn of 1862 he joined the Army of the Potomac as a volunteer surgeon, and applied ether to more than two thousand wounded soldiers during the battles of Fredericksburg, Chancellorsville, and the Wilderness. At the same time Senator Wil- [*printer's error--double line and missing text] revive the gratuity for Morton in Congress, but the decision of the French Academy was in men's minds, and a vicious precedent proved stronger than reason.

I saw Doctor Morton for the last time about nine months before his death; and the impression his appearance made on me was indelible. He was walking in the path before his house with his eldest daughter, and he seemed like the victim of an old Greek tragedy--a noble Oedipus who had solved the Sphynx's riddle, attended by his faithful Antigone.

In July, 1868, a torrid wave swept over the Northern States which carried off many frail and delicate persons in the large cities, and Doctor Morton was one of those who suffered from it. He happened to be in New York City at the time, and went to Central Park to escape the feeling of suffocation which oppressed him, but never returned alive. He now lies in Mount Auburn Cemetery, with a modest monument over his grave erected by his Boston friends, with this epitaph composed by Dr. Jacob Bigelow:

WILLIAM T. G. MORTON

INVENTOR AND REVEALER OF ANAESTHETIC INHALATION BY WHOM, PAIN IN SURGERY WAS ARRESTED AND ANNULLED BEFORE WHOM, IN ALL TIME, SURGERY WAS AGONY SINCE WHOM, SCIENCE HAS CONTROL OF PAIN

Doctor Morton was a self-made man, but not a rough diamond,--rather one of

Nature's gentlemen. The pleasant urbanity of his manner was so conspicuous that no person of sensibility could approach him without being impressed by it. His was a character such as those who live by academic rules would be more likely to misjudge than to comprehend.

The semi-centennial of painless surgery was celebrated, in 1896, in Boston, New York, London, and other cities, and the credit of its discovery was universally awarded to William T. G. Morton. About the same time it happened that the Massachusetts State House was reconstructed, and William Endicott, as Commissioner, and a near relative of Robert Rantoul, had Morton's name emblazoned in the Hall of Fame with those of Franklin, Morse, and Bell. This may be said to have decided the controversy; but, like many another benefactor of mankind, Doctor Morton's reward on earth was a crown of thorns.

LEAVES FROM A ROMAN DIARY

February, 1869
(Rewritten in 1897)

As I look out of P----'s windows on the Via Frattina every morning at the plaster bust of Pius IX., I like his face more and more, and feel that he is not an unworthy companion to George Washington and the young Augustus.[23] I think there may be something of the fox, or rather of the *crow*, in his composition, but his face has the wholeness of expression which shows a sound and healthy mind,--not a patchwork character. I was pleased to hear that he was originally a liberal; and the first, after the long conservative reaction of Metternich, to introduce reforms in the states of the Church. The Revolution of 1848 followed too quickly, and the extravagant proceedings of Mazzini and Garibaldi drove him into the ranks of the conservatives, where he has remained ever since. Carlyle compared him to a man who had an old tin-kettle which he thought he would mend, but as soon as he began to tinker it the thing went to pieces in his hands. The Revolution of 1848 proved an unpractical experiment, but it opened the way for Victor Emanuel and a more sound liberalism in 1859.

We attended service at the Sistine Chapel yesterday in company with two young ladies from Philadelphia, who wore long black veils so that Pius IX. might not catch the least glimpse of their pretty faces. I was disappointed in my hope of obtaining a view of the Pope's face. Cardinal Bonaparte sat just in front of us, a man well worth observing. He looks to be the ablest living member of that family, and bears a decided resemblance to the old Napoleon. His features are strong, his eyes keen, and he wears his red cap in a jaunty manner on the side of his head. When the blessing was passed around the conclave of Cardinals, Bonaparte transferred it

---

23   Three busts in a row.

to his next neighbor as if he meant to put it through him. It is supposed that he will be the successor of Pius IX.; but, as Rev. Samuel Longfellow says, that will depend very much upon whether Louis Napoleon is alive at the time of the election.

The singing in the Sistine Chapel is not worth listening to, besides having unpleasant associations; so during the service we had an excellent opportunity to study Michael Angelo's Last Judgment--for there was nothing else to be done.

Kugler considers the picture an inharmonious composition, and that nothing could be more disagreeable than the stout figure of St. Bartholomew holding a flaying knife in one hand and his own mortal hide in the other. This is not a pleasant spectacle; but Michael Angelo did not paint for other people's pleasure, but rather to satisfy his own conscience. It was customary to introduce St. Bartholomew in this manner, for there was no other way in which he could be identified. We found the towering form of St. Christopher on the left side of the Saviour rather more of an eyesore than St. Bartholomew, whose expression of awe partially redeems his appearance.

The Saviour has a herculean frame, but his face and head are magnificent. He has no beard, and his hair is arranged in festoons which gives the impression of a wreath of grape leaves. The expression of his face is the noblest I have seen in any work of art in Rome; the face that has risen through suffering; calm, compassionate, immutable. The Madonna seems like a girl beside this stalwart form, and she draws close to her son with naive timidity at the vast concourse which crowds about them. Her face is expressive of resignation and compassion rather than any joyful feeling.

The left side of this vast painting, in which the bodies of men and women are rising from their graves, is less interesting than the right side, where the saints and blessed are gathered together above and the sinners are hurled down below. Michael Angelo's saints and apostles look like vigorous men of affairs, and are all rather stout and muscular. The attitudes of some of them are by no means conventional, but they are natural and unconstrained. St. Peter, holding forth the keys, is a magnificent figure. The group of the saved who are congregated above the saints is the pleasantest portion of the picture. Here Damion and Pythias embrace each other; a young husband springs to greet the wife whom he lost too early; a poor unfortunate to whom life was a curse is timidly raising his eyes, scarcely believing that he is in paradise; men with fine philosophic heads converse together; and a number of honest serving- women express their astonishment with such gestures as are customary among that class of persons.

In the lunettes above, wingless angels are hovering with the cross, the column, and other instruments of Christ's agony, which they clasp with a loving devotion. In the lower right-hand corner, Charon appears (taken from pagan mythology) with a boat-load of sinners, whom he smites with his oar according to Dante's description. He is truly a terrible demon, and his fiery eyes gleam across the length of the chapel. Minos, who receives the boat-load in the likeness of Biagio da Cesena, the pope's master of ceremonies, is another to match him. A modern fop with banged hair is stepping from the boat to the shore of hell. This is said to be the best painted portion of the picture,--most life-like and free from mannerism. It is a mighty work, and too little appreciated, like many other works of art, chiefly owing to the critics, who do not understand it, and write a lingo of their own which is not easy to make out and does not come to much after all.[24]

After the service we went into St. Peter's with the ladies, and walked the whole circuit of the church. Our ladies talked meanwhile exactly as they might at an American watering-place, without apparently observing anything about them. When we came to the statue of St. Peter, P---- said, pointing to the big toe: "You see there the mischief that can be done by too much kissing." Nearly a third of the toe has been worn away by the oscular applications of the faithful.

Feb. 4.--Dr. B. B. Appleton, an American resident of Florence, is here on a flying visit. We have heard from many sources of the kindness of this man to American travellers, especially to young students. In fact, he took P---- into his house while at Florence, and entertained him in the most generous manner. He has done the same for Mrs. Julia Ward Howe and many others. He lives with an Italian family who were formerly in the service of the Grand Duke of Tuscany, and who were ruined by the recent change of rulers. Dr. Appleton boards with them, and helps to support them in other ways. In spite of his goodness he does not seem to be happy.

One of his chief friends in Florence is Fraulein Assig, who was banished from Prussia together with her publisher for editing Von Humboldt's memoirs, which

---

24 All this shows what a heart there was in Michael Angelo, and dissipates the assertion of a recent English biographer that Michael Angelo painted masks instead of faces, with little or no expression.

were perhaps too severely critical of the late king of Prussia. The book, however, had an excellent sale, and she now lives contentedly in Florence, where she is well acquainted both with prominent liberals and leading members of the government. Dr. Appleton reports that a cabinet officer lately said to her, "We may move to Rome at any time."

Louis Napoleon is the main-stay of the papacy, and the only one it has. The retrocession of Venetia to Italy has separated Austria effectually from the states of the Church, and the Spaniards are too much taken up with their internal affairs to interfere at present in the pope's behalf. Napoleon's health is known to be delicate, and prayers for his preservation are offered up daily in Roman churches. If he should die before his son comes of age great political changes may be looked for.

Meanwhile murmurs of discontent are heard on all sides. The city is unclean and badly cared for. The civil offices are said to be filled mainly with **nephews** of cardinals and other prelates. Even Italians of the lower classes know enough of political economy to foresee that if Rome was the capital of Italy it would be more prosperous than it is at present. The value of land would rise, and all the small trades would flourish. This is what is really undermining the power of Pius IX. A most curious sign of the times is the general belief among the Roman populace that the Pope has an evil eye. How long since this originated I have not been able to learn; but it is not uncommon for those who chance to see the pope in his carriage, especially women, to go immediately into the nearest church for purification. A few days since the train from Rome to Florence ran into a buffalo, and the locomotive was thrown off the track. Even this was attributed to the fact that the engineer had encountered the pope near the Quirinal the previous Sunday.

Dr. Appleton told us a story at dinner about the youth of Louis Napoleon. His Florentine housekeeper, Gori, remembers Hortense and her two sons very distinctly; for Louis once met him in the Boboli Gardens and insisted on his smoking a cigar, in order to laugh at him when it had made him sick,--as it was Gori's first experience with tobacco. He also says that on one occasion when the young princes had some sort of a feast together, the others all gave the caterer from five to ten francs as a **pour-boir**, but Louis Napoleon gave him a twenty-franc piece. When his companions expressed their surprise at this Louis said: "It is only right that I should do so, for some day I shall be Emperor."

As a rule few Italian men attend church. The women go; but the men, if not heretical, are at least rather indifferent, on the subject of religion. Macaulay refers to this fact in his essay on Macchiavelli, and Dr. Appleton, who has lived among them, knows it to be true. To make amends for it, English and American ladies are returning to the fold of St. Peter in large numbers; and many of them bring their male relatives eventually with them. I believe this to be largely a matter of fashion. They have always accepted the Protestant creed as a matter of course, and coming here, where they are separated from all previous associations, they find themselves out of tune with their surroundings. They feel lonely, as all travellers do at times, and being in need of sympathy are easily impressed by those about them. Most of them have Catholic maids, who often serve as stepping-stones to the acquaintance of the priest. Conversion gives them a kind of importance, which Catholic ladies of rank know how to make the most of. The external grandeur of Catholicism as we see it here has also its due influence.

Feb. 9.--I was greatly disgusted last evening while calling on two New England ladies, who were formerly my schoolmates, to have a pompous priest walk in and take possession of the parlor, spoiling my pleasant *tete-a-tete*. He sat in the middle of the room like a pail of water, and stared about in the most ill-mannered way. My friends remarked that he was the *abbate* of the Pantheon, and he inquired if I had been to see it; to which I replied that I had, and that I considered it the noblest building in Rome. This seemed to be a new idea to him, and one which he did not altogether like. Not long since I came upon a priest drinking wine with some young artists, and laughing at jokes for which a stage-driver might be ashamed. There are fine exceptions among them, but as a class they appear to me coarse and even vicious,--by no means spiritually attractive. Monks are not attractive either, but in their way they are much more interesting. Religion seems to be meat and drink to them.

P---- and I were invited to dine by an American Catholic lady who was formerly a friend of Margaret Fuller, and who having been incautiously left in Rome by her husband, embraced Catholicism before he was fairly across the Atlantic,-- to his lasting sorrow and vexation. Being in an influential position she has made many converts, and it is said that she has come to Rome on the present occasion to be sainted by the pope. She has already loaned P---- a biography of Father Lacordaire, which he has not had leisure to read. He referred to it, as soon as politeness permitted, with a shrewd inquiry as to whether the book did not give rather a rose-colored view of practical Catholicism. Mrs. X---- turned to her daughters and said with all imaginable sweetness: "Just hear him,-- the poor child!" Then she went off into a long, eloquent, and really interesting discourse on the true, sole, and original Christian Church. She admitted, however, that during the sixteenth century the Christian faith had much fallen into decay, and that Martin Luther was not to be blamed for his exhortations against the evil practices of popes and cardinals. Now that the Church had been reformed it was altogether different. She told us how she became converted. It came to her like a vision on a gloomy winter day, while she was looking into the embers of a wood-fire.

Then she talked about Margaret Fuller, whom she called the most brilliant woman she had ever known. She had never loved another woman so much; but it was a dangerous love. If she wrote a rather gushing letter to Margaret, she would receive in reply, "How could you have written so beautifully! You must have been inspired." This, she said, had all the effect of flattery without being intended for it, and was so much the more mischievous. "Emerson and Margaret Fuller," said Mrs. X----, "put inspiration in the place of religion. They believed that some people had direct communication with the Almighty." P---- and I thought this might be true of Miss Fuller, but doubted it in Emerson's case.

Miss X---- told me that she had lately ascended to the rotunda of the Capitol, from which the pope's flag flies all day, and that she had asked the Swiss guard what he would do if she hoisted the tricolor there. He replied: "I should shoot you." Nothing could be more kind or truly courteous than the manner in which these ladies treated us.

Another distinguished convert here is Mrs. Margaret Eveleth, a rare, spirituelle woman, who was born within a mile of my father's house. She was formerly a Unitarian, but soon became a Catholic on coming to Rome. While she was in process of transition from one church to the other she wrote a number of letters to her former pastor in New York, requesting information on points of faith. Not one of these letters was ever answered, and it is incredible to suppose that they would not have been if he had received them. It is highly probable that they never left Rome. I have myself been warned to attach my stamps to letters firmly, so that they may not be stolen in passing through the Post-office. Postage here is also double what it is in Florence.

Feb. 12.--I have been looking for some time to find a good picture of Marcus Aurelius, and have generally become known among Roman photographers as the man who wants the *Marc Aureli*. This morning I had just left my room when I discovered Rev. Samuel Longfellow in a photograph shop in the Via Frattina. "I was just coming to see you," he said; "and I stopped here to look for a photograph of Marcus Aurelius." He laughed when I told him that I had been on the same quest, and suggested that we should walk to the Capitol together and look at the statue and bust of our favorite emperor. "I think he was the greatest of the Romans," said Mr. Longfellow, "if not the noblest of all the ancients."

So we walked together--as we never shall again--through the long Corso with its array of palaces, past the column of Aurelius and the fragments of Trajan's forum, until we reached the ancient Capitol of Rome, rearranged by Michael Angelo. Here we stood before the equestrian statue of Marcus Aurelius, and considered how it might be photographed to advantage. "I do not think," said Rev. Mr. Longfellow, "that we can obtain a satisfactory picture of it. The face is too dark to be expressive, and it is the man's face that I want; and I suppose you do also."

I asked him how he could explain the creation of such a noble statue in the last decline of Greek art; he said he would not attempt to explain it except on the ground that things do not always turn out as critics and historians would have them. It was natural that the arts should revive somewhat under the patronage of Hadrian and the Antonines.

We went into the museum of the Capitol to look for the bust of the young Aurelius, which shone like a star (to use Homer's expression) among its fellows, but we discovered from the earth-stains on portions of it why the photographers had not succeeded better with it. We decided that our best resource would be to have Mr. Appleton's copy of it photographed, and Rev. Mr. Longfellow agreed to undertake the business with me in the forenoon of the next day.

The busts of the Roman emperors were interesting because their characters are so strongly marked in history. The position would seem to have made either brutes or heroes of them. Tiberius, who was no doubt the natural son of Augustus, resembles him as a donkey does a horse. Caligula, Nero, and Domitian had small, feminine features; Nero a bullet-head and sensual lips, but the others quite refined. During the first six years of Nero's reign he was not so bad as he afterwards became; and I saw an older bust of him in Paris which is too horrible to be looked at more than once. Vespasian has a coarse face, but wonderfully good-humored; and Titus, called "the delight of mankind," looks like an improvement on Augustus. The youthful Commodus bears a decided resemblance to his father, and there is no indication in his face to suggest the monster which he finally became.

Early in the next forenoon I reached the Hotel Costanzi in good season and inquired for the Rev. Mr. Longfellow. He soon appeared, together with Mr. T. G. Appleton, who was evidently pleased at my interest in the young Aurelius, and remarked that it was a more interesting work than the young Augustus. The bust had been sent to William Story's studio to be cleaned, and thither we all proceeded in the best possible spirits.

We found a photographer named Giovanni Braccia on the floor a *piano* above Mr. Story; and after a lengthy discussion with him, in which Mr. Longfellow was the leading figure, he agreed to take the photographs at two napoleons a dozen. [25] When the bust was brought in Mr. Longfellow called my attention to the incisions representing pupils in the eyes, which he said were a late introduction in sculpture, and not generally considered an improvement. After this Mr. Appleton called to us to come with him to the studio of an English painter in the same building, whose name I cannot now recollect. He was the type of a graceful, animated young artist, and had just finished a painting representing ancient youths and maidens in a procession with the light coming from the further side, so that their faces were mostly in shadow, with bright line along the profile,--an effect which it requires skill to render.

On returning to the street we looked into Mr. Story's outer room again, where the casts of all his statues were seated in a double row like persons at a theatre. Mr. Appleton was rather severe in his criticism of them, though he admitted that the Cleopatra (which I believe was a replica) had a finely modulated face.

Feb. 15.--Warrington Wood invited P---- and myself to lunch with him in his studio, and at the appointed time a waiter appeared from the *Lapre* with a great tin

---

25   These pictures proved to be fine reproductions, and are still to be met with in Boston and Cambridge parlors.

box on his shoulder filled with spaghetti, roast goat, and other Italian dishes. We had just spread these on a table in front of the clay model of Michael and Satan, when Wood's marble- cutter rushed in to announce the King and Queen of Naples. Wood hastily threw a green curtain over the dishes, while P---- and I retreated to the further end of the room.

The Queen of Naples is a fine-looking and spirited person, still quite young, and talks English well. She conversed with Wood and asked him a number of questions about his group, and also about the stag-hound, Eric, that was standing sentinel. The King said almost nothing, and moving about as if he know not what to do with himself, finally backed up against the table where our lunch was covered by the green cloth. I think he had an idea of sitting down on it, but the dishes set up such a clatter that he beat a hasty retreat. The King did not move a muscle of his countenance, but the Queen looked around and said something to him in Italian, laughing pleasantly. She is said to be friendly to Americans and is quite intimate with Miss Harriet Hosmer. She is at least a woman of noble courage, and when Garibaldi besieged Naples she went on to the ramparts and rallied the soldiers with the shells bursting about her.

They subscribed themselves in Wood's register under the name of Bourbon, and after their departure we found our lunch cold, but perhaps we relished it better for this visitation of royalty. Then we all went to the carnival, where an Italian *lazzaroni* attempted to pick Wood's pocket, but was caught in the act and soundly kicked by Wood.

This was the most entertaining event of the afternoon. The best part of the carnival was the quantity of fresh flowers that were brought in from the country and sold at very moderate prices. P---- distinguished himself throwing bouquets to ladies in the balconies. It is said that he has an admirer among them. For the first hour or so I found it entertaining enough, but after that I became weary of its endless repetition. Eighty years since Goethe, seated in one of these balconies, was obliged to ask for paper and pencil to drive away *ennui*, as he afterwards confessed. The carnival now is almost entirely given up to the English and Americans; while many of the lower class of Italians mix in it disguised in masks and fancy dresses. Four masked young women greeted us with confetti and danced about me on the sidewalk. One tipped up my hat behind and another whispered a name in my ear which I did not suppose was known in Europe. I have not yet discovered who they were.

Feb. 19.--I have had the pleasure of dining with that remarkable woman and once distinguished actress, Miss Charlotte Cushman. Her nephew was consul at Rome, appointed by William II. Seward, who was one of her warmest American friends. She is still queen of the stage, and of her own household, and unconsciously gives orders to the servants in a dramatic manner which is sometimes very amusing. So it was to hear her sing, "Mary, call the cattle home," as if she were sending for the heavy artillery. She impresses me, however, as one of the most genuine of womankind; and her conversation is delightful,--so sympathetic, appreciative, full of strong good sense, and fresh original views. She has small mercy on newly-converted Catholics. "The faults of men," she said, "are chiefly those of strength, but the faults of my own sex arise from weakness." I happened to refer to Mr. Appleton's bust of Aurelius, and she said she was surprised he had purchased it, for it did not seem to her a satisfactory copy; a conclusion that I had been slowly coming to myself. She has a bronze replica of Story's "Beethoven" which, like most of his statues, is seated in a chair, and a rather realistic work, as Miss Cushman admitted. I judged from the conversation at table that she is not treated with full respect by the English and American society here, although looked upon as a distinguished person. The reason for this may be more owing to the social position of her relatives than her former profession. Mrs. Trelawney, the wife of Byron's eccentric friend, spoke of her to me a few days ago in terms of the highest esteem. She is a great-hearted woman, and her presence would be a moral power anywhere.

There is snobbishness enough in Rome--English, American, and Italian. Doolittle, who is the son of a highly respectable New York lawyer, went to the hunt last week, as he openly confessed, to give himself distinction. A young lady was thrown from her horse, and he was the first person to come to her assistance. She thanked him for it at the time, but two days afterwards declined to recognize his acquaintance. This was probably because he was an artist, or rather sets up for one, for he is more like a gentleman of leisure.

MY LAST VISIT TO THE LONGFELLOWS.

The Longfellow party will soon depart for Naples, and I went to the Costanzi to make my final call. Mr. Henry W. Longfellow was alone in his parlor cutting the leaves of a large book. He said that his brother had gone to the Pincion with the ladies, but would probably return soon. Everything this man says and does has the same grace and elevated tone as his poetry. I took a chair and pretty soon he said to me, "How do you like your books, Mr. S----? For my part, I prefer to cut the leaves of a book, for then I feel as if I had earned the right to read it." I replied that I liked books with rough edges if they were printed on good paper; and then he said, "See this remarkable picture."

I drew my chair closer to him, and he showed me a large colored chart of Hell and Purgatory, according to the theory that prevailed in Dante's time. Satan with his three faces was represented in the centre, and on the other side rose the Mount of Purgatory.

"It is an Italian commentary," he said, "on the ***Divina Commedia***," which had been sent to him that day; and he added that some of the information in it was of a very curious sort.

I asked him if he could read Italian as easily as English. "Very nearly," he replied; "but the fine points of Italian are as difficult as those of German."

He inquired how I and my friends spent our evenings in Rome, and I said, "In all kinds of study and reading, but just now P---- was at work on Browning's 'Ring and the Book.'"

Mr. Longfellow laughed. "I do not wonder you call it work," he said. "It seems to me a story told in so many different ways may be something of a curiosity--not much of a poem."[26]

I remarked that Rev. Mr. Longfellow had a decided partiality for Browning. "Yes," he said; "Sam likes him, and my friend John Weiss prefers him to Tennyson. My objection is to his diction. I have always found the English language sufficient for my purpose, and have never tried to improve on it. Browning's 'Saul' and 'The Ride from Ghent to Aix' are noble poems."

"Carlyle also," I said, "has a peculiar diction." "That is true," he replied, "but one can forgive anything to a writer who has so much to tell us as Carlyle. Besides, he writes prose, and not poetry."

He took up a photograph which was lying on the table and showed it to me,

26   I have since observed that poets as a class are not fair critics of poetry; for they are sure to prefer poetry which is like their own. This is true at least of Lowell, Emerson, or Matthew Arnold; but when I came to read "The Ring and the Book" I found that Longfellow's objection was a valid one.

saying, "How do you like Miss Stebbins's 'Satan'?" I told him I hardly knew how to judge of such a subject. Then we both laughed, and Mr. Longfellow said: "I wonder what our artists want to make Satans for. I doubt if there is one of them that believes in the devil's existence."

I noticed on closer examination that the features resembled those of Miss Stebbins herself. Mr. Longfellow looked at it closely, and said, "So it does,--somewhat." Then I told him that I asked Warrington Wood how he obtained the expression for his head of Satan, and that he said he did it by looking in the glass and making up faces. Mr. Longfellow laughed heartily at this, saying, "I suppose Miss Stebbins did the same, and that is how it came about. Our sculptors should be careful how they put themselves in the devil's place. Wood has modelled a fine angel, and his group (Michael and Satan) is altogether an effective one."

Rev. Mr. Longfellow and the ladies now came in, and as it was late I shook hands with them all.

It is reported that when Mr. Longfellow met Cardinal Antonelli he remarked that Rome had changed less in the last fifteen years than other large cities, and that Antonelli replied, "Yes; God be praised for it!"

Feb. 25.--The elder Herbert[27] has painted a fine picture, and we all went to look at it this afternoon, as it will be packed up to-morrow for the Royal Exhibition at London. He has chosen for his subject the verse of a Greek poet, otherwise unknown:

"Unyoke your oxen, you fellow,   And take the coulter out of your plough; For you are ploughing amid the graves of men,   And the dust you turn up is the dust of your ancestors."

Herbert has substituted buffalos for oxen as being more picturesque, though they were not imported into Italy until some time in the Middle Ages. It is generally predicted that Herbert will become an R. A. like his father; but the subject is even more to his credit than his treatment of it. It is discussed at the *Lapre* whether this verse has been equalled by Tennyson or Longfellow, and the conclusion was: "Not proven."

March 1.--The Longfellows are gone, and Rome is filling up with a different class of people who have come here to witness the fatiguing spectacles of Easter.

---

27   The elder of two brothers, sons of an English artist.

One look at Michael Angelo's "Last Judgment" would be worth the whole of it to me.

P---- is said to have captured his young lady, and it seems probable, for I see very little of him now. He disappears after breakfast, rushes through his dinner, and returns late in the evenings. So all the world changes.

CENTENNIAL CONTRIBUTIONS

THE ALCOTT CENTENNIAL

Read at the Second Church, Copley Square, Boston, Wednesday, November 29, 1899

A hundred years ago A. Bronson Alcott was born, and thirty-three years later his daughter Louisa was born, happily on the same day of the year, as if for this very purpose,--that you might testify your appreciation of the good work they did in this world, at one and the same moment. It was a fortunate coincidence, which we like to think of to-day, as it undoubtedly gave pleasure to Bronson Alcott and his wife sixty-seven years ago.

How genuine were Mr. Alcott and his daughter, Louisa! "All else," says the sage, "is superficial and perishable, save love and truth only." It is through the love and truth that was in these two that we still feel their influence as if they were living to-day. How well I recollect Mr. Alcott's first visit to my father's house at Medford, when I was a boy! I had the same impression of him then that the consideration of his life makes on me now,--as an exceptional person, but one greatly to be trusted. I could see that he was a man who wished well to me, and to all mankind; who had no intention of encroaching on my rights as an individual in any way whatever; and who, furthermore, had no suspicion of me as a person alien to himself. The criticism made of him by my young brother held good of him then and always,--that "he looked like one of Christ's disciples." His aspect was intelligently mild and gentle, unmixed with the slightest taint of worldly self-interest.

He heard that Goethe had said, "We begin to sin as soon as we act;" but he did not agree to this, and was determined that one man at least should live in this world without sinning. He carried this plan out so consistently that, as he once confessed to me, it brought him to the verge of starvation. Then he realized that in order to play our part in the general order of things,--in order to obviate the perpetual tendency in human affairs to chaos,--we are continually obliged to compromise. However, to the last he would never touch animal food. Others might murder sheep and oxen, but he, Bronson Alcott, would not be a partaker in what he considered a serious transgression of moral law. This brought him into antagonism with the current of modern opinion, which considers man the natural ruler of this earth, and that it is both his right and his duty to remodel it according to his ideas of usefulness and beauty.

It brought him into a life-long conflict with society, but how gallantly, how amiably he carried this on you all know. It cannot be said that he was defeated, for his spirit was unconquerable. His purity of intention always received its true recognition; and wherever Bronson Alcott went he collected the most earnest, high-minded people about him, and made them more earnest, more high-minded by his conversation.

How different was his daughter, Louisa,--the keen observer of life and manners; the witty story-teller with the pictorial mind; always sympathetic, practical, helpful--the mainstay of her family, a pillar of support to her friends; forgetting the care of her own soul in her interest for the general welfare; heedless of her own advantage, and thereby obtaining for herself as a gift from heaven, the highest of all advantages, and the greatest of all rewards!

And yet, with so wide a difference in the practical application of their lives, the well-spring of Louisa's thought and the main-spring of her action were identical with those of her father, and may be considered an inheritance from him. For the well-spring of her thought was ***truth***, and the main-spring of her action was ***love***. There can be no fine art, no great art, no art which is of service to mankind, which does not originate on this twofold basis. We are told that when she was a young girl, on a voyage from Philadelphia to Boston, her face suddenly lighted up with the true brightness of genius, as she said, "I love everybody in this whole world!" If, afterwards, a vein of satire came to be mingled with this genial flow of human kindness, it was not Louisa's fault.

In like manner, Bronson Alcott rested his argument for immortality on the ground of the family affections. "Such strong ties," he reasoned, "could not have been made merely to be broken." Let us share his faith, and believe that they have not been broken.

THE EMERSON CENTENNIAL

EMERSON AND THE GREAT POETS

Read in the Town Hall, Concord, Mass., July 23, 1903

On his first visit to England, Emerson was so continually besieged with invitations that, as he wrote to Carlyle, answering the notes he received "ate up his day like a cherry;" and yet I have never met but one Englishman, Dr. John Tyndall, the chemist, who seemed to appreciate Emerson's poetry, and few others who might be said to appreciate the man himself. Tyndall may have recognized Emerson's keen insight for the poetry of science in such verses as:

> "What time the gods kept carnival;
>   Tricked out in gem and flower;
> And in cramp elf and saurian form
>   They swathed their too much power."

A person who lacks some knowledge of geology would not be likely to understand this. Matthew Arnold and Edwin Arnold had no very high opinion of Emerson's poetry; and even Carlyle, who was Emerson's best friend in Europe, spoke of it in rather a disparaging manner. The "Mountain and the Squirrel" and several others have been translated into German, but not those which we here consider the best of them.

On the other hand, Dr. William H. Furness considered Emerson "heaven-high above our other poets;" C. P. Cranch preferred him to Longfellow; Dr. F. H. Hedge looked upon him as the first poet of his time; Rev. Samuel Longfellow and Rev. Samuel Johnson held a very similar opinion, and David A. Wasson considered Emerson's "Problem" one of the great poems of the century.

These men were all poets themselves, though they did not make a profession of it, and in that character were quite equal to Matthew Arnold, whose lecture on Emerson was evidently written under unfavorable influences. They were men who had passed through similar experiences to those which developed Emerson's mind and character, and could therefore comprehend him better than others. We all feel that Emerson's poetry is sometimes too abstruse, especially in his earlier verses, and that its meaning is often too recondite for ready apprehension; but there are passages in it so luminous and so far-reaching in their application that only the supreme poets of all time have equalled them.

Homer's strength consists in his pictorial descriptions, but also sometimes in pithy reflections on life and human nature; and it is in these latter that Emerson often comes close to him. Most widely known of Homer's epigrams is that reply of Telemachus to Antiochus in the Odyssey, which Pope has rendered:

"True hospitality is in these terms expressed,
Welcome the coming, speed the parting guest."

To which the following couplet from "Woodnotes" seems almost like a continuation:

"Go where he will, the wise man is at home,
His hearth the earth,--his hall the azure dome;"

The wise man carries rest and contentment in his own mental life, and is equally himself at the Corona d'Italia and on a western ranch; while the weakling runs back to earlier associations like a colt to its stable. But Homer is also Emersonian at times. What could be more so than Achilles's memorable saying, which is repeated by Ulysses in the Odyssey: "More hateful to me than the gates of death is he who thinks one thing and speaks another;" or this exclamation of old Laertes in the last book of the Odyssey: "What a day is this when I see my son and grandson contending in excellence!"

It seems a long way from Dante to Emerson, and yet there are Dantean passages in "Woodnotes" and "Voluntaries." They are not in Dante's matchless measure, but they have much of his grace, and more of his inflexible will. This warning against mercenary marriages might be compared to Dante's answer to the embezzling Pope Nicholas III. in Canto XIX. of the Inferno:

> "He shall be happy in his love,
> Like to like shall joyful prove;
> He shall be happy whilst he woos,
> Muse-born, a daughter of the Muse.
> But if with gold she bind her hair,
> And deck her breast with diamond,
> Take off thine eyes, thy heart forbear,
> Though thou lie alone on the ground.
> The robe of silk in which she shines,
> It was woven of many sins;
> And the shreds
> Which she sheds
> In the wearing of the same,
> Shall be grief on grief,
> And shame on shame."

There is a Spartan-like severity in this, but so was Dante very severe. It was his mission to purify the moral sense of his countrymen in an age when the Church no longer encouraged virtue; and Emerson no less vigorously opposed the rank materialism of America in a period of exceptional prosperity.

The next succeeding lines are not exactly Dantean, but they are among Emerson's finest, and worthy of any great poet. The "Pine Tree" says:

"Heed the old oracles,
Ponder my spells;
Song wakes in my pinnacles
When the wind swells.
Soundeth the prophetic wind,
The shadows shake on the rock behind,
And the countless leaves of the pine are strings
Tuned to the lay the wood-god sings."

Again we are reminded of Dante in the opening passages of "Voluntaries":

"Low and mournful be the strain,
  Haughty thought be far from me;
Where a captive lies in pain
  Moaning by the tropic sea.
Sole estate his sire bequeathed--
  Hapless sire to hapless son--
Was the wailing song he breathed,
  And his chain when life was done."

It is still more difficult to compare Emerson with Shakespeare, for the one was Puritan with a strong classic tendency, and the other anti- Puritan with a strong romantic tendency; but allowing for this and for Shakespeare's universality, it may be affirmed that there are few passages in King Henry IV. and Henry V. which take a higher rank than Emerson's description of Cromwell:

"He works, plots, fights 'mid rude affairs,
With squires, knights, kings his strength compares;
Till late he learned through doubt and fear,
Broad England harbored not his peer:
Unwilling still the last to own,
The genius on his cloudy throne."

Emerson learned a large proportion of his wisdom from Goethe, as he frequently confessed, but where in Goethe's poetry will you find a quatrain of more penetrating beauty or wider significance than this from "Woodnotes":

"Thou canst not wave thy staff in air
  Nor dip thy paddle in the lake,
 But it carves the bow of beauty there,
   And ripples in rhyme the oar forsake."

Or this one from the "Building of the House"--considered metaphorically as the life structure of man:

"She lays her beams in music,
  In music every one,
 To the cadence of the whirling world
   Which dances round the sun."

There is a flash as of heaven's own lightning in some of his verses, and his name has become a spell to conjure with.

THE HAWTHORNE CENTENNIAL

HAWTHORNE AS ART CRITIC

When the "Marble Faun" was first published the art criticism in it, especially of sculptors and painters who were then living, created a deal of discussion, which has been revived again by the recent centennial celebration. Hawthorne himself was the most perfect artist of his time as a man of letters, and the judgment of such a person ought to have its value, even when it relates to subjects which are beyond the customary sphere of his investigations, and for which he has not made a serious preparation. In spite of the adage, "every man to his own trade," it may be fairly asserted that much of Hawthorne's art criticism takes rank among the finest that has been written in any language. On the other hand, there are instances, as might be expected, in which he has failed to hit the mark.

These latter may be placed in two classes: Firstly, those in which he indicates a partiality for personal acquaintances; and secondly, those in which he has followed popular opinion at the time, or the opinion of others, without sufficient consideration.

American society in Rome is always split up into various cliques,--which is not surprising in view of the adventitious manner in which it comes together there,-- and in Hawthorne's time the two leading parties were the Story and the Crawford factions. The latter was a man of true genius, and not only the best of American sculptors, but perhaps the greatest sculptor of the nineteenth century. His statue of Beethoven is in the grand manner, and instinct with harmony, not only in attitude and expression, but even to the arrangement of the drapery. Crawford's genius was only too well appreciated, and he was constantly carrying off the prizes of his art from all competitors. Consequently it was inevitable that other sculptors should be jealous of him, and should unite together for mutual protection. Story was a man of talent, and not a little of an amateur, but he was the gentlemanly entertainer of those Americans who came to the city with good letters of introduction. Hawthorne evidently fell into Story's hands. He speaks slightingly of Crawford, and praises Story's statue of Cleopatra in unqualified terms; and yet there seems to have been an undercurrent of suspicion in his mind, for he says more than once in the "Marble Faun" that it would appear to be a failing with sculptors to speak unfavorably of the work of other sculptors, and this, of course, refers to those with whom he was acquainted, and whom he sometimes rated above their value.

Warrington Wood, the best English sculptor of thirty years ago, praised Story's "Cleopatra" to me, and I believe that Crawford also would have praised it. Neither has Hawthorne valued its expression too highly--the expression of worldly splendor incarnated in a beautiful woman on the tragical verge of an abyss. If she only were beautiful! Here the limitations of the statue commence. Hawthorne says: "The sculptor had not shunned to give the full, Nubian lips, and other characteristics of the Egyptian physiognomy." Here he follows the sculptor himself, and it is remarkable that a college graduate like William Story should have made so transparent a mistake. Cleopatra was not an Egyptian at all. The Ptolemies were Greeks, and it is simply impossible to believe that they would have allied themselves with a subject and alien race. This kind of small pedantry has often led artists astray, and was peculiarly virulent during the middle of the last century. The whole figure of Story's "Cleopatra" suffers from it. He says again: "She was draped from head to foot in a costume minutely and scrupulously studied from that of ancient Egypt." In fact, the body and limbs of the statue are so closely shrouded as to deprive the work of that sense of freedom of action and royal abandon which greets us in Shakespeare's and Plutarch's "Cleopatra." Story might have taken a lesson from Titian's matchless "Cleopatra" in the Cassel Gallery, or from Marc Antonio's small woodcut of Raphael's "Cleopatra."

Hawthorne was an idealist, and he idealized the materials in Story's studio, for literary purposes, just as Shakespeare idealized Henry V., who was not a magnanimous monarch at all, but a brutal, narrow-minded fighter. The discourse on art, which he develops in this manner, forms one of the most valuable chapters in the "Marble Faun." It assists us in reading it to remember that Story was not the model for Hawthorne's "Kenyon," but a very different character. The passage in which he criticises the methods of modern sculptors has often been quoted in later writings on that subject; and I suppose the whole brotherhood of artists would rise up against me if I were to support Hawthorne's condemnation of nude Venuses and "the guilty glimpses stolen at hired models."

They are not necessarily guilty glimpses. To an experienced artist the customary study from a naked figure, male or female, is little more than what a low-necked dress would be to others. Yet the instinct of the age shrinks from this exposure. We can make pretty good Venuses, but we cannot look at them through the same mental and moral atmosphere as the cotemporaries of Scopas, or even with the same eyes that Michael Angelo did. We feel the difference between a modern Venus and an ancient one. There is a statue in the Vatican of a Roman emperor, of which every one says that it ought to wear clothes; and the reason is because the face has such a modern look. A raving Bacchante may be a good acquisition to an art museum, but it is out of place in a public library. A female statue requires more or less drapery to set off the outlines of the figure and to give it dignity. We feel this even in the finest Greek work--like the Venus of Cnidos.

In this matter Hawthorne certainly exposes his Puritanic education, and he also places too high a value on the carving of buttonholes and shoestrings by Italian workmen. Such things are the fag-ends of statuary.

His judgment, however, is clear and convincing in regard to the tinted Eves and Venuses of Gibson. Whatever may have been the ancient practice in this respect, Gibson's experiment proved a failure. Nobody likes those statues; and no other sculptor has since followed Gibson's example.

Hawthorne overestimates the Apollo Belvidere, as all the world did at that time; but his single remark concerning Canova is full of significance: "In these precincts which Canova's genius was not quite of a character to render sacred, though it certainly made them interesting," etc.

He goes to the statue gallery in the Vatican and returns with a feeling of dissatisfaction, and justly so, for the vast majority of statues there are merely copies, and many of them very bad copies. He recognizes the Laocoon for what it really is, the abstract type of a Greek tragedy. He notices what has since been proved by severe archaeological study, that most of the possible types and attitudes of marble statues had been exhausted by the Greeks long before the Christian era. Miss Hosmer's Zenobia was originally a Ceres, and even Crawford's Orpheus strongly resembles a figure in the Niobe group at Florence.

But Hawthorne's description of the Faun of Praxiteles stands by itself. As a penetrative analysis of a great sculptor's motive it is unequalled by any modern writer on art, and this is set forth with a grace and delicacy worthy of Praxiteles himself. The only criticism which one feels inclined to make of it is that it *too* Hawthornish, too modern and elaborate; but is not this equally true of all modern criticism? We cannot return to the simplicity of the Greeks any more than we can to their customs. If Hawthorne would seem to discover too much in this statue, which is really a poor Roman copy, he has himself given us an answer to this objection. In Volume II., Chapter XII., he says: "Let the canvas glow as it may, you must look with the eye of faith, or its highest excellence escapes you. There is always the necessity of helping out the painter's art with your own resources of sensibility and imagination." His cursory remarks on Raphael are not less pertinent and penetrating. Of technicalities he knew little, but no one, perhaps, has sounded such depths of that clairvoyant master's nature, and so brought to light the very soul of him.

The "Marble Faun" may not be the most perfect of Hawthorne's works, but it is much the greatest,--an epic romance, which can only be compared with Goethe's "Wilhelm Meister."

HAWTHORNE AND HAMLET.

A Reply to Professor Bliss Perry.

To compare a person in real life with a character in fiction is not uncommon, but it is more conducive to solidity of judgment to compare the living with the living, and the imaginary with the imaginary. The chief difficulty, however, in Hamlet's case, is that he only appears before us as a person acting in an abnormal mental condition. The mysterious death of his father, the suspicion of his mother's complicity in crime, which takes the form of an apparition from beyond the grave, is too much of a strain for his tender and impressible nature. His mental condition has become well known to physicians as *cerebral hyperaemia*, and all his strange speeches and eccentric actions are to be traced to this source; and it is for this reason that the dispute has arisen as to whether Hamlet was not partially insane. If the strain continued long enough he would no doubt have become insane.

As well as we can penetrate through this adventitious *nimbus*, we discover Hamlet to be a person of generous, princely nature, high-minded and chivalrous. He is cordial to every one, but always succeeds in asserting the superiority of his position, even in his conversation with Horatio. If he is mentally sensitive he shows no indication of it. He never appears shy or reserved, but on the contrary, confident and even bold. This may be owing to the mental excitement under which he labors; but the best critics from Goethe down have accredited him with a lack of resolution; and it is this which produces the catastrophe of the play. He must have realized, as we all do, that after the scene of the players in which he "catches the conscience of a king," his life was in great danger. He should either have organized a conspiracy at once, or fled to the court of Fortinbras; but he allows events to take their course, and is controlled by them instead of shaping his own destiny. Instead of planning and acting he philosophizes.

Of Hawthorne, on the contrary, we know nothing except as a person in a perfectly normal condition. His wife once said that she had rarely known him to be indignant, and never to lose his temper. He was the most sensitive of men, but he also possessed an indomitable will. It was only his terrible determination that could make his life a success. Emerson, who had little sympathy with him otherwise, always admired the perfect equipoise of his nature. A man could not be more thoroughly himself; but, such a reticent, unsociable character as Hawthorne could never be used as the main-spring of a drama, for he would continually impede the progress of the plot. A dramatic character needs to be a talkative person; one that either acts out his internal life, or indirectly exposes it. Hawthorne's best friends do not appear to have known what his real opinions were. This perpetual reserve, this unwillingness to assimilate himself to others, may have been necessary for the perfection of his art.

The greater a writer or an artist, the more unique he is,--the more sharply defined from all other members of his class. Hawthorne certainly did not resemble Scott, Dickens, or Thackeray, either in his life or his work. He was perhaps more like Auerbach than any other writer of the nineteenth century, but still more like Goldsmith. The "Vicar of Wakefield" and the "House of the Seven Gables" are the two perfect romances in the English tongue; and the "Deserted Village," though written in poetry, has very much the quality of Hawthorne's shorter sketches. "And tales much older than the ale went round" is closely akin to Hawthorne's humor; yet there was little outward similarity between them, for Goldsmith was often gay and sometimes frivolous; and although Hawthorne never published a line of poetry he was the more poetic of the two, as Goldsmith was the more dramatic. He also resembled Goldsmith in his small financial difficulties.

In his persistent reserve, in the seriousness of his delineation, and in his indifference to the opinions of others, Hawthorne reminds us somewhat of Michael Angelo; but he is one of the most unique figures among the world's geniuses.

The Codes Of Hammurabi And Moses
W. W. Davies

QTY

The discovery of the Hammurabi Code is one of the greatest achievements of archaeology, and is of paramount interest, not only to the student of the Bible, but also to all those interested in ancient history...

Religion   **ISBN: *1-59462-338-4***

Pages:132
MSRP $12.95

The Theory of Moral Sentiments
Adam Smith

QTY

This work from 1749. contains original theories of conscience amd moral judgment and it is the foundation for systemof morals.

Philosophy **ISBN: *1-59462-777-0***

Pages:536
MSRP $19.95

Jessica's First Prayer
Hesba Stretton

QTY

In a screened and secluded corner of one of the many railway-bridges which span the streets of London there could be seen a few years ago, from five o'clock every morning until half past eight, a tidily set-out coffee-stall, consisting of a trestle and board, upon which stood two large tin cans, with a small fire of charcoal burning under each so as to keep the coffee boiling during the early hours of the morning when the work-people were thronging into the city on their way to their daily toil...

Childrens   **ISBN: *1-59462-373-2***

Pages:84
MSRP $9.95

My Life and Work
Henry Ford

QTY

Henry Ford revolutionized the world with his implementation of mass production for the Model T automobile. Gain valuable business insight into his life and work with his own auto-biography... "We have only started on our development of our country we have not as yet, with all our talk of wonderful progress, done more than scratch the surface. The progress has been wonderful enough but..."

Biographies/   **ISBN: *1-59462-198-5***

Pages:300
MSRP $21.95

The Art of Cross-Examination
Francis Wellman

QTY

I presume it is the experience of every author, after his first book is published upon an important subject, to be almost overwhelmed with a wealth of ideas and illustrations which could readily have been included in his book, and which to his own mind, at least, seem to make a second edition inevitable. Such certainly was the case with me; and when the first edition had reached its sixth impression in five months, I rejoiced to learn that it seemed to my publishers that the book had met with a sufficiently favorable reception to justify a second and considerably enlarged edition. ..

Reference   **ISBN:** *1-59462-647-2*

Pages:412

MSRP $19.95

On the Duty of Civil Disobedience
Henry David Thoreau

QTY

Thoreau wrote his famous essay, On the Duty of Civil Disobedience, as a protest against an unjust but popular war and the immoral but popular institution of slave-owning. He did more than write—he declined to pay his taxes, and was hauled off to gaol in consequence. Who can say how much this refusal of his hastened the end of the war and of slavery ?

Law   **ISBN:** *1-59462-747-9*

Pages:48

MSRP $7.45

Dream Psychology Psychoanalysis for Beginners
Sigmund Freud

QTY

Sigmund Freud, born Sigismund Schlomo Freud (May 6, 1856 - September 23, 1939), was a Jewish-Austrian neurologist and psychiatrist who co-founded the psychoanalytic school of psychology. Freud is best known for his theories of the unconscious mind, especially involving the mechanism of repression; his redefinition of sexual desire as mobile and directed towards a wide variety of objects; and his therapeutic techniques, especially his understanding of transference in the therapeutic relationship and the presumed value of dreams as sources of insight into unconscious desires.

Psychology   **ISBN:** *1-59462-905-6*

Pages:196

MSRP $15.45

The Miracle of Right Thought
Orison Swett Marden

QTY

Believe with all of your heart that you will do what you were made to do. When the mind has once formed the habit of holding cheerful, happy, prosperous pictures, it will not be easy to form the opposite habit. It does not matter how improbable or how far away this realization may see, or how dark the prospects may be, if we visualize them as best we can, as vividly as possible, hold tenaciously to them and vigorously struggle to attain them, they will gradually become actualized, realized in the life. But a desire, a longing without endeavor, a yearning abandoned or held indifferently will vanish without realization.

Self Help   **ISBN:** *1-59462-644-8*

Pages:360

MSRP $25.45

☐	**The Rosicrucian Cosmo-Conception Mystic Christianity** *by Max Heindel*	ISBN: *1-59462-188-8*	**$38.95**

The Rosicrucian Cosmo-conception is not dogmatic, neither does it appeal to any other authority than the reason of the student. It is: not controversial, but is: sent forth in the, hope that it may help to clear...
New Age/Religion Pages 646

☐ **Abandonment To Divine Providence** *by Jean-Pierre de Caussade* — ISBN: *1-59462-228-0* **$25.95**
"The Rev. Jean Pierre de Caussade was one of the most remarkable spiritual writers of the Society of Jesus in France in the 18th Century. His death took place at Toulouse in 1751. His works have gone through many editions and have been republished...
Inspirational/Religion Pages 400

☐ **Mental Chemistry** *by Charles Haanel* — ISBN: *1-59462-192-6* **$23.95**
Mental Chemistry allows the change of material conditions by combining and appropriately utilizing the power of the mind. Much like applied chemistry creates something new and unique out of careful combinations of chemicals the mastery of mental chemistry...
New Age Pages 354

☐ **The Letters of Robert Browning and Elizabeth Barret Barrett 1845-1846 vol II** — ISBN: *1-59462-193-4* **$35.95**
by Robert Browning and Elizabeth Barrett
Biographies Pages 596

☐ **Gleanings In Genesis (volume I)** *by Arthur W. Pink* — ISBN: *1-59462-130-6* **$27.45**
Appropriately has Genesis been termed "the seed plot of the Bible" for in it we have, in germ form, almost all of the great doctrines which are afterwards fully developed in the books of Scripture which follow...
Religion/Inspirational Pages 420

☐ **The Master Key** *by L. W. de Laurence* — ISBN: *1-59462-001-6* **$30.95**
In no branch of human knowledge has there been a more lively increase of the spirit of research during the past few years than in the study of Psychology, Concentration and Mental Discipline. The requests for authentic lessons in Thought Control, Mental Discipline and...
New Age/Business Pages 422

☐ **The Lesser Key Of Solomon Goetia** *by L. W. de Laurence* — ISBN: *1-59462-092-X* **$9.95**
This translation of the first book of the "Lernegton" which is now for the first time made accessible to students of Talismanic Magic was done, after careful collation and edition, from numerous Ancient Manuscripts in Hebrew, Latin, and French...
New Age/Occult Pages 92

☐ **Rubaiyat Of Omar Khayyam** *by Edward Fitzgerald* — ISBN:*1-59462-332-5* **$13.95**
Edward Fitzgerald, whom the world has already learned, in spite of his own efforts to remain within the shadow of anonymity, to look upon as one of the rarest poets of the century, was born at Bredfield, in Suffolk, on the 31st of March, 1809. He was the third son of John Purcell...
Music Pages 172

☐ **Ancient Law** *by Henry Maine* — ISBN: *1-59462-128-4* **$29.95**
The chief object of the following pages is to indicate some of the earliest ideas of mankind, as they are reflected in Ancient Law, and to point out the relation of those ideas to modern thought.
Religiom/History Pages 452

☐ **Far-Away Stories** *by William J. Locke* — ISBN: *1-59462-192-2* **$19.45**
"Good wine needs no bush, but a collection of mixed vintages does. And this book is just such a collection. Some of the stories I do not want to remain buried for ever in the museum files of dead magazine-numbers an author's not unpardonable vanity..."
Fiction Pages 272

☐ **Life of David Crockett** *by David Crockett* — ISBN: *1-59462-250-7* **$27.45**
"Colonel David Crockett was one of the most remarkable men of the times in which he lived. Born in humble life, but gifted with a strong will, an indomitable courage, and unremitting perseverance...
Biographies/New Age Pages 424

☐ **Lip-Reading** *by Edward Nitchie* — ISBN: *1-59462-206-X* **$25.95**
Edward B. Nitchie, founder of the New York School for the Hard of Hearing, now the Nitchie School of Lip-Reading, Inc, wrote "LIP-READING Principles and Practice". The development and perfecting of this meritorious work on lip-reading was an undertaking...
How-to Pages 400

☐ **A Handbook of Suggestive Therapeutics, Applied Hypnotism, Psychic Science** — ISBN: *1-59462-214-0* **$24.95**
by Henry Munro
Health/New Age/Health/Self-help Pages 376

☐ **A Doll's House: and Two Other Plays** *by Henrik Ibsen* — ISBN: *1-59462-112-8* **$19.95**
Henrik Ibsen created this classic when in revolutionary 1848 Rome. Introducing some striking concepts in playwriting for the realist genre, this play has been studied the world over.
Fiction/Classics/Plays 308

☐ **The Light of Asia** *by sir Edwin Arnold* — ISBN: *1-59462-204-3* **$13.95**
In this poetic masterpiece, Edwin Arnold describes the life and teachings of Buddha. The man who was to become known as Buddha to the world was born as Prince Gautama of India but he rejected the worldly riches and abandoned the reigns of power when... Religion/History/Biographies Pages 170

☐ **The Complete Works of Guy de Maupassant** *by Guy de Maupassant* — ISBN: *1-59462-157-8* **$16.95**
"For days and days, nights and nights, I had dreamed of that first kiss which was to consecrate our engagement, and I knew not on what spot I should put my lips..."
Fiction/Classics Pages 240

☐ **The Art of Cross-Examination** *by Francis L. Wellman* — ISBN: *1-59462-309-0* **$26.95**
Written by a renowned trial lawyer, Wellman imparts his experience and uses case studies to explain how to use psychology to extract desired information through questioning.
How-to/Science/Reference Pages 408

☐ **Answered or Unanswered?** *by Louisa Vaughan* — ISBN: *1-59462-248-5* **$10.95**
Miracles of Faith in China
Religion Pages 112

☐ **The Edinburgh Lectures on Mental Science (1909)** *by Thomas* — ISBN: *1-59462-008-3* **$11.95**
This book contains the substance of a course of lectures recently given by the writer in the Queen Street Hall, Edinburgh. Its purpose is to indicate the Natural Principles governing the relation between Mental Action and Material Conditions...
New Age/Psychology Pages 148

☐ **Ayesha** *by H. Rider Haggard* — ISBN: *1-59462-301-5* **$24.95**
Verily and indeed it is the unexpected that happens! Probably if there was one person upon the earth from whom the Editor of this, and of a certain previous history, did not expect to hear again...
Classics Pages 380

☐ **Ayala's Angel** *by Anthony Trollope* — ISBN: *1-59462-352-X* **$29.95**
The two girls were both pretty, but Lucy who was twenty-one who supposed to be simple and comparatively unattractive, whereas Ayala was credited, as her Bombwhat romantic name might show, with poetic charm and a taste for romance. Ayala when her father died was nineteen... Fiction Pages 484

☐ **The American Commonwealth** *by James Bryce* — ISBN: *1-59462-286-8* **$34.45**
An interpretation of American democratic political theory. It examines political mechanics and society from the perspective of Scotsman James Bryce
Politics Pages 572

☐ **Stories of the Pilgrims** *by Margaret P. Pumphrey* — ISBN: *1-59462-116-0* **$17.95**
This book explores pilgrims religious oppression in England as well as their escape to Holland and eventual crossing to America on the Mayflower, and their early days in New England...
History Pages 268

QTY

The Fasting Cure by *Sinclair Upton*　　　　　　　　　ISBN: *1-59462-222-1*　**$13.95**
*In the Cosmopolitan Magazine for May, 1910, and in the Contemporary Review (London) for April, 1910, I published an article dealing with my experi-
ences in fasting. I have written a great many magazine articles, but never one which attracted so much attention...　New Age/Self Help/Health Pages 164*

Hebrew Astrology by *Sepharial*　　　　　　　　　　ISBN: *1-59462-308-2*　**$13.45**
*In these days of advanced thinking it is a matter of common observation that we have left many of the old landmarks behind and that we are now pressing
forward to greater heights and to a wider horizon than that which represented the mind-content of our progenitors...　Astrology Pages 144*

Thought Vibration or The Law of Attraction in the Thought World　ISBN: *1-59462-127-6*　**$12.95**
by *William Walker Atkinson*　　　　　　　　　　　　　　　　　*Psychology/Religion Pages 144*

Optimism by *Helen Keller*　　　　　　　　　　　　ISBN: *1-59462-108-X*　**$15.95**
*Helen Keller was blind, deaf, and mute since 19 months old, yet famously learned how to overcome these handicaps, communicate with the world, and
spread her lectures promoting optimism. An inspiring read for everyone...　Biographies/Inspirational Pages 84*

Sara Crewe by *Frances Burnett*　　　　　　　　　　ISBN: *1-59462-360-0*　**$9.45**
*In the first place, Miss Minchin lived in London. Her home was a large, dull, tall one, in a large, dull square, where all the houses were alike, and all the
sparrows were alike, and where all the door-knockers made the same heavy sound...　Childrens/Classic Pages 88*

The Autobiography of Benjamin Franklin by *Benjamin Franklin*　ISBN: *1-59462-135-7*　**$24.95**
*The Autobiography of Benjamin Franklin has probably been more extensively read than any other American historical work, and no other book of its kind
has had such ups and downs of fortune. Franklin lived for many years in England, where he was agent...　Biographies/History Pages 332*

Name	
Email	
Telephone	
Address	
City, State ZIP	

☐ **Credit Card**　　　　　☐ **Check / Money Order**

Credit Card Number	
Expiration Date	
Signature	

*Please Mail to:　Book Jungle
PO Box 2226
Champaign, IL 61825
or Fax to:　　　630-214-0564*

ORDERING INFORMATION

web: *www.bookjungle.com*
email: *sales@bookjungle.com*
fax: *630-214-0564*
mail: *Book Jungle　PO Box 2226　Champaign, IL 61825*
or PayPal *to sales@bookjungle.com*

Please contact us for bulk discounts

DIRECT-ORDER TERMS

**20% Discount if You Order
Two or More Books**
Free Domestic Shipping!
Accepted: Master Card, Visa,
Discover, American Express